The Chronicle of Leopold and Molly Bloom

The Chronicle of
Leopold and Molly Bloom

Ulysses as Narrative

JOHN HENRY RALEIGH

UNIVERSITY OF CALIFORNIA PRESS

BERKELEY · LOS ANGELES · LONDON

University of California Press
Berkeley and Los Angeles, California

University of California Press, Ltd.
London, England

Copyright ©1977 by
The Regents of the University of California

ISBN 0-520-03301-9
Library of Congress Catalog Card Number: 76-20025
Printed in the United States of America

MEMORY OF L B:

a very long time I was going to bed somewhere and there was a
squareshaped or was it when I was where was that.
Philip Herring, *Joyce's "Ulysses" Notesheets
in the British Museum* (Charlottesville, 1972), p. 91

But tomorrow is a new day will be. Past was is today. What
now is will then tomorrow as now was be past yester.
Leopold Bloom, *Ulysses* (515)

There are sins or (let us call them as the world calls them)
evil memories which are hidden away by man in the darkest
places of the heart but they abide there and wait. He may suffer
their memory to grow dim, let them be as though they had not
been and all but persuade himself that they were not or at least
were otherwise. Yet a chance word will call them forth suddenly
and they will rise up to confront him in the most various
circumstances, a vision or a dream, or while timbrel and harp
soothe his senses amid the cool silver tranquility of the evening
or at the feast at midnight when he is now filled with wine. Not
to insult over him will the vision come as over one that lies
under her wrath, not for vengeance to cut off from the living but
shrouded in the piteous vesture of the past, silent, remote,
reproachful.

(421)

Contents

Preface

I am chiefly indebted to five allies: Anita Lynn, my typist, for her painstaking typing of an intricate manuscript; my wife, Jo, and my daughter, Lydia, for the accurate checking and rechecking of quotations; Fritz Senn for his careful and knowledgable reading of the original manuscript and his intelligent corrections and suggestions; and my copy editor, Karen McClung, for her care, good sense, and creative ideas on matters of format.

I wish also to thank Mr. James Joyce for providing me with an unaccountable number of enjoyable hours of circling, backtracking, recircling around and around in his maze following my own Ariadne's thread.

I give my thanks to Mr. Karl Gay, Curator of the Poetry Collection at the Lockwood Memorial Library of the State University of New York at Buffalo, for his kindness and help to me when I was examining the Joyce manuscripts there.

Acknowledgement is made to Clive Hart and Leo Knuth for permission to reproduce some Dublin maps published in their *A Topographical Guide to James Joyce's "Ulysses"* (Colchester, 1975).

Acknowledgment is made to Random House, Inc. for permission to quote from *Ulysses* by James Joyce. Copyright 1914, 1918 by Margaret Caroline Anderson and renewed 1942, 1946 by Nora Joseph Joyce.

Abbreviations

The following books are cited in the text by the first initials given below:

A.—Robert Martin Adams, *Surface and Symbol* (New York, 1967).

E.—Richard Ellmann, *James Joyce* (New York, 1959).

G.—Don Gifford with Robert J. Seidman, *Notes for Joyce* (New York, 1974).

H.—Philip Herring, *Joyce's "Ulysses" Notesheets in the British Museum* (Charlottesville, 1972).

H. & K.—Clive Hart and Leo Knuth, *A Topographical Guide to James Joyce's "Ulysses"* (Colchester, 1975).

L.—*Letters of James Joyce,* Vol. I, ed. by Stuart Gilbert; Vols. II and III, ed. by Richard Ellmann (New York, 1966).

T.—Weldon Thornton, *Allusions in "Ulysses"* (Chapel Hill, 1968).

The indispensable book for this project has been Miles Hanley's *Word Index to James Joyce's "Ulysses"* (Madison, 1957).

Introduction

The assembling of the present work was begun as a hobby to keep me in direct touch with scholarship during a period when I was a full-time administrator, Vice Chancellor for Academic Affairs of the Berkeley campus of the University of California. Just prior to assuming this office, I had become interested in the chronologies of the lives of the Blooms which Joyce had scattered—and thus in a sense buried—throughout *Ulysses*. I was quite sure that these chronologies had been carefully put together before they were shredded and the pieces distributed randomly throughout the book to the respective memories of the Blooms. It was not until I had been able to reconstruct, and set in chronological order, the greater part of the Blooms' past by working only with the text of *Ulysses* that I turned to investigate the known chronologies for the book that Joyce himself had left behind in manuscript form. These are all in the Poetry Collection of the Lockwood Memorial Library of the State University of New York at Buffalo.

In the Buffalo collection of Joyce manuscripts there are three chronologies for the past of Molly and Leopold Bloom. Even the longest one is rather brief, and its notations are not always followed in *Ulysses* itself. Either Joyce's memory was even more exact and tenacious than we already know it was, and he was thus able to keep in his head the precise and multitudinous details of the chronologies of the lives of his characters, or he had worked out an extensive chronology for the Blooms, and others, which has since been destroyed or lost. Or perhaps, most likely, he had some kind of private code or notation to keep his chronologies correct and congruent. There are also some dates, again not always adhered to in the novel itself, in the British Museum *Notesheets,* which have been published by Philip Herring. Joyce did make some errors, as will be pointed out in the text, but they are remarkably few. And at times he makes the Blooms misremember in order to show that they are human and fallible (this can be demonstrated too). The three chronologies are distributed as follows, using the code devised by Peter Spielberg in his *James Joyce's Manuscripts and Letters at the University of Buffalo* (Buffalo, 1962): two in VI.C.7 "Finnegans Wake: Transcriptions of Workbooks"; and one in V.A.8 "Ulysses Holograph M.S.S.: Cyclops." VI.C.7 contains the longest chronology, which I have designated as VI.C.7 (1), and also a shorter one, which I have designated as VI.C.7 (2). Both of the chronologies in VI.C.7 are transcriptions made from Joyce's hand by his copyist Mme. France Raphael, who in a letter to Spielberg, dated August 6, 1959, said that she had been Joyce's amanuensis from about 1933 to the end of 1936 (Spielberg, p. 96, footnote 4). Anyone who has wrestled with Joyce's handwriting can readily understand why there are mistakes in Mme. Raphael's transcriptions. The very brief chronology in V.A.8 is in Joyce's hand in pencil and is on the inside of the front cover of the blue notebook that Joyce employed for some of his Cyclops material. It is not in one vertical column, as are the other two, but is in two more or less vertical parallel columns, which in their lower reaches are very difficult to decipher.

The following collation then represents, to the best of

my knowledge, the only extant material there is, in Joyce's
notes, on the chronologies of the lives of the Blooms. I
have made some changes in the order of V.A.8; I am
indebted to Philip Herring for its deciphering. I have also
silently corrected Mme. Raphael's mistranscriptions, Anglicized her notations, and listed her notes for each year in
a vertical order, which she does not always do. A question
mark in a bracket indicates my uncertainty about the
proper rendering.

	VI.C.7(1)	VI.C.7(2)	V.A.8	
1866	L.B. b.	L B b. 66.	L B born 1866	born 1866
1867				
1868				
1869				
1870				
1871	M B b. 8/9/921.			
1872				
1873				
1874				
1875				
1876				
1877				
1878				
1879				
1880	= LB leaves HS.	left school 1880	left school 1880	left school 1880
				entered ? Thom 1880
1881				
1882	= S.D. b.			
1883				
1884				
1885				
1886	LB Thams			
	R B d.			
	Clanbrassil			
	Charade			
	Dolphin's Barn			
1887	Mat Dillons		L B married ~~1887~~	
1888	L B and M B m.		R B born 1888	
	Hely's			
	Raymond Terrace			
1889	Milly, b.		Milly born 1889	
1890	L B's Mother ?			
1892	Rudy conceived			
	Greystones			
1893	Rudy b. and d.			
1894	Arnott's fire			
	Val Dillon L M [that is,			
	Lord Mayor]			
	Phil Gilligan d.			
	hotter [?]			
	Goodwin's concert			
	M B choir			
	left Lamb St.			
	Glencree			

	VI.C.7(1)	VI.C.7(2)	V.A.8
1895	Holles St.	Hely's 1895	Hely's 1895
	Ben Dollard's concert		
	M Coffee Palace		
	City Arms Hotel		
1896	LB in Drimmies'	Cuffe's 1896-7	Cuffe's 1896-7
1897			
1898			
1899			
1900			
1901		[?] Insurance 1901-2	Insurance 1901-1902
		[indecipherable]	
1902		Freeman 1902-04	Freeman 1902-1904
1903	LB Freeman's		
	Eccles St.		
1904	Milly Mullingar		

There are some bedrock certainties in these chronologies about Joyce's plans for the lives of the Blooms that are borne out by the novel itself: for example, that Bloom was to have been born in 1866 and was to leave high school in 1880; that the Blooms were to marry in 1888; that Milly was to be born in 1889; that they were to be in Holles Street in 1895 and that a memorable concert involving Ben Dollard was to take place that same year; and that Milly was to go to Mullingar in 1904.

But there are changes of mind as well. In VI.C.7(1) Molly is born on September 8, 1871, and in a letter Joyce said the same thing: "Molly Bloom was born in 1871" (L. I, p. 170). But in the novel itself she is born on September 8, 1870. The Blooms were not on Raymond Terrace in 1888, as VI.C.7(1) indicates, but in 1893. Rudy is not to be conceived and born in 1892 and to die in 1893 [VI.C.7(1)], but in 1893 and 1894. Bloom did not work for Joe Cuffe in 1896 and 1897 [VI.C.(2)] but in 1893 and 1894. There are other such changes of plans.

There are likewise some suggested events that never turn up in the novel. For example VI.C.7(1) has an entry for 1890: "LB's mother?" My guess is that Joyce intended at one time to have her die in that year. But in the novel nothing is explicitly said about the date of her death, although it is reasonably clear from the general context that she died before her husband Rudolph, who in the novel dies in 1886. Again in VI.C.7(1), for 1894 there is a note for the Blooms to leave Lamb Street. But in *Ulysses* they never live on Lamb Street. There is the possibility, of course, that Lombard Street (West) was meant here and that "Lamb" is Mme. Raphael's mistranscription.

But there is at least one unmistakable congruence between the chronologies and the chronological facts of *Ulysses* itself. Of all the entries the one for the year 1894 in VI.C.7(1) contains the largest number of separate notations, and in *Ulysses* (154) this same constellation, plus other matters, constitutes Bloom's largest single and most complicated remembrance of factual things past. Its complexities are discussed in detail in my entry for the year 1894.

The present work has multiple purposes. First, it is meant to serve as an introduction to Joyce for the uninitiated who are, understandably, intimidated by the bulk and complexity of *Ulysses* in toto. Second, it attempts to provide answers for some factual problems concerning the lives of the Blooms that have perplexed close students of the book; i.e., the years in which Bloom held his various jobs, and the years in which the Blooms lived at their various residences; the month that Bloom proposed to Molly; the year in which the Blooms moved to Eccles Street; and so on. In addition it extracts from the great atemporal flux of *Ulysses* certain episodes in the lives of the Blooms that even the most careful reader might miss, as, for example, what I call the "Gardiner St.-Old Glynn —*Stabat Mater*" complex, which took place in 1903 or 1904 and involved Father Conmee, Father Bernard Vaughan, Father Farley, Bloom, and a superb performance by Molly of Rossini's "Stabat Mater" in a Jesuit Church (see pp. 213-215 below). Beyond this the book addresses itself to some of the many leg-pulls, purposeful mystifications, and, admittedly sometimes virtually insoluble enigmas that Joyce put into the book. For example, I think it is reasonably certain that "Major" Tweedy, Molly's father, was in fact not an officer but a sergeant major (see pp. 78-80 below).

More importantly, the present endeavor highlights, as no other method could, the immense and detailed naturalistic base upon which *Ulysses* is constructed. Ever since its publication, more than a half century ago, it has been its Blakean or symbolic side that has attracted the attention or concern of both readers and critics. My concern is to lay out in chronological order the Defoe-esque or narrative side, and in addition to point up how much of the novel is "remembrance of things past." I estimate that roughly 50,000 of the 350,000 words of *Ulysses* are given to that past. In this buried narrative of *Ulysses* both the spirit and the method of Defoe are manifest. In 1912 Joyce delivered a lecture on Defoe in Trieste, and his description of Defoe's methods is a forecast of the naturalistic side of *Ulysses*. In analyzing Defoe's "The Storm" Joyce speaks of Defoe's prelude, an inquiry into the causes of winds, famous storms in human history, the successive piling up of information and details, until, "finally the narrative, like a great snake, begins to crawl slowly through a tangle of letters and reports."[1] At last the storm itself is completely, utterly, uniquely evoked: "By dint of repetitions, contradictions, details, figures, noises, the storm has come alive, the ruin is visible."[2]

1. James Joyce, "Daniel Defoe," ed. and trans. Joseph Prescott, *Buffalo Studies* I (December 1964), p. 15.
    2. *Ibid.*, p. 16.

Repetitions, contradictions, details, figures, noises: all these help to make the great snake of the Chronicle of the Blooms crawl along.

In keeping with my naturalistic bias, I have tried to confine most of my quotations to the actual train of thought of each Bloom; that is to say, the bulk of the quotations are from Calypso, Lotus Eaters, Hades, Lestrygonians, Sirens, Nausicaa and Penelope. However, since many memories of Bloom are dramatized in Circe, I cite from that section as well, and from Cyclops, whose narrator, the Nameless One, is a rhetorician of Dublinese without peer. Relevant material from such sections as Ithaca or Oxen of the Sun or Eumaeus is often, although not always, either paraphrased or merely cited by page number and line(s). The Chronicle is thus in great part a compendium of the Blooms' own thoughts on their respective and mutual pasts, given in their own unique vocabularies, idioms, and styles of rhetoric. Bloom's thought is sometimes paraphrasable, although rather seldom, and Molly's is virtually never so. In her simplest and shortest statements the inimicable and meaningful rhetorical touch is always there. I have come to believe that only her pronouns and articles carry no extra message, and even amongst these abstractions the defining touch at times appears. Thus amidst the enormous number of "he's" (Bloom, Boylan, Mulvey, Dedalus, and so on) that punctuate her monologue there are a few "He's," i.e., Jesus Christ. Only she can speak for herself, and I always allow her to do so.

Most importantly, Bloom takes on new dimensions when viewed chronologically. In fact, there are some six Blooms in *Ulysses,* for Joyce has carefully woven into his character's history a Proustian curve, a continuing series of metamorphoses. Bloom number six, of June 16, 1904, whom I do not attempt to set forth in the Chronology for obvious reasons, is not the same Bloom as the other Blooms who lie concealed or obscured in the dark backward and abysm of time and text. Readers, of course, must judge these matters for themselves, but I should point out the major periods: first, the child-boy-adolescent from 1866 to the 1880s; second, the twenty-one- to twenty-two-year-old suitor for Molly's hand in 1887-1888; third, the happy husband of the early married years, 1888-1893; fourth, the most un-Bloomlike Bloom, the aggressive maladroit of the years 1893-1894; fifth, the protean, complex, and many-sided Bloom that arises before the reader's eyes only at the end of *Ulysses* in the Penelope section, Molly's final monologue, the lengthiest, most complicated, and most detailed picture of a husband by a wife in literature. In turn Molly's portrayal of her husband has, generally, three chronological dimensions. First, there are the remembrances, almost wholly favorable, of the Bloom of the courtship years; second, there are her long-term opinions of him, some favorable, some unfavorable, some intuited early on, some learned only by long experience; third, there are her opinions of her husband in the present, in the early morning hours of June 17, 1904.

As for Molly herself, the Chronicle greatly enlarges her role over what it is in the novel itself. For throughout the whole of the Chronicle her voice is constantly heard, as one supposes it must often have been heard by her husband during the seventeen years, sixteen of them married, in which he has had the inestimable pleasure of her incomparable company. Just as she dominates the end of *Ulysses* by virtue of being the sole voice left, so she dominates the end of the Chronicle by virtue of the fact that her thoughts, plans, hopes, fantasies about the future, beginning with the morning of June 17, far outnumber those of her husband, as he had adumbrated them throughout his day and night. One could say that this discrepancy is the result only of the simple fact that she is awake and he is asleep. True, but this is still how it works out. If Molly occupies around 6 percent (45 of 783 pages) of *Ulysses,* she occupies more than 50 percent of the Chronicle. As *Ulysses* is Bloom's book, the Chronicle is in a sense hers. At least she's not all huddled at the back.

When Molly's menstrual comes on her, she exclaims, "O Jamsey let me up out of this" (769), a phrase that has often been taken as her asking her creator, Jamsey, to let her out of the book (an interpretation echoed by many a Joyce scholar, including, at times, the present one). The Chronicle provides at least a partial release of this un-sentimental, shrewd, and rather formidable woman who, unlike her gentle archetype, Homer's Penelope, is able to, and does, slaughter, verbally, the suitors; for in Joyce's version of the return of Odysseus to his home and his wife it is Penelope rather than her husband who strings the bow and wings the suitors. To give a few examples: John Henry Menton, who in 1887 was one of Bloom's rivals for her affections, "of all the big stupoes I ever met and thats called a solicitor" (739); Lenehan, who on a winter's night in an open carriage in 1894 got very close to her Junoesque person, "that sponger he was making free with me after the Glencree dinner coming back that long joult over the featherbed mountain" (750); Hugh Boylan, with whom she has just been in bed on the late afternoon and early evening of June 16, 1904, "of course hes right enough in his way to pass the time as a joke sure you might as well be in bed with what with a lion God Im sure hed have something better to say for himself an old Lion would" (776). Ulysses-Bloom is winged repeatedly (although never mortally), as is the male genus (Irish branch) and a few desultory females here and there.

However, it should be added that the Chronicle also distorts the meaning of the novel since in *Ulysses* itself Molly at the conclusion of her great monologue is no longer scattering verbal darts but is in the grip of a powerful secular vision, an affirmation of the beauties of nature and of romantic love, all culminating in her final, reverberating, reconciling "Yes." But the roots of the vision go back to her experiences with Mulvey in 1886 and with Bloom in 1888, and thus the vision itself appears in 1886 and 1888 in the Chronicle.

All of which is to say that the Chronicle is no substitute for the novel, merely an introduction.

Matters Genealogical

The genealogies of the main characters of *Ulysses* present some interesting problems and mysteries. Did Joyce intend plain mystification? or did he bury the answers to the mysteries in other parts of the book or in notes for the book or in other works (*Finnegans Wake* is a possible repository)? or did he just make plain errors by not always tying up his loose ends? The answers to these questions I do not at present know.

The first of Bloom's ancestors who is mentioned in the book (724:27-28), his great-grandfather, was an eighteenth-century man and was said to have actually seen the Empress Maria Theresa (1717-1780), Empress of Austria and Queen of Hungary. His son, Leopold Bloom's grandfather, first appears in 1852 along with his son Rudolph, Leopold's father, in a faded daguerreotype which was executed in the portrait atelier of a cousin of theirs, Stefan Virag of Szesfehervar (properly Székesfhérvar), Hungary, and which is in Bloom's drawer at 7 Eccles Street: "An indistinct daguerreotype of Rudolph Virag and his father Leopold Virag" (723). But Bloom's grandfather has already appeared in Circe, only not as Leopold Virag but first as Lipoti Virag (511:20) and second as Virag Lipoti (511:29). The first confusion comes here. Whether Joyce was playing some elaborate game or

The Genealogies of Leopold and Molly Bloom

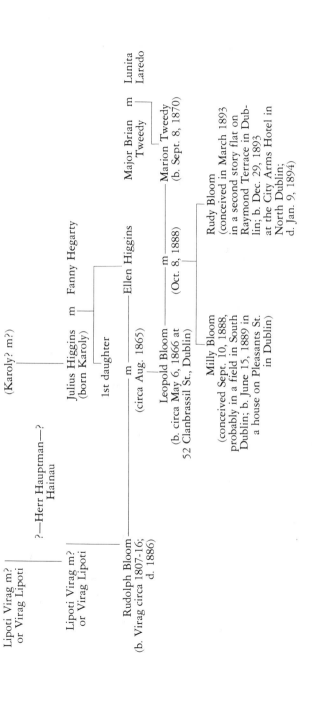

whether he was not too familiar with Hungarian nomenclature I shall leave to the reader to decide.

For Joyce's Hungarian I have relied on three Hungarian-speaking colleagues at the University of California: Professors Julia Bader, Andrew Janos, and Charles Tobias. They did not always agree on the exact meaning of Hungarian words and phrases in *Ulysses,* and since all these words and phrases are a transliteration into English from the Magyar, or Finno-Ugric, language, it is difficult to get two experts to agree upon just what were Joyce's intentions in this matter. I was assured, however, that Joyce's Hungarian was less than exact.

I present then alternative explanations.

In Hungarian nomenclature the family name always comes first, and sometimes ends in an "i," and the given name comes last. Lipot is Hungarian for Leopold and becomes a family name by virtue of the addition of "i." However, Lipot is also a place name, and when a person is designated as "Lipoti" it could mean "from or of Lipot." Virag means "flower," is not usually a given name, and is never such for a man. There are several possible interpretations of all this. In *Ulysses,* as pointed out above, this familial name is put both ways: "Lipoti Virag" (342, 511) and "Virag Lipoti" (511). It appears then that Joyce gave Bloom's paternal ancestors two family names rather than a family name and a given name, and that he may not have known that in Hungarian the family name comes first. The presumption is he did not since he refers to Bloom's father and grandfather as "Rudolph Virag" and "Leopold Virag" and to Rudolph's cousin as "Stefan Virag" (723). However, there is a possibility that Joyce's Hungarian was correct and that "Virag" was meant to be the family name. Jews were often designated by the place they came from plus their family name. Thus "Lipoti Virag" could mean a

Jew named Virag who came from Lipot. The trouble with this interpretation is that Rudolph Bloom did not come from Lipot, at least we are not told so. A further complication is that Lipot is the name of the Jewish community of Budapest, and by extension can be the name of any Jewish community. For a Jew living in Budapest, where Rudolph Virag once lived, "Lipoti" would tell others that he was Jewish. "Virag" was probably a Hungarianization of the German "Blum."

Szombathely, Rudolph Bloom's home town, means literally "Saturday place." Szesfehervar (properly, Székesfhérvar"), where the daguerreotype of Leopold Virag and Rudolph Virag (Bloom) was taken (723), is an ancient and important, though small, town in Hungary and a bishop's seat.

All my informants told me that Joyce consistently mistransliterated his Hungarian. Thus when Bloom flees Barney Kiernan's pub, all are invited to "bid farewell to Nagyaságos (properly "Nagysàgos") uram Lipóti Virag" (342), meaning, "Your greatness, My Lord." Bloom is also given a Hungarian salutation: "*Visszontlátásra* [properly "Viszontlàtàsra"] *Kedvés* [properly "kedves"] *baráton* [properly "baràton"]! *Visszontlátásra!*" (343), which means "Goodbye ("see you again") my dear fellow! Goodbye!" This is one of a number of conventional Hungarian salutations which were carefully adjusted to one's class standing and were strictly observed. The one accorded to Bloom indicates he is a middle-class man, not an "eminence" or "dignitary." In the eighteenth century the phrase meant something like "Your Highness," but became debased by overuse. Still it is an honorific accorded only to a professional or a man of means.

There is just one indisputable fact here: Joyce wanted to name his hero "Leopold Bloom" and may or may not have found the proper Hungarian correlative nomenclature for his hero's ancestry.

When Rudolph Bloom dies in 1886, he is said to be a septuaginarian (724:6), which means he could have been any age from seventy to seventy-nine. [In Cyclops the Nameless One calls him "old Methusalem Bloom" (336).] This means that Rudolph must have been born sometime between 1807 and 1816. (We never, of course, get a month and a day for him.) In 1852 then, when the daguerreotype was taken, he would have been somewhere between thirty-six and forty-five. Sometime after 1852 he must have left his ancestral home in Hungary to begin his middle phase as the Wandering Jew: "Szombathely, Vienna, Budapest, Milan, London, and Dublin" (682); "Dublin, London, Florence, Milan, Vienna, Budapest, Szombathely" (724). In 1865 he finally turned up in London: "Year before I [Leopold] was born that was sixtyfive" (76). By this time Bloom Sr. must have been between forty-nine and fifty-eight years of age. Sometime that year, either in London or Dublin, he met and married, we suppose, one Ellen Higgins. Leopold Bloom, their first and only child, was born sometime around May 6, 1866, which means that he must have been conceived in August of 1865.[1] His father would have been between fifty and

1. In the cabman's shelter, the men are talking about the Phoenix Park murders and Bloom reminisces: "when it took the civilised world by storm, figuratively speaking, early in the eighties, eightyone to be correct, when he was just turned fifteen." (629) There is a famous goof or spoof here, known to all Joyceans and never satisfactorily explained. Earlier in the book, in the newspaper office, Myles Crawford also misdates the Phoenix Park murders: "That was in eightyone, sixth of May, time of the invincibles, murder in the Phoenix Park [...]" (136). Actually the Phoenix Park murders occurred on May 6, 1882. Bloom is correct, however, in saying that he would have turned fifteen on his birthday in May 1881 since he was born in 1866, and the May 6 gives us the month and approximate day of his birth. Why both Bloom

fifty-nine when Leopold was born. Leopold Bloom is thus the only child of a rather elderly man. All of this, of course, adds to the pathos of the story of the Blooms, father and son, and points to the extinction of the male line in little Rudy.

About the time of Leopold Bloom's birth—it is not quite clear exactly when—Rudolph Virag, by now living on Clanbrassil Street in Dublin, changed his name to Bloom (723:18-22). In any event the infant Bloom is baptized "Leopold Paula Bloom" (723).

Rudolph Bloom's wife Ellen was the second daughter of Julius Higgins (born Karoly) and Fanny Hegarty (682:11-13). Fanny Hegarty was obviously Irish, but Julius Higgins was not. Leopold Bloom is thus one-quarter Irish through his maternal grandmother. "Karoly" is an extremely common Hungarian name. It was the name of a distinguished aristocratic Hungarian family, the most famous member of which was Count Mihaly Karolyi (1875-1955), a liberal-socialist political leader who spent much of his later life in exile. In the final "yi" of Karolyi the "y" belongs to the preceding "l," and when an

---

and Crawford would be a year off on the correct date of this gory event in fairly recent Irish history I do not know. Studies of human memory demonstrate that among the dates we remember most accurately are those of great national events, especially calamities, as with the date of the Japanese attack on Pearl Harbor for many living Americans. Myles Crawford's slip is even more egregious, for he is talking to Stephen Dedalus, and he goes on to say "before you were born." (136) Well, Stephen Dedalus (or James Joyce) was born in February 1882 and certainly knew that the Phoenix Park murders occurred in May of that same year. Moreover, other Irishmen, some of them professional, are listening to this conversation in the newspaper office and none of them correct Crawford's mistake. The only explanation I can think of is that this is Joyce's way of saying that while these people are very retrospective and memory-mongering, they are not certain of—and couldn't care less about—their facts.

"i" is added, the name signifies an aristocratic family. Bloom's maternal grandfather "Karoly" is thus a non-aristocratic bearer of this name. For a bearer of the name of Karoly there are three possibilities: he could have been a Hungarian; he could—most likely—have been a Hungarian Jew; and he could have been a Hungarian Jew, originally with a Jewish name, who bought the name of Karoly during the period when the Jews were forced to give up their Jewish ones and adopt, with appropriate payment, German ones. My own guess is that Karoly was probably Jewish, thus making Leopold Bloom (with an infusion of something else, as will be shown below) approximately three-quarters Hungarian Jew and the offspring of *two* Hungarian Jews who moved to Ireland, married Irish women and changed their names. I further suspect, knowing Joyce, that Karoly was not the original name which the father of Higgins changed to Karoly. With Higgins then, if I am correct here, we have three names: the original Jewish name of Karoly's father, Karoly, and Higgins.[2]

Ellen Higgins, the second daughter of Julius and Fanny Higgins and the mother of Leopold Bloom, is thus half Irish and half Hungarian Jewess. This fact perhaps helps to explain her marriage—rather strange on the face of it—to Rudolph Bloom, a foreigner in his fifties whom she met and married in 1865.

Molly Bloom, born September 8, 1870 (736:5), is the daughter, so it is alleged, of Major Brian Tweedy and

2. In the genealogy of Higgins (above) I have put his presumed father in parentheses, viz. "Karoly? m?," because he is never mentioned in the book, the word Karoly appearing only once. What this man's real name was we cannot be sure, or whom he married. Thus the question mark for his wife. Similarly, we know nothing of the wives of the two Lipoti Virags, and hence the question marks there in the genealogy.

Lunita Laredo (761:39), evidently a demimondaine. There
might have been no marriage here, and Molly might be
illegitimate. In fact it is possible that she may not have
been the daughter of Tweedy. According to Molly's testimony her mother was a very active woman in her professional endeavors. Thinking of the Prince of Wales' visit to
Gibraltar "the year I was born" (Molly must have been
conceived in December, 1869), Molly asserts, "he [the
Prince of Wales] planted the tree he planted more than
that in his time he might have planted me too if hed come
a bit sooner then I wouldnt be here as I am" (752).[3] If
Lunita Laredo could have been the object of the tender
affections of the Prince of Wales, then she must have been
a member of the aristocracy of her profession. Molly
makes one other, rather enigmatic statement about her
mother: "he [Bloom] thinks nothing can happen without
him knowing he hadnt an idea about my mother till we
were engaged otherwise hed never got me so cheap as he
did he was 10 times worse himself" (745-46). I do not
know quite what to make of this statement. One's suspi-
cions about Tweedy's paternity are increased by Molly's
assertion that she got her eyes and figure from her mother
while all she got from her "father" was his brogue
(762:43-763:2). However, there is the counter-assertion
of Molly when she mentions having "the map of it
[Ireland] all" on her face (748). Finally, to add a further
complication, Molly is not absolutely certain that Lunita
Laredo was, in fact, her mother: "my mother whoever she

3. The Prince of Wales, later Edward VI, visited Gibraltar in 1859
and 1876, but not in 1870. In 1870 he visited Egypt but did not pass
through Gibraltar; instead he went overland across Europe and then
sailed south across the Mediterranean to Egypt, returning in the same
fashion. Joyce's reference here is one of not a few factual obscurities or
mysteries in the book.

was" (761). In short, Molly's heritage is a tangle of ambiguities.

Leopold and Molly had sexual intercourse on September 10, 1888—they were married on October 8, 1888—and conceived Milly, their first and only surviving child (736:7-9). Milly was born on June 15, 1889 (736:6-7, and elsewhere). Now Milly turns out to be blond although both of her parents are dark-haired. A bit of murky light is thrown on this anomaly by a catechismal statement in Ithaca:

> 15 June 1889. A querulous newborn female infant crying to cause and lessen congestion [. . .] blond, born of two dark, she had blond ancestry, remote, a violation, Herr Hauptmann Hainau, Austrian army, proximate, a hallucination, lieutenant Mulvey, British Navy. (693)

I do not quite know what to make of the ambiguous reference to Mulvey. Joyce himself calls Mulvey's part in Milly's blondness a "hallucination." Further there was no sexual intercourse between Molly and Mulvey: "O yes I pulled him off into my handkerchief" (760), and finally the encounter to which she refers happened on Gibraltar in May of 1886: "May yes it was May when the infant king of Spain was born" (760).[4]

This leaves us with Herr Hauptmann Hainau of the Austrian army, who has to be a remote ancestor of Bloom rather than of Molly, who has, so far as we know, no central European connections in her family history—unless Lunita Laredo got over there in 1870 and got back very quickly. Furthermore, in Circe when Joe Hynes asks

4. This is a reference to Alphonso XIII, posthumous son of Alphonso XII, born in May 1886.

Bloom: "Why aren't you in uniform?" Bloom replies:
"When my progenitor of sainted memory wore the uniform of the Austrian despot in a dank prison where
was yours?" (488). Thus certain biological traits introduced into Bloom's genetic code by Herr Hainau but
which are recessive in him have become dominant in
Milly. Her blondness is underscored elsewhere, as in Circe
(542:13, 17). Milly is also completely indifferent to, and
has no talent for, music, a gift of her mother and a love
and preoccupation of her father. Thus Bloom in thinking
of music muses: "Milly no taste. Queer because we both
I mean" (278). On the other hand, Milly is *in esse*
very much a combination of a Bloom and a Tweedy (?), or,
especially, a Laredo (?). Bloom's father and grandfather
both had a taste for photography and Bloom, evidently,
thinks this penchant hangs on in Milly, which is why he
had encouraged her to go to Mullingar to work as a "photo
girl": "Now photography. Poor papa's daguerreotype
atelier he told me of. Hereditary taste" (155). Molly does
not agree with Bloom's judgment here: "such an idea for
him to send the girl down there to learn to take photographs on account of his grandfather" (766). But then
parents often disagree on what are the real traits of their
progeny and which side of the family the alleged traits
come from. Above all Milly is her mother's and grandmother's child, sexually precocious and sexually attractive,
and both parents dwell on this aspect in their memories of
her. Moreover, she has just turned fifteen on June 15 and is
thus the same age as her mother was when she had her
first experience with Mulvey. Bannon, her boyfriend in
Mullingar, will presumably play the same role with Milly
that Mulvey did with Molly. Milly's genetic inheritance
thus derives from Molly through perhaps Lunita Laredo
and whoever sired Molly, possibly Tweedy, and through

Bloom and his complex of forebears, with a "sport" element deriving from Hainau. The question here is whether Hainau came in on the Lipoti side or the Karoly side, but it is clear that one of Bloom's female ancestors had an interlude with Hainau.[5] How all this could have been achieved biologically and provide Bloom with an Austrian blood quotient exceeds my genetic grasp. In any event Hainau complicates things considerably, genetically speaking.

Thus Bloom finally turns out to be one-quarter Irish, something less than three-quarters Hungarian-Jewish, with an unspecified quotient of Austrian. And Milly turns out to be a kind of walking United Nations: Hungarian-Jewish-Austrian-Spanish-Irish.

One final thing about Bloom's family and inheritance: Joyce evidently intended it to be very strange and very complex, as indeed it turns out to be. Thus in Circe J. J. O'Molloy, Bloom's defender, says:

> I would deal in especial with atavism. There have been cases of shipwreck and somnambulism in my client's family. If the accused could speak he could a tale unfold one of the strangest that have ever been narrated between the covers of a book. (463)

Finally, as is customary in *Ulysses* for many matters, there is a dialectic between the mysterious and the absurd. The mysteries of the genealogies I have traced out above. But there is also a mock, pseudo-Biblical genealogy provided for Bloom, at some length, in Circe (495:34-496:8).

5. Haynau was the name of a man infamous in Hungarian history. When the revolution of 1848 was finally put down in 1849, and the reaction set in, Haynau was the state butcher: "the Hyena of Brescia."

A Note on the Typographical Format
of The Chronicle

In an attempt to keep the text as uncluttered as possible, I have adopted the following policy on ellipses. When an ellipsis occurs in a quotation from Joyce, it is his unless the ellipses points are in square brackets. Since there are no ellipses in Molly's monologue in Penelope, any ellipses that do occur in quotations from Penelope are mine even though I do not bracket them in the text. To avoid the multiplication of my own ellipses at the beginnings or the ends of fragments taken from sections of the book where the sentences tend to be long, as in Eumaeus, I have adopted the following policy: if a quotation begins with a small letter, it is not the beginning of a sentence but a fragment from a sentence. If the fragment begins with a capital letter, as happens infrequently, I insert an ellipsis to indicate that fact. As for the ends of fragments from Joyce's sentences: if there is no punctuation at all, or a comma, or any other mark of punctuation except a period, then one knows that the sentence continues on after my quotation has ceased. Every quotation and paraphrase is preceded by a colon. Joyce, or whoever was responsible, was not absolutely consistent about leaving out all punctuation, except for the final period, in Molly's monologue. There are a few apostrophes and periods, and I leave them in.

The citations are to the Random House 1961 edition of *Ulysses*, by page for quotations and by page and line number for paraphrases.

The Chronicle of Leopold and Molly Bloom

and Some of Their Friends and Acquaintances,
Together With the Chronology of Certain Events
Occurring On The Rock of Gibraltar and
In Dublin and Environs Long Antecedent To, Prior To,
And On the Day of June 16, 1904, Anno Domini,
In Holy Roman Catholic Ireland.

DOMINUS VOBISCUM   ORA PRO NOBIS

The narrative of the past; the contemplation of the present; and the expectations of the future.

EIGHTEENTH CENTURY

1. Leopold Bloom's great grandfather, Lipoti Virag, sees Maria Theresa (1717-1780), Empress of Austria and Queen of Hungary (724:27-28).

2. Bloom's grandfather follows certain immemorial Hebrew practices: "And the tephilim no what's this they call it poor papa's father had on his door to touch. That brought us out of the land of Egypt and into the house of bondage." (378) [Bloom here mistakes the tephilim for the mezuzah, a scroll affixed to the right side of the door of the Jewish home. It is to be touched or kissed as one passes through (G. and T.).]

3. One of Bloom's female ancestors goes over the fence with an Austrian, Herr Hauptmann Hainau (693:6-8). Herr Hauptmann Hainau is incarcerated in Austria (488: 22-24).

Nineteenth Century

c. 1807-1816. Rudolph Virag is born (said to be a septuagenarian when he dies in 1886) (724:6).

1852. A daguerreotype is taken of Rudolph Virag (age thirty-six to forty-five) with his father Leopold Virag in the portrait atelier of Stefan Virag, a cousin, in Szesfehervar, Hungary (723:25-28).

1850s. Simon Dedalus (b. 1849) as a boy hears the Italians singing in Queenstown harbor (278:38-279:2).

1850s and subsequently. Joseph Nannetti's father hawks religious articles on the streets of Dublin: "By Cantwell's offices roved Greaseabloom [Leopold], by Ceppi's virgins, bright of their oils. Nannetti's father hawked those things about, wheedling at doors as I. Religion pays. Must see him about Keyes's par." (260) [Nannetti (1851-1915) was a Dublin master printer and an M.P. Bloom talks to him in the office and printing establishment of the *Freeman's Journal* at noon on June 16, 1904, about his ad for Alexander Keyes, and he evidently plans to talk to him about it again. Ceppi, P. & Sons was a picture-frame and looking-glass factory and statuary manufacturer.]

c. 1852-1865. Rudolph Bloom as the Wandering Jew; leaves his native Szombathely for Vienna, Budapest, Milan, London and Dublin (682:10-11); Dublin, London, Florence, Milan, Vienna, Budapest (724:25-26). In Vienna he sees the great actress Ristori play in "Leah" and he is later to tell his son, repeatedly, of the power of the play:

And Ristori in Vienna. What is this the right name is? By Mosenthal it is. Rachel, is it? No. The scene he was always talking about where the old blind Abraham recognizes the voice and puts his fingers on his face.

—Nathan's voice! His son's voice! I hear the voice of Nathan who left his father to die of grief and misery in my arms, who left the house of his father and left the God of his father.

Every word is so deep, Leopold. (76)

[Both G. and T. discuss certain mistakes made here.]

1865. THE CHRONICLE PROPER BEGINS

1. Rudolph Virag turns up in London: "Year before I was born that was: sixty five." (76)

2. Rudolph sees the great actress Kate Bateman play Hamlet: "Poor papa! How he used to talk about Kate Bateman in that! Outside the Adelphi in London waited all the afternoon to get in." (76) [Star actresses in the nineteenth century did, on occasion, play male roles.]

3. Rudolph Virag, by now in Dublin, is converted to the Irish Protestant Church by the Society for Promoting Christianity Among the Jews (716:23-27): "Society over the way papa went to for the conversion of poor jews." (180)

4. July. Leopold Bloom is conceived; by this time Rudolph Virag has married Fanny Higgins, second daughter of Julius (born Karoly) and Fanny (born Hegarty) Higgins (682:9-13).

1866

1. A star appears for Leopold Bloom's birth (700:41-701:3). [A nova, T. Coronae Borealis, did appear in May 1866 (G.).]

2. c. May 6. Leopold Bloom (his father being between ages fifty and fifty-nine) is born in Ireland: "Year before I was born that was: sixtyfive," (76) "Ireland my country." (118)—"What is your nation if I may ask, says the citizen.—Ireland, says Bloom. I was born here. Ireland." (331) [For the month and day of Bloom's birth see the

discussion in footnote 1, pp. 15-16 above.] The ill-effects of Bloom's having been born in Ireland:

> [he] is at his best an exotic tree which, when rooted in its native orient, throve and flourished and was abundant in balm but, transplanted to a clime more temperate, its roots have lost their quondam vigour while the stuff that comes away from it is stagnant, acid and inoperative. (410)

3. Rudolph Virag changes his name to Bloom and settles down at 52 Clanbrassil Street in Dublin. A press clipping of the change of name still resides in Bloom's desk in 1904 (723:18-22).

The name-change of the Blooms is also alluded to by Martin Cunningham in a discussion of Bloom in Barney Kiernan's pub (337:36-38), by Bloom in an hallucination in Bella Cohen's brothel (455:27), and by Bloom in a conversation with Stephen Dedalus in Skin-the-Goat's cab shelter (623:2).

4. Leopold Bloom is baptized as a Protestant in the Church of Saint Nicholas Without, Coombe, by the reverend Mr. Gilmer Johnston, M.A. (682:18-20).

1869

December. Marion Tweedy conceived, probably out of wedlock, perhaps of a union between Lunita Laredo and, possibly, Major Brian Cooper Tweedy in Gibraltar.

1870

Molly.

1. September 8. Marion Tweedy born (736:5): "my mother whoever she was might have given me a nicer name the Lord knows after the lovely one she had Lunita Laredo" (761) "Ive my mothers eyes and figure anyhow he [her father] always said" (763)

2. HRH, then the Prince of Wales, later Edward VII, visits Gibraltar (752:8). [See footnote 3, p. 18 above.]

1872

Bloom.

1. Rudolph (now between ages fifty-six and sixty-five) tells Leopold (age six) of his migratory life and gives his son some financial advice: "(having taken care of pence, the pounds having taken care of themselves)." (724) Leopold follows his father's narrative by reference to a map of Europe and exhibits a precocious interest in commercial enterprise:

> Leopold Bloom (aged 6) had accompanied these narrations by constant consultation of a geographical map of Europe (political) and by suggestions for the establishment of affiliated business premises in the various centres mentioned. (724) [This constitutes Bloom's earliest remembrance of his father.]

1874

Bloom.

1. Leopold (age eight) begins to ponder a life-long question: "Where was Moses when the candle went out?" (729)

1870s

Molly, as a child on Gibraltar.

1. Motherless: "hadnt all a mother to look after them what I never had" (778)

2. The thunderbolts: "like those awful thunderbolts in Gibraltar" (741)

3. The heat:

Gibraltar my goodness the heat there before the levanter
came on black as night and the glare of the rock standing up
in it like a big giant compared with their 3 Rock mountain [a
mountain south of Dublin] they think is so great with the red
sentries here and there the poplars and they all whitehot and
the mosquito nets and the smell of the rainwater in those
tanks watching the sun all the time weltering down on you
(755)

4. The sea and the fishermen:

because the smell of the sea excited me of course the sardines
and the bream in Catalan bay round the back of the rock they
were fine all silver in the fishermens baskets old Luigi near a
hundred they said came from Genoa and the tall old chap
with the earrings (765)

5. The exotic names:

like those names in Gibraltar Delapaz Delagracia they had
the devils queer names there father Vial plana of Santa
Maria that gave me the rosary Rosales y OReilly in the Calle
las Siete Revueltas and Pisimbo and Mrs Opisso in Governor
street O what a name Id go and drown myself in the first
river if I had a name like her O my and all the bits of streets
Paradise ramp and Bedlam ramp and Rodgers ramp and
Crutchetts ramp and the devils gap steps (779)

6. Regiments on Parade:

I love to see a regiment pass in review the first time I saw the
Spanish cavalry   at La Roque it was lovely after looking
across the bay from Algeciras all the lights of the rock like
fireflies . . . the Black Watch with their kilts in time at the
march past the 10th hussars the prince of Wales own or the
lancers O the lancers theyre grand or the Dublins that won
Tugela (749)

7. Little education:

> instead of sending her [Milly] to Skerrys academy where shed have to learn not like me getting all at school (766) [Skerry's was a commercial school in Dublin which taught shorthand and typing (G.).] well small blame to me if I am a harumscarum I know I am a bit I declare to God I dont feel a day older than then I wonder could I get my tongue round any of the Spanish como esta usted muy bien gracias y usted see I havent forgotten it all I thought I had only for the grammar a noun is the name of any person place or thing pity I never tried to read that novel cantankerous Mrs Rubio lent me (779) [The Spanish means, "How are you? Very well, thank you, and you?" Mrs. Rubio, an elderly woman, was a servant of the Tweedys (G.).]

8. Sham battles: "or those sham battles on the 15 acres" (749) [Molly appears to be fusing separate memories here, as the fifteen acres is a well-known section of Phoenix Park in Dublin where, as G. points out, military reviews and exercises were occasionally held. Both of the Blooms have fusion memories, that is, in their remembrance of things past two events separate in time but similar in circumstance sometimes coalesce.]

9. Funerals: "if they saw a real officers funeral thatd be something reversed arms muffled drums the poor horse walking behind in black" (773)

Bloom as a child at 52 Clanbrassil St.

1. A bed wetter (537:9-10).

2. Attends Mrs. Ellis's day school and plays marbles: "And once I played marbles when I went to that old dame's school. She liked mignonette. Mrs Ellis's. And Mr?" (77)

3. His nightly ritual:

> Because the odour [of toe-jams] inhaled corresponded to other odours inhaled of other unguical fragments, picked and lacerated by Master Bloom, pupil of Mrs Ellis's juvenile school, patiently each night in the act of brief genuflection and nocturnal prayer and ambitious meditation. (712)

4. Makes anagrams on his name:

> Leopold Bloom
> Ellpodbomool
> Molldopeloob.
> Bollopedoom
> Old Ollebo, M.P. (678)

5. Looks out of the window of 52 Clanbrassil:

Because in middle youth he had often sat observing through a rondel of bossed glass of a multicoloured pane the spectacle offered with continual changes of the thoroughfare without, pedestrians, quadrupeds, velocipedes, vehicles, passing slowly, quickly, evenly, round and round and round the rim of a round precipitous globe. (681)

1877

Bloom.

1. Aged eleven, he composes his first verse, in an attempt to win one of three prizes offered by the *Shamrock,* a weekly newspaper, in a poetry contest:

> *An ambition to squint*
> *At my verses in print*
> *Makes me hope that for these you'll find room.*
> *If you so condescend*
> *Then please place at the end*
> *The name of yours truly, L. Bloom.* (678)

2. The battle of Plevna. Joyce said of his work, "I've put in so many enigmas and puzzles that it will keep the professors busy for centuries arguing over what I meant, and that's the only way of insuring one's immortality." (E., p. 535.) There are thus many leg-pulls in the novel, and the frequent references to the battle of Plevna constitute one of them. Major Tweedy claimed to have been at Plevna and to have risen from the ranks for his conduct during the battle (56:32-33). Plevna is also recalled by Bloom in an hallucination in Bella Cohen's (484:4-7), and in a quiet retrospective in his own home before he retires, just after he looks at his library, which contains, among other items, Hozier's *History of the Russo-Turkish War* (710:1-11). Molly also remembers her father and a friend discussing battles, Plevna being one (757:21).

Plevna, in Bulgaria, was the site of three battles, and a siege, between the Russians and the Turks in 1877. It became world renowned because of the tenacity of the Turks who, occupying Plevna, held off three assaults by the Russians during the summer and fall of that year. They finally did capitulate on December 10. It would have been impossible for the Royal Dublin Fusiliers, Tweedy's regiment, to have participated in this affair. There were individuals of European nationality, volunteers, fighting with the Turks. One of them, Frederick William Von Herbert, a British subject, wrote a book about it, *The Defence of Plevna* (London, 1911). Von Herbert says there were quite a few foreign surgeons: three Germans, three English, one French, one Swiss, one Austrian, ten or twelve Jewish (Austrian, Polish, Hungarian). But so far as I know, Russian armies employed only Russian nationals or those whom the government deemed Russian nationals.

Plevna captured the imagination of the Western world because of its David-and-Goliath or Jack-the-Giant-Killer aspect: little Turkey holding off huge Russia. The appeal to Joyce, an Irishman, should be obvious.

1878

Molly.

November 17. Molly (age eight) hears the guns booming for Ulysses S. Grant's visit to Gibraltar:

> their damn guns bursting and booming all over the shop especially the Queens birthday [May 24] and throwing everything down in all directions if you didnt open the windows when general Ulysses Grant whoever he was or did supposed to be some great fellow landed off the ship and old Sprague the consul that was there from before the flood dressed up poor man and he in mourning for the son (757) [Grant arrived in Gibraltar by boat from Cadiz on November 17, 1878. The American Consul, Mr. Sprague, met him.]

1878, 1879, 1880

Bloom in Dublin High School.

1. Learns a smattering of classics: "I call that patriotism. *Ubi patria,* as we learned a small smattering of in our classical day in *Alma Mater, vita bene.* Where you can live well, the sense is, if you work." (644)

2. Writes moral essays: "essays on various subjects or moral apothegms (e.g. *My Favourite Hero* or *Procrastination is the Thief of Time*) composed during school-years," (685)

3. Is most impressed by, and remembers or mis-remembers (and mixes up) the most from, Vance, the physics teacher: "Vance in High school cracking his

fingerjoints, teaching. The college curriculum. Cracking curriculum." (72)

[Vance laid the foundations for Bloom's life-long interest in science which was later supplemented by the reading of popular books of scientific explanation.]

Gravity:

> Where was the chap I saw in that picture somewhere? Ah, in the dead sea, floating on his back, reading a book with a parasol open. Couldn't sink if you tried: so thick with salt. Because the weight of the water, no, the weight of the body in the water is equal to the weight of the. Or is it the volume is equal of the weight? It's a law something like that [. . . .] What is weight really when you say the weight? Thirtytwo feet per second, per second. Law of falling bodies: per second, per second. They all fall to the ground. The earth. It's the force of gravity of the earth is the weight. (72)

Gravity surfaces in Bloom's mind periodically throughout the day and night of June 16 (152:28-29; 486:24; 528:17-18; 550:11-12).

Roygbiv, the rays of the spectrum: "Some light still [it is evening]. Red rays are longest. Roygbiv Vance taught us: red, orange, yellow, green, blue, indigo, violet." (376) [Vance taught his pupils a handy way to memorize the spectrum: "Red, Orange, Yellow, Green, Blue, Indigo, Violet" spells "Roygbiv."]: "(*He* [Bloom] *performs juggler's tricks, draws red, orange, yellow, green, blue, indigo and violet silk handkerchiefs from his mouth.*) Roygbiv." (486)

Acoustics (plus gravity):

> O, look we are so! Chamber music. Could make a kind of pun on that. It is a kind of music I often thought when she [that is, when Molly tinkles in the chamber pot]. Acoustics

that is. Tinkling. Empty vessels make most noise. Because the acoustics, the resonance changes according as the weight of the water is equal to the law of falling water. (282)

Properties of light: "Clearly I can see today. Moisture about gives long sight perhaps." (74)

Conduction of heat: "Be a warm day I fancy. Specially in these black clothes feel it more. Black conducts, reflects (refracts is it?), the heat." (57) [The question of whether black conducts, reflects, or refracts heat is never decided definitively by Bloom on June 16 (267:29-30; 374:32-33; 443:8-9). Actually, black absorbs heat.]

Archimedes:

Howth a while ago amethyst. Glass flashing. That's how that wise man what's his name with the burning glass. Then the heather goes on fire. It can't be tourists' matches. What? Perhaps the sticks dry rub together in the wind and light. Or broken bottles in the furze act as a burning glass in the sun. Archimedes. I have it! My memory's not so bad. (378)

Magnetism:

Also that now is magnetism. Back of everything magnetism. Earth for instance pulling this and being pulled. That causes movement. And time? Well that's the time the movement takes. Then if one thing stopped the whole ghesabo would stop bit by bit. Because it's arranged. Magnetic needle tells you what's going on in the sun, the stars. Little piece of steel iron. When you hold out the fork. Come. Come. Tip. Woman and man that is. Fork and steel. Molly, he [Boylan]. (374)

Computations: "As a physicist he had learned that of the 70 years of complete human life at least 2/7ths, viz., 20 years passed in sleep." (720)

A mélange: "Confused light confuses memory. Red influences lupus. Colours affect women's characters, any they have. This black makes me sad." (526)

4. Is a poor athlete: "Course I never could throw anything straight at school. Crooked as a ram's horn." (373) "He flung his wooden pen away. The stick fell in silted sand, stuck. Now if you were trying to do that for a week on end you couldn't. Chance." (382) But he is good on the parallel bars (681:31-35).

5. Bloom and his friends, Apjohn and Goldberg, play at being monkeys: "Apjohn, myself and Owen Goldberg up in the trees near Goose green playing the monkeys. Mackerel they called me." (162)

6. Not much luck with girls: "(*With pathos.*) No girl would when I went girling. Too ugly. They wouldn't play . . ." (550)

7. A Peeping Tom:

Lotty Clarke, flaxenhaired, I saw at her night toilette through ill-closed curtains, with poor papa's operaglasses. The wanton ate grass wildly. She rolled downhill at Rialto Bridge to tempt me with her flow of animal spirits. She climbed their crooked tree and I . . . A saint couldn't resist it. The demon possessed me. Besides, who saw? (549)

8. Either urinates or defecates or masturbates, or all three, in the cattle creep behind Killbarrack, under the Ballybough bridge, and in the devil's glen:

A CRAB
(*In bushranger's kit.*) What did you do in the cattlecreep behind Kilbarrack?
A FEMALE INFANT
(*Shakes a rattle.*) And under Ballybough bridge?
A HOLLY BUSH
And in the devil's glen?
BLOOM
(*Blushes furiously all over from front to nates, three tears falling from his left eye.*) Spare my past. (496)

9. Masturbates: "I was precocious. Youth. The fauns. I
sacrificed to the god of the forest. The flowers that bloom
in the spring. It was pairing time." (549) "Simply satisfy-
ing a need." (550)

10. A fellow student, Wilkins, draws Venus on the
blackboard: "never meet one like that Wilkins in the high
school drawing a picture of Venus with all his belongings
on show." (371)

11. Aspires to be a shoefitter at Mansfield's:

(*Murmurs lovingly.*) To be a shoefitter in Mansfield's was
my love's young dream, the darling joys of sweet button-
hooking, to lace up crisscrossed to kneelength the dressy kid
footwear satinlined, so incredibly small, of Clyde Road
ladies. Even their wax model Raymonde I visited daily to
admire her cobweb hose and stick of rhubarb toe, as worn in
Paris. (529)

1880

Bloom's last year in Dublin High.

1. That winter it snows: "(*Hobbledehoy, warmgloved,
mammamufflered, stunned with spent snowballs, strug-
gles to rise.*) Again! I feel sixteen! What a lark! Let's ring
all the bells in Montague Street. (*He cheers feebly.*)
Hurray for the High School!" (548) [Actually in the
winter of 1880 Bloom was thirteen; by the time of his
graduation he was fourteen.]

2. Bloom walking to school of a brisk morning:

That young figure of then is seen, precociously manly,
walking on a nipping morning from the old house in
Clambrassil street to the high school, his book satchel on
him bandolierwise, and in it a goodly hunk of wheaten loaf, a
mother's thought. (413) [Clanbrassil is misspelled here in
the text.]

3. Bloom wins a contest by urinating higher than any of his 210 classmates (703:3-5). Joyce's note on this extraordinary affair is, "urine = sea (girls who longest, boys who highest)" (H., p. 417.)

4. Bloom confesses to Percy Apjohn, evidently his best friend, his disbelief in Irish Protestantism (716:22-24). Sometime in the early eighties, after his abjuration of Irish Protestantism, occurred Bloom's second and secular baptism by James O'Connor, Philip Gilligan and James Fitzpatrick, together, under a pump in the village of Swords (682:20-21). There is some logic for Joyce having chosen Swords, a village north of Dublin, for the second baptism of his hero. "Swords" is an anglicized corruption of "Sord," meaning a pure well, and, in this instance, one which St. Columcille (Columbanus) is said to have blessed.

5. Sexually excitable:

(*Pigeonbreasted, bottleshouldered, padded, in nondescript juvenile grey and black striped suit, too small for him, white tennis shoes, bordered stockings with turnover tops, and a red school cap with badge.*) I was in my teens, a growing boy. A little then sufficed, a jolting car, the mingling odours of the ladies' cloakroom and lavatory, the throng penned tight on the old Royal stairs, for they love crushes, instincts of the herd, and the dark sexsmelling theatre unbridles vice. Even a pricelist of their hosiery. And then the heat. (548) [This recollection is tied to 1880 because at the conclusion of it he mentions the end of school—see No. 8 below.]

6. Encounters (no intercourse) a prostitute, Bridie Kelly, on a rainy night in Hatch St.:

He thinks of a drizzling night in Hatch street, hard by the bonded stores there, the first. Together (she is a poor waif, a child of shame, yours and mine and of all for a bare shilling and her luckpenny), together they hear the heavy tread of the watch as two raincaped shadows pass the new royal university [established in 1880]. Bridie! Bridie Kelly! He will never forget the name, ever remember the night, first night, the bridenight. They are entwined in nethermost darkness, the willer with the willed, and in an instant (*fiat!*) light shall flood the world. Did heart leap to heart? Nay, fair reader. In a breath 'twas done but—hold! Back! It must not be! In terror the poor girl flees away through the murk. She is the bride of darkness, a daughter of night. She dare not bear the sunny-golden babe of day. No, Leopold! Name and memory solace thee not. That youthful illusion of thy strength was taken from thee and in vain. (413) [Joyce's style here is meant to be imitative of that of the Gothic novel. Bridie Kelly reappears in an hallucination in Bella Cohen's (441:20-27).]

7. Acquaintance with Gerald, a homosexual, who imparts to young Leopold a fetish for female clothes; Bloom impersonates a female in a high school play, '*Vice Versa*':

(*Her* [Bloom is now a female] *hands and features working.*) It was Gerald converted me to be a true corsetlover when I was female impersonator in the High School play *Vice Versa*. It was dear Gerald. He got that kink, fascinated by sister's stays. Now dearest Gerald uses pinky grease-paint and gilds his eyelids. Cult of the beautiful. (536-537) Who's Ger Ger? Who's dear Gerald? O, I much fear he shall be most badly burned. (516-517) [uttered by Bloom's grandfather, in an hallucination at Bella Cohen's.]

8. A school picnic at Poulaphouca Falls, where Bloom retires to masturbate:

THE YEWS
(*Murmuring.*) Who came to Poulaphouca with the high school excursion? Who left his nutquesting classmates to seek our shade? (548)

9. School spirit, school friends, end of school, and summer:

There were sunspots that summer. End of school. And typsycake. Halcyon days.

(*Halcyon Days, high school boys in blue and white football jerseys and shorts, Master Donald Turnbull, Master Abraham Chatterton, Master Owen Goldberg, Master Jack Meredith, Master Percy Apjohn, stand in a clearing of the trees and shout to Master Leopold Bloom.*)

THE HALCYON DAYS

Mackerel! Live us again. Hurray!

(*They cheer.*) (548)

10. Apjohn takes Bloom's picture: "reclined laterally, left, with right and left legs flexed, the indexfinger and thumb of the right hand resting on the bridge of the nose, in the attitude depicted on a snapshot photograph made by Percy Apjohn," (737)

1880-1881

Molly (age ten) experiences a cold winter and contracts a continuing fear of gas:

> better than having him [Bloom] leaving the gas on all night I couldnt rest easy in my bed in Gibraltar even getting up to see why am I so damned nervous about that though I like it in the winter its more company O Lord it was rotten cold too that winter when I was only about ten was I yes I had the big doll with all the funny clothes dressing her up and undressing that icy wind skeeting across from those mountains the something Nevada sierra nevada standing at the fire with the little bit of a short shift I had up to heat myself I loved dancing about in it then make a race back into bed (763)

1881

Bloom goes to work as a salesman for his father:

Or it is the same figure, a year or so gone over [after high school], in his first hard hat (ah, that was a day!), already on the road, a fullfledged traveller for the family firm, equipped with an orderbook, a scented handkerchief (not for show only), his case of bright trinketware (alas, a thing now of the past!), and a quiverful of compliant smiles for this or that halfwon housewife reckoning it out upon her fingertips or for a budding virgin shyly acknowledging (but the heart? tell me!) his studied baisemoins. The scent, the smile but more than these, the dark eyes and oleaginous address brought home at duskfall many a commission to the head of the firm seated with Jacob's pipe after like labours in the paternal ingle (a meal of noodles, you may be sure, is aheating), reading through round horned spectacles some paper from the Europe of a month before. (413)

EARLY 1880s

Molly in adolescence.

1. A spirit of independence: "I was just like that [her daughter Milly] myself they darent order me about the place" (768)

2. Captain Groves, Tweedy's best friend:

drunken old devil with his grog on the windowsill catch him leaving any of it picking his nose trying to think of some other dirty story to tell up in a corner but he never forgot himself when I was there sending me out of the room on some blind excuse paying his compliments the Bushmills whiskey talking of course but hed do the same to the next woman that came along I supposed he died of galloping drink ages ago (757)

3. Coming home on the night boat from Tarifa:

where softly sighs of love the light guitar where poetry is in the air the blue sea and the moon shining so beautifully coming back on the nightboat from Tarifa the lighthouse at Europa point the guitar that fellow played was so expressive will I never go back there again all new faces two glancing eyes a lattice hid (775)

4. Tweedy gets a corner in stamps from an American who owns a squirrel:

> some liquor Id like to sip those richlooking green and yellow expensive drinks those stagedoor johnnies drink with the opera hats I tasted one with my finger dipped out of that American that had the squirrel talking stamps with father (741)

Bloom: "Hard as nails at a bargain, old Tweedy [....] Still he had brains enough to make that corner in stamps. Now that was farseeing." (56)

5. Tweedy buys her a second-hand bed:

> the lumpy old jingly bed always reminds me of old Cohen I suppose he scratched himself in it often enough and he [Bloom] thinks father bought it from Lord Napier that I used to admire when I was a little girl (772) O I like my bed (772) Im sick of Cohens old bed (780)

Bloom:

> He heard then a warm heavy sigh, softer, as she turned over and the loose brass quoits of the bedstead jingled. Must get them settled really. Pity. All the way from Gibraltar [....] Wonder what her father gave for it. Old style. Ah yes, of course. Bought it at the governor's auction. Got a short knock. Hard as nails at a bargain, old Tweedy. (56)

[The subject of the origin of Molly's bed constitutes a characteristic Joycean deflation. Molly has told Bloom that it had originally belonged to Lord Napier who had been governor of Gibraltar from 1876 to 1883. After his departure, presumably, the belongings and furnishings he left behind were auctioned off. Thus, as far as Bloom is concerned, the bed was purchased by Tweedy at the governor's auction in 1883. It is only at the end of the book that we learn that this bed (through the agency of *Ulysses* now become—along with its archetype, the bed of Odysseus and Penelope—one of the most celebrated beds in history) was in reality bought from "old Cohen," a pawn broker or used-furniture dealer, presumably. One David A. Cohen did keep a shop on Gibraltar (G.).]

6. "I always liked poetry when I was a girl" (775)

Bloom.

1. Sometime during this period, probably, Bloom works for Kellet's, a mail order house: "I can make a true black knot. Learned when I served my time and worked the mail order line for Kellet's. Experienced hand. Every knot says a lot." (529)

1882

Bloom.

1. Intends to devote the year of 1882 to a study of the religious problem and in attempts to square the circle and win a million pounds (514:33-515:2).

2. Advocates colonialism and evolutionism during nighttime walks to his friends Francis Wade and Daniel Magrane, who in this year emigrated from Ireland (716: 29-35).

3. The Phoenix Park murders and the Invincibles. In the fall of 1881 a group of Irish extremists, to be known as the Invincibles, organized. Their aim was assassination and their target was to be William Forster, a member of the English Parliament and Chief Secretary for Ireland. However, William Gladstone, who had become the British Prime Minister for the second time in 1880, with a virtual mandate to settle the "Irish question," had reached in the spring of 1882 a compromise agreement with Charles Stewart Parnell, the leader of the Irish party in Parliament. Forster regarded the settlement as too leni-

ent to the Irish. In consequence he resigned and was replaced by Lord Frederick Cavendish. By this time, apparently, the Invincibles' target was T. H. Burke, an under-secretary at Dublin castle, an Irishman himself, and therefore, doubly hateful. On May 6, 1882, Burke and Lord Frederick Cavendish, who had just arrived in Dublin, were walking in Phoenix Park where they were assassinated, by knife in broad daylight. Although the Invincibles were twenty in number, the actual killings were carried out by two young men, Joe Brady and Tim Kelly. Brady struck down the two men with powerful stabs and Tim Kelly cut the throats of the dying men as they lay on the ground. The assassins made their escape in one cab, and another cab driven by a man named Fitzharris acted as a decoy. Fitzharris is described by Tom Corfe in *The Phoenix Park Murders* (London, 1968) as "a coarsely cheerful, robust, and elderly man, well-known to Dubliners as 'Skin-the-Goat' because of a tale about his selling the hide of a pet animal to pay his drinking debts" (p. 144). At the subsequent trial in 1883, Skin-the-Goat was sentenced to life imprisonment, but was released in 1902.

Skin-the-Goat.

Bloom and Dedalus stop at a cabman's shelter for refreshment shortly after midnight (now June 17). The proprietor is rumored to be the legendary Skin-the-Goat, although this was most unlikely. No matter, the memory of the Invincibles lives on, and they and their deeds are discussed more in this section of the book, Eumaeus, than in any other. The difficulties of paraphrasing anything from the Eumaeus section are discussed in connection with Parnell (see pp. 111-112 below).

1. As the pair enters the cab shelter Bloom tells Stephen that it is rumored that the proprietor is the

famous "Skin-the-Goat" Fitzharris, but he won't vouch for it (621:33-39).

2. Someone in the shelter remarks on the fact that the Invincibles had perpetrated their deed with cold steel, a most un-Irish act which had fostered the initial suspicion that the assassins were foreigners. The remark leads Stephen and Bloom to look at the proprietor once more and Bloom to think back to the celebrated deed itself which he misdates as happening in 1881 (629:7-29).

3. The rumor again that the proprietor is Skin-the-Goat (641:40-41).

4. A Bloom soliloquy on violence in the cause of politics and love, leading once more to Skin-the-Goat and his escape from the gallows (642:10-31).

The Invincibles.

At twelve noon on June 16, 1904, there is a gathering of Dublin "bon vivants" in the offices of the *Freeman's Journal,* for which Bloom works as a canvasser of ads. Stephen Dedalus is also there. Myles Crawford, the editor of *Freeman's,* regales the assembled wits with the story of how Gallaher, a legendary newspaper reporter who had been introduced into Joyce's world in "A Little Cloud" in the *Dubliners,* sent an account of the murders by cable and in code to the *New York World.* Like Bloom, Crawford misdates the murders as occurring in 1881: "That was eightyone, sixth of May, time of the invincibles, murder in the Phoenix park, before you [Stephen Dedalus] were born, I suppose." (136)

Crawford's explanation of Gallaher's exploit runs, with interruptions, from 135:30 to 137:20. Myles Crawford's recital of Gallaher's feat further compounds the errors in the dating of the Phoenix Park murders in *Ulysses*; for he gives the impression that Gallaher cabled the whole story, in code, to the *New York World* right after the twin assassinations. But the true story of what happened did not come out until 1883 when the Invincibles were apprehended and convicted, as will be explained below. So if Myles Crawford is one year off on the date of the murders (1881 rather than 1882), he is two years off (1881 rather than 1883) on the revelation of who the Invincibles were and how they carried out their scheme. The trial itself was public, and its relevations were carried in all newspapers, in Ireland and elsewhere.

My only explanation is that it all constitutes some kind of insane hint—not at all unlikely for Joyce—that Galla-her was such a determined, clever, resourceful, and un-scrupulous pressman that he had insinuated himself into the circle of the Invincibles and was thus a party not only to their plans but to the execution of those plans. It all sounds like a precursor of Hecht's and MacArthur's *The Front Page*.

Probably, and most likely, it is a kind of wild satire on modern journalism. In addition, Myles Crawford is drunk, even more than usual—at least for this time of day:

—He's pretty well on, Professor MacHugh said in a low voice.

—Seems to be, J. J. O'Molloy said, (130)

Long before 1904, and continuing on after 1904, Brady, Kelly and the others had become heroes and martyrs in Irish and Irish-American memory.

J. J. O'Molloy informs the gathering in the newspaper office that in February 1903, postcards commemorating the Invincibles were being sold right outside of the viceregal lodge, where Cavendish would have lived, had he lived, in Phoenix Park itself (138:3-8).

Still later in the day, at 5:00 P.M., a group of Dublin

stalwarts gather in Barney Kiernan's pub to drink, converse, and listen to the rumblings of a ferocious Irish nationalist known as the Citizen: "So of course the citizen was only waiting for the wink of the word and he starts gassing out of him about the invincibles" [and other patriotic matters] (305).

5. Bloom tells Stephen that a score of years ago he was a quasi aspirant to Parliament in the Buckshot Forster days:

> Though they [Stephen and Bloom] didn't see eye to eye in everything, a certain analogy there somehow was, as if both their minds were travelling, so to speak, in the one train of thought. At his age when dabbling in politics roughly some score of years previously when he had been a *quasi* aspirant to parliamentary honours in the Buckshot Foster days he too recollected in retrospect (which was a source of keen satisfaction in itself) he had a sneaking regard for those same ultra ideas. (656)

There is a tissue of errors in this elaborate persiflage, as befits a section of *Ulysses* where everything is mysterious, nothing known for certain, and every assertion is suspect. As Bloom mistakes the year of the Phoenix Park murders (1881 instead of 1882), he gets everything else wrong as well. A "score" signifies twenty, so "some score of years previously" would translate about 1884. But William E. Forster (not "Foster," as Bloom has it) left the post of Irish Chief Secretary in 1882, as explained above, and it was his replacement, Lord Frederick Cavendish, who was assassinated by the Invincibles in Phoenix Park. It should be observed that, historically, Forster had earned the nickname of "Buckshot" not for his cruelty but for his humanity: he ordered the police to use buckshot rather than live ammunition when dispersing crowds. Bloom says that at the time of the Buckshot Forster days, he was

Stephen's age, which is twenty-two. But Bloom did not turn twenty-two until 1888. Finally, we are told elsewhere, Bloom was once involved in politics, worked for Alderman John Hooper, and was considered as a possible candidate for an M.P., but all this transpired about the time he met and courted Molly, in 1886 or 1887-1888.

Bloom continues to tell Stephen of his radical younger days, and how he supported the Land League and was once, even, twitted for being more radical on the land question than Michael Davitt (656:41-657:9). [Michael Davitt (1846-1906) established the Land League in October 1879. Its purpose was nationalization of Irish land, i.e., Irish ownership of Irish land. Parnell became the first president of the League. The Land League was prominent, and effective, in Irish and Anglo-Irish politics in the 1880s. Molly remembers that during the days when Bloom was courting her, 1887-1888, he delivered himself of a lot of: "blather about home rule and the land league" (771).]

6. Bloom (age sixteen) falls in with some harriers, gets drunk (for the first and last time), engages in a foot race, falls, cuts his hand and muddies his attire, and returns home to face paternal wrath and maternal sorrow (438:1-439:2). [The date of this incident is given in relation to the scar on Bloom's hand, said in 1904 to have been the result of a cut suffered twenty-two years before: "(*Points to his hand.*) That weal there is an accident. Fell and cut it twenty-two years ago. I was sixteen." (563) [In Notesheet No. 2 for Circe: "L.B. memory of only spree" (H., p. 275).]

1883

1. James Carey, an Invincible, turns Queen's evidence, and the Invincibles are tried, found guilty, and some are

executed [Bloom has trouble getting Carey's name straight]:

> That fellow that turned queen's evidence on the invincibles he used to receive the [Bloom is attending a mass], Carey was his name, the communion every morning. This very church. Peter Carey. No, Peter Claver I am thinking of. Denis Carey. And just imagine that. Wife and six children at home. And plotting that murder all the time. (81)

2. The welter of Dublin informers and their methods:

> Never know who you're talking to. Corny Kelleher he has Harvey Duff [an informer in a play by Dion Boucicault] in his eye. Like that Peter or Denis or James Carey that blew the gaff on the invincibles. Member of the corporation too. Egging raw youths on to get in the know. All the time drawing secret service pay from the castle. Drop him like a hot potato. Why those plain clothes men are always courting slaveys. Easily twig a man used to uniform. Square-pushing up against a backdoor. Maul her a bit. Then the next thing on the menu. And who is the gentleman does be visiting there? Was the young master saying anything? Peeping Tom through the keyhold. Decoy duck. Hotblooded young student fooling round her fat arms ironing.
>   —Are those yours, Mary?
>   —I don't wear such things ... Stop or I'll tell the missus on you. Out half the night.
>   —There are great times coming, Mary. Wait till you see.
>   —Ah, get along with your great times coming.
>   Barmaids too. Tobacco shopgirls. (163) there always being the offchance of a Dannyman [an informer] coming forward and turning queen's evidence—or king's now—like Denis or Peter Carey, (642)

Joe Brady, the Invincible, is hung, with memorable side-effects:

—God's truth, says Alf. I heard that from the head warder that was in Kilmainham when they hanged Joe Brady, the invincible. He told me when they cut him down after the drop it [his penis] was standing up in their faces like a poker. (304)

1884

c. December 8: Molly (Bloom's memory of Molly's memory).

Bloom is thinking of Milly's first menstruation, on September 15, 1903, three months to the day after her fourteenth birthday. If Milly was following her mother's pattern, a not-at-all unlikely parallel for Joyce, then Molly would have first menstruated on December 8, 1884, three months after her fourteenth birthday, September 8:

Frightened she was when her nature came on her first. Poor child! Strange moment for the mother too. Brings back her girlhood. Gibraltar. Looking from Buena Vista. O'Hara's tower. The seabirds screaming. Old Barbary ape that gobbled all his family. Sundown, gunfire for the men to cross the lines. Looking out over the sea she told me. Evening like this, but clear, no clouds. I always thought I'd marry a lord or a gentleman with a private yacht. *Buenas noches, señorita. El hombre ama la muchacha hermosa.* (380) [Buena Vista and O'Hara's Tower are peaks on Gibraltar. The Barbary ape is a monkey, tailless and terrestrial, that inhabits the Rock. These monkeys live in packs and are dominated by a fierce old male. The Spanish means, "Good evening, young lady. The man loves the beautiful young girl" (G.).]

Bloom.

1. Bloom discusses his favorite topics with Owen Goldberg and Cecil Turnbull in nocturnal rambles between Longwood Avenue and Leonard's corner, and Leonard's

corner and Synge Street, and Synge Street and Bloomfield Avenue (667:15-20). [All places in Bloom's boyhood neighborhood. See map, p. 138 below.]

The favorite topics being:

> Music, literature, Ireland, Dublin, Paris, friendship, woman, prostitution, diet, the influence of gaslight or the light of arc and glow-lamps on the growth of adjoining paraheliotropic trees, exposed corporation emergency dustbuckets, the Roman catholic church, ecclesiastical celibacy, the Irish nation, jesuit education careers, the study of medicine, the past day, the maleficent influence of the presabbath, Stephen's collapse. (666) [These last items were added on June 16, 1904.]

2. The black Maria peels off Bloom's shoe at Leonard's corner: "Heel easily catch in tracks or bootlace in a cog. Day the wheel of the black Maria peeled off my shoe at Leonard's corner." (435)

1884-1885

Molly and sex. [Some of these experiences could have happened to Molly earlier. I group them here for convenience.]

1. Some of the girls on Gibraltar wear no drawers: "and half the girls in Gibraltar never wore them either naked as God made them that Andalusian singing her Manola she didnt make much secret of what she hadnt yes" (750)

2. Scatology in Gibraltar [during their courtship in 1888 Bloom had written Molly a letter with some dirty words in it and later asked her if she knew what the words meant (746:43-747:4)]:

> and if I knew what it meant of course I had to say no for form sake dont understand you I said and wasnt it natural so it is of

course it used to be written up with a picture of a womans on that wall in Gibraltar with that word I couldnt find anywhere only for children seeing it too young (747)

3. Performs in the nude for the man across the way:

Im sure that fellow opposite used to be there the whole time watching with the lights out in the summer and I in my skin hopping around I used to love myself then stripped at the washstand dabbing and creaming only when it came to the chamber performance I put out the light too so then there were 2 of us (763)

4. Sees young men swimming in the nude off Margate Strand:

besides hes [Stephen] young those fine young men I could see down in Margate strand bathing place from the side of the rock standing up in the sun naked like a God or something and then plunging into the sea with them why arent all men like that thered be some consolation for a woman (775) [Margate was a beach on Gibraltar reserved for male bathers (G.).]

5. Is aware of a red-light district on Irish Street: "they [men] can pick and choose what they please a married woman or a fast widow or a girl for their different tastes like those houses round behind Irish street" (777) [There is no Irish Street in either Dublin or Gibraltar. But there are sections of Gibraltar and Dublin called Irish Town (G.).]

6. Two soldiers expose themselves to her:

that disgusting Cameron highlander behind the meat market or that other wretch with the red head behind the tree where the statue of the fish used to be when I was passing pretending he was pissing standing out for me to see it with his babyclothes up to one side the Queens own they were a nice lot its well the Surreys relieved them theyre always trying to show it to you every time (753)

[The Cameron Highlanders were stationed on Gibraltar from June 1879 to August 1882 when they were relieved by the first East Surreys; the statue of the fish is in the center of the Alameda Gardens on Gibraltar (G.). It should be added that the voice and attitude here sound like the Molly of 1904 and not the young virgin of the Gibraltar days.]

7. Tries to masturbate with a banana: "after I tried with the Banana but I was afraid it might break and get lost up in me somewhere yes because they once took something down out of a woman that was up there for years covered with limesalts" (760)

8. Is warned of certain dangers: "or leave me with a child embarazada that old servant Ines told me that one drop even if it got into you at all" (760)

9. Morals on Gibraltar are breaking down: "that old Bishop that spoke off the altar his long preach about womans higher functions about girls now riding the bicycle and wearing peak caps and the new woman bloomers God send him sense and me more money" (761)

10. Hester, a first "love":

> then a girl Hester we used to compare our hair mine was thicker than hers she showed me how to settle it at the back when I put it up and whats this else how to make a knot on a thread with the one hand we were like cousins what age was I then the night of the storm I slept in her bed she had her arms around me then we were fighting in the morning with the pillow what fun . . . it wouldnt have been nice on account of her but I could have stopped it in time (756)

11. And novels:

> she gave me the Moonstone to read that was the first I read of Wilkie Collins East Lynne I read and the shadow of Ashlydyat Mrs Henry Wood Henry Dunbar by that other

woman . . . and Lord Lytton Eugene Aram Molly bawn she
gave me by Mrs Hungerford on account of the name I dont
like books with a Molly in them (756) [Wilkie Collins, Mrs.
Henry Wood, Edward Bulwer-Lytton (Baron Lytton), and
Mrs. Hungerford, were all popular nineteenth-century English novelists.]

12. And hot nights:

I used to be weltering then in the heat my shift drenched
with the sweat stuck in the cheeks of my bottom on the chair
when I stood up they were so fattish and firm when I
got up on the sofa cushions to see with my clothes up and
the bugs tons of them at night and the mosquito nets I
couldnt read a line Lord how long ago it seems centuries
of course (756)

Molly and the Stanhopes.

1. Molly becomes friendly with the Stanhopes ("fathers
friend Mrs. Stanhope" [755]), a younger woman married
to an older man, whom she calls "wogger"; whether
Hester is also Mrs. Stanhope is not exactly clear from the
text. A. and G. think the two are the same, and that the
Hester of *Ulysses* is thus the namesake of Lady Hester
Stanhope, the famous Victorian eccentric who retired to a
monastery in the Middle East. On the other hand, Molly
identifies Mrs. Stanhope as father's friend, and not as her
friend Hester. On the third hand, Mrs. Stanhope is much
younger than her husband, making it possible for her to
have been Hester: "she didnt look a bit married just like a
girl he was years older than her wogger" (755)

2. The Stanhopes take Molly to a bull fight:

he was awfully fond of me when he held down the wire
with his foot for me to step over at the bullfight at La
Linea when that matador Gomez was given the bulls ear
clothes we have to wear whoever invented them . . . all

staysed up you cant do a blessed thing in them in a crowd run or jump out of the way thats why I was afraid when that other ferocious old Bull began to charge the banderillos with the sashes and the 2 things in their hats and the brutes of men shouting bravo toro sure the women were as bad in their nice white mantillas ripping all the whole insides out of those poor horses I never heard of such a thing in all my life (755)

3. The friendship of Molly and Mrs. Stanhope (this is Mrs. Stanhope, now living in Paris, reminiscing by letter to Molly): "my dearest Doggerina . . . wd give anything to be back in Gib and hear you sing in old Madrid or Waiting Concone . . . will always think of the lovely teas we had together scrumptious currant scones and raspberry wafers I adore" (755)

4. The Stanhopes leave Gibraltar to go to Paris:

people were always going away and we never I remember that day with the waves and the boats with their high heads rocking and the swell of the ship those Officers uniforms on shore leave made me seasick he didnt say anything he was very serious I had the high buttoned boots on and my skirt was blowing she kissed me six or seven times didnt I cry yes I believe I did or near it my lips were taittering when I said goodbye she had a Gorgeous wrap of some special kind of blue colour on her for the voyage made very peculiarly to one side like and it was extremely pretty (756-757) [Both Blooms, as noted above, have fusion memories. Here Molly is conflating her leave-taking of the Stanhopes ("she kissed me six or seven times") with her leave-taking of Lieutenant Mulvey in May 1886 ("he didnt say anything he was very serious").]

5. After the Stanhopes leave, boredom sets in:

it got as dull as the devil after they went I was almost planning to run away mad out of it somewhere . . . then the same old reveille in the morning and drums rolling and the unfortunate poor devils of soldiers walking about with mess-tins smelling the place more than the old longbearded jews in their jellibees and levites assembly and sound clear and gunfire for the men to cross the lines and the warden marching with his keys to lock the gates and the bagpipes and only Captain Groves and father talking about Rorkes drift and Plevna and sir Garnet Wolseley and Gordon at Khartoum lighting their pipes for them everytime they went out [Rorkes Drift was the site of a celebrated defense by a small number of British troops against a large number of Zulus in the Zulu War in 1879; for Plevna see above pp. 33-34; Sir Garnet Wolseley was commander-in-chief of the British forces in the Zulu War; the English General Charles George Gordon was killed, along with all his forces, when the city, Khartoum, which he was holding, fell to Moslem forces in January, 1885. The Stanhopes then must have left Gibraltar sometime in 1884 since the date is now, Khartoum being discussed, after January 1885.] . . . not a letter from a living soul except the odd few I posted to myself with bits of paper in them so bored sometimes I could fight with my nails listening to that old Arab with the one eye and his heass of an instrument singing his heah heah aheah all my compriments on your hotchapotch of your heass as bad as now (757)

6. Mrs. Stanhope writes her a letter and sends her a frock, which was subsequently faded by the Gibraltar sun:

the sun all the time weltering down on you faded all that lovely frock fathers friend Mrs Stanhope sent me from the B Marche Paris what a shame my dearest Doggerina she wrote on what she was very nice whats this her other name was just a P C to tell you I sent the little present have just had a jolly warm bath and feel a very clean dog now enjoyed it wogger . . . well now dearest Doggerina be sure and write soon kind she left out regards to your father also Captain Grove with love yrs affly x x x x x (755)

7. And that ends that: "of course they never come back and she didnt put her address right on it either she may have noticed her wogger" (756)

1885

Bloom.

1. Discusses his "favorite topics" with Percy Apjohn reclining against a wall between Gibraltar villa and Bloomfield house in Crumlin, barony of Uppercross (667: 20-22).

2. Political views:

> In 1885 he had publicly expressed his adherence to the collective and national economic programme advocated by James Fintan Lalor, John Fisher Murray, John Mitchel, J. F. X. O'Brien and others, the agrarian policy of Michael Davitt, the constitutional agitation of Charles Stewart Parnell (M. P. for Cork City), the programme of peace, retrenchment and reform of William Ewart Gladstone (M.P. for Midlothian, N.B.) (716) [The list would indicate that Bloom was a radical and a strong Irish nationalist in his political outlook. Both T. and G. identify each person named. Parnell, an important "ghost" in 1904 Dublin, will be discussed below, pp. 108-121]

1886

Molly—first love in the spring.

1. At this time the Tweedys have as a governess or a housekeeper an old Spanish woman named Mrs. Rubio who tries, unsuccessfully, to interest Molly in higher things. Literature: "pity [Molly is regretting the loss of her speaking Spanish] I never tried to read that novel cantankerous Mrs Rubio lent me by Valera with the questions in it all upside down" (779)

[Juan Valera y Alcala Galiano (1824-1905) was a Spanish writer and man of public affairs. In Spanish questions begin (¿) and end (?) (G.).] Religion:

> and because I didn't run into mass often enough in Santa Maria to please her with her shawl up on her except when there was a marriage on with all her miracles of the saints and her black blessed virgin with the silver dress and the sun dancing 3 times on Easter Sunday morning and when the priest was going by with the bell bringing the vatican to the dying blessing herself for his Majestad (759)

2. The English Atlantic fleet comes in:

> ah horquilla disobliging old thing and it staring her in the face with her switch of false hair on her and vain about her appearance ugly as she was near 80 or a 100 her face a mass of wrinkles with all her religion domineering because she never could get over the Atlantic fleet coming in half the ships of the world and the Union Jack flying with all her carabineros because 4 drunken English sailors took all the rock from them (759) [Gibraltar was captured by the British and the Dutch on July 24, 1704. Actually, the attackers considerably outnumbered the attacked (G.).]

3. Mulvey, a young English naval officer, a lieutenant, sees Molly:

> he was watching me whenever he got an opportunity at the band on the Alameda esplanade when I was with father and Captain Grove (756) if ever they [the young ladies of present day Dublin] got a chance of walking down the Alameda on an officers arm like me on the bandnight my eyes flash my bust (762) I looked up at the church first and then at the windows then down and our eyes met I felt something go through me like all needles my eyes were dancing I remember after when I looked at myself in the glass hardly recognized myself the change I had a splendid

skin from the sun and the excitement like a rose and I didn't
get a wink of sleep (756)

Molly and Mulvey see one another on the street: "I
wanted to pick him up when I saw him following me
along the Calle Real in the shop window then he tipped
me just in passing I never thought hed write making an
appointment" (759)

A missive is sent:

> Mulveys was the first when I was in bed that morning
> and Mrs Rubio brought it in with the coffee she stood there
> standing when I asked her to hand me and I pointing at
> them I couldnt think of the word a hairpin to open it with
> . . . an admirer he signed it I near jumped out of my skin
> . . . I had it inside my petticoat bodice all day reading it up
> in every hole and corner while father was up at the drill in-
> structing to find out by the handwriting or the language of
> stamps singing I remember shall I wear a white rose and I
> wanted to put on the old stupid clock to near the time (759)

4. First assignation, the kiss under the Moorish Wall:

> he was the first man kissed me under the Moorish wall my
> sweetheart when a boy it never entered my head what kis-
> sing meant till he put his tongue in my mouth his mouth
> was sweetlike young I put my knee up to him a few times to
> learn the way what did I tell him I was engaged for fun to
> the son of a Spanish nobleman named Don Miguel de la
> Flora and he believed that I was to be married to him in
> 3 years time theres many a true word spoken in jest there is
> a flower that bloometh a few things I told him true about
> myself just for him to be imagining the Spanish girls he
> didnt like I suppose one of them wouldnt have him I got him
> excited he crushed all the flowers on my bosom he brought
> me he couldnt count the pesetas and the perragordas till I
> taught him Cappoquin he came from he said on the Black-

water (759) [Mulvey has trouble with Spanish coins; he comes from a small Irish town, Cappoquin, on the River Blackwater in County Wexford (G.).] and Gibraltar as a girl where I was a Flower of the mountain yes when I put the rose in my hair like the Andalusian girls used or shall I wear a red yes and how he kissed me under the Moorish wall and I thought well as well him as another (783)

[At this point in Molly's monologue the memory of Mulvey, of May 1886, fuses with her memory of Bloom kissing her and proposing to her on Howth in May of 1888. The phrase "well as well him as another" refers both to the kiss—reciprocated—by Mulvey and the kiss and the proposal of marriage—accepted—by Bloom.

Although the matter is not crystal clear from the text, Molly appears to have two distinct remembrances of her romance with Mulvey. The first was the kiss under the Moorish Wall in the middle section of Gibraltar; the second, longer and more intimate, occurred on one of the more southerly heights of the Rock, near O'Hara's Tower. Joyce's sense of the Gibraltar geography is indicated by his own sketch (see p. 65 below), reproduced from No. 3 of the Penelope Notesheets (H., p. 500). Joyce's geography is inaccurate in many respects—which does not matter— and the exact timing and sequence of the Molly-Mulvey ambulatory romance are difficult to decipher from the text. Geographically they range from the middle of the Rock at the Moorish Wall, which is not in actuality as far north as Joyce puts it on his map, to the southernmost tip, Europa point. The distances involved are not great. The peninsula itself juts out a distance of two and three-quarters miles from the mainland (Captain Sayer, *History of Gibraltar* [London, 1862], p. 444). The distance between the Moorish Wall and Europa point would be a good deal less than this. Young people of the 1880s would have thought nothing of traversing this territory in one day or one afternoon. Thus everything could have occurred in one afternoon; the kiss under the Moorish Wall, the encounter by O'Hara's Tower, which is further south than Joyce puts it, the walk out to Europa point, and the walk back. My own idea is that there are two occasions from her romance with Mulvey that Molly here recalls (implying that there were others that she does not). The first was the first kiss, under the Moorish Wall. The second, on the day before Mulvey left, was her first physical intimacy (although without consummation) with a man, on Gibraltar's southerly heights. Also on that same afternoon they walked out to and back from Europa Point. My theory is that they first walked out to the Point, walked back to O'Hara's Tower where they stopped— Molly: "I said I was tired" (760)—and where they had their dalliance, and then walked back to the town. The next day Mulvey sailed for India. Molly in 1904 thinks Mulvey would now be about forty, or about six or seven years older than she, who is now thirty-three going on thirty-four. Thus in 1886 Mulvey would have been twenty-one or twenty-two to her fifteen.]

5. The first sexual experience c. May 17: "but it was too short then the day before he left May yes it was May when the infant king of Spain was born" (759-760) [Alphonse XIII, posthumous son of Alphonse XII, was born on May 17, 1886.]

Going out to Europa Point:

> the fun we had running along Willis road to Europa point twisting in and out all round the other side of Jersey they were shaking and dancing about in my blouse like Millys little ones now when she runs up the stairs I loved looking down at them I was jumping up at the pepper trees and the white poplars pulling the leaves off and throwing them at him (761-762)

On the southerly heights, first they talk, while Molly tells him of matters Gibraltarian:

> Im always like that in the spring Id like a new fellow every year up on the tiptop under the rockgun near OHaras tower I told him it was struck by lightning and all about the old Barbary apes they sent to Clapham without a tail career-ing all over the show on each others back Mrs Rubio said she was a regular old rock scorpion robbing the chickens out of Inces farm and throw stones at you if you went anear (760)

[A mixup in geography: the rockgun, Rock G, was a signal gun mounted on the highest part of the northern face of the rock, while O'Hara's Tower was the southern high point (G.). All indications are that Molly and Mulvey are south rather than north. G. has a full explanation for each of Molly's references.]

Intimacy and gratification:

> he was looking at me I had that white blouse on open at the front to encourage him as much as I could without too openly they were just beginning to be plump I said I was tired we lay over the firtree cove a wild place I suppose it must be the highest rock in existence the galleries and case-mates and those frightful rocks and Saint Michaels cave with the icicles or whatever they call them hanging down and ladders all the mud plotching my boots Im sure thats the way down the monkeys go under the sea to Africa when they die the ships out far like chips that was the Malta boat passing yes the sea and the sky you could do what you liked lie there for ever he caressed them outside they love doing that its the roundness there I was leaning over him with my white ricestraw hat to take the newness out of it the left side of my face the best my blouse open for his last day transparent kind of shirt he had I could see his chest pink he wanted to touch mine with his for a moment but I wouldn't let him he was awfully put out first for fear you never know consumption or leave me with a child

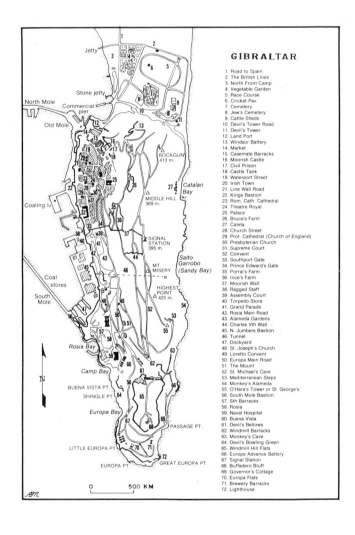

GIBRALTAR

1. Road to Spain
2. The British Lines
3. North Front Camp
4. Vegetable Garden
5. Race Course
6. Cricket Pav.
7. Cemetery
8. Jew's Cemetery
9. Cattle Sheds
10. Devil's Tower Road
11. Devil's Tower
12. Land Port
13. Windsor Battery
14. Market
15. Casemate Barracks
16. Moorish Castle
17. Civil Prison
18. Castle Tank
19. Waterport Street
20. Irish Town
21. Line Wall Road
22. Kings Bastion
23. Rom. Cath. Cathedral
24. Theatre Royal
25. Palace
26. Bruce's Farm
27. Caleta
28. Church Street
29. Prot. Cathedral (Church of England)
30. Presbyterian Church
31. Supreme Court
32. Convent
33. Southport Gate
34. Prince Edward's Gate
35. Porral's Farm
36. Ince's Farm
37. Moorish Wall
38. Ragged Staff
39. Assembly Court
40. Torpedo Store
41. Grand Parade
42. Rosia Main Road
43. Alameda Gardens
44. Charles Vth Wall
45. N. Jumbers Bastion
46. Tunnel
47. Dockyard
48. St. Joseph's Church
49. Loretto Convent
50. Europa Main Road
51. The Mount
52. St. Michael's Cave
53. Mediterranean Steps
54. Monkey's Alameda
55. O'Hara's Tower or St. George's
56. South Mole Bastion
57. Sth Barracks
58. Rosia
59. Naval Hospital
60. Buena Vista
61. Devil's Bellows
62. Windmill Barracks
63. Monkey's Cave
64. Devil's Bowling Green
65. Windmill Hill Flats
66. Europa Advance Battery
67. Signal Station
68. Buffadero Bluff
69. Governor's Cottage
70. Europa Flats
71. Brewery Barracks
72. Lighthouse

Jetty
North Mole
Stone jetty
Commercial pier
Old Mole
Coaling I.
Coal stores
South Mole
Rosia Bay
Camp Bay
BUENA VISTA PT.
SHINGLE PT.
Europa Bay
LITTLE EUROPA PT.
EUROPA PT.
GREAT EUROPA PT.
PASSAGE PT.

ROCKGUN
413 m.

Catalan Bay

MIDDLE HILL
369 m.

SIGNAL STATION
395 m.

Salto Garrobo
(Sandy Bay)

MT. MISERY

HIGHEST POINT
425 m.

N

0   500 KM

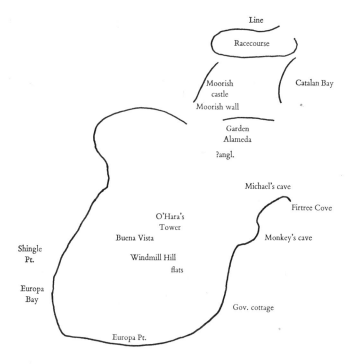

Philip Herring's copy of Joyce's sketch of Gibraltar, in the
Penelope notesheets in the British Museum. H. p. 500.

embarazada . . . theyre all mad to get in there where they come out of youd think they could never get far enough up and then theyre done with you in a way till the next time yes because theres a wonderful feeling there all the time so tender how did we finish it off yes O yes I pulled him off into my handkerchief pretending not to be excited but I opened my legs I wouldnt let him touch me inside my petticoat I had a skirt opening up the side I tortured the life out of him first tickling him . . . his eyes shut and a bird flying below us he was shy all the same I liked him like that morning I made him blush a little when I got over him that way when I unbuttoned him and took his out and drew back the skin it had a kind of eye in it theyre all Buttons men down the middle on the wrong side of them Molly darling he called me what was his name Jack Joe Harry Mulvey was it yes I think a lieutenant he was rather fair he had a laughing kind of a voice so I went around to the whatyoucallit everything was whatyoucallit moustache had he he said hed come back Lord its just like yesterday to me and if I was married hed do it to me and I promised him yes faithfully Id let him block [copulate with] me now flying perhaps hes dead or killed or a Captain or admiral its nearly 20 years [actually eighteen] if I said firtree cove he would if he came up behind me and put his hands over my eyes to guess who I might recognise him hes young still about 40 perhaps hes married some girl on the black water [reference to Mulvey's home town] and is quite changed they all do they havent half the character a woman has she little knows what I did with her beloved husband before he ever dreamt of her in broad daylight too in the sight of the whole world you might say they could have put an article about it in the Chronicle (760-761)

6. Aftermath. The walk back:

I was a bit wild after when I blew out the old bag the biscuits were in from Benady Bros and exploded it Lord what a bang all the woodcocks and pigeons screaming coming back the same way that we went over middle hill round by the old guardhouse and the jews burial place pretending to read out the Hebrew on them I wanted to fire his pistol he said he hadnt one he didnt know what to make of me with his peaked cap on that he always wore crooked as often as I settled it straight H M S Calypso swinging my hat (761) [If they passed the Jew's cemetery, they must also have walked up to the northern part of the peninsula.]

7. A time of farewells: "he went to India he was to write the voyages those men have to make to the ends of the world and back its the least they might get a squeeze or two at a woman while they can going out to be drowned or blown up somewhere" (762)

8. Molly watches the fleet leave on a Sunday morning:

I went up windmill hill to the flats that Sunday morning with Captain Rubios that was dead spyglass like the sentry had he said hed have one or two from on board I wore that frock from the B Marche Paris and the coral necklace the straits shining I could see over to Morocco almost the bay of Tangier white and the Atlas mountain with snow on it and the straits like a river so clear Harry Molly Darling (762)

9. Mementos of Mulvey—a memory, a soiled handkerchief, a Claddagh ring, a photograph and some elemental wisdom.

The handkerchief and the ring:

I was thinking of him on the sea all the time after at mass when my petticoat began to slip down at the elevation weeks and weeks I kept the handkerchief under my pillow for the smell of him there was no decent perfume to be got in that Gibraltar only that cheap peau despagne that faded and left a stink on you more than anything else I wanted to give him a memento he gave me that clumsy Claddagh ring for luck (762)

[Claddagh, from the Gaelic "cladach" or "clodach," signi-fying a flat, stony seashore, was the name of the Irish part of Galway in Norman times. In more recent times it has been the suburb of Galway inhabited by fishermen. A Claddagh ring, made of gold and decorated with a heart supported by two hands, was thought to be an ancient Celtic design (G.).]

The Photo: "and the shadow of Ashlydyat Mrs Henry Wood Henry Dunbar by that other woman I lent him [Bloom—we are now in 1887 or 1888 and Molly is loaning a book to Leopold] afterwards with Mulveys photo in it so as he see I wasnt without" (756)

The wisdom of experience: "I knew more about men and life when I was 15 than theyll [the young women of present-day Dublin] all know at 50" (762)

Bloom remembers Molly's memory of Mulvey:

> Young kisses: the first. Far away now past. Mrs Marion [Bloom walking on a Dublin street thinks of what his wife is doing at home.] Reading lying back now, counting the strands of her hair, smiling, braiding. (67) First kiss does the trick. The propitious moment. Something inside them goes pop. Mushy like, tell by their eye, on the sly. First thoughts are best. Remember that till their dying day. Molly, lieutenant Mulvey that kissed her under the Moorish wall beside the gardens. Fifteen she told me. But her breasts were developed. Fell asleep then. After Glencree dinner that was when we drove home the featherbed mountain. [This occurred in the winter of 1894; see the chronology below.] Gnashing her teeth in sleep. (371)

c. September 8. On or about her sixteenth birthday Molly makes her debut as a singer, whether in Gibraltar or Dublin is not clear from the text (652:41-653:2). Some time in 1886 or 1887 the Tweedys removed themselves, along with old Cohen's bed and Tweedy's trunk, from

Gibraltar to Dublin: "I always knew wed go away in the end" (779) The trunk still resides in the bedroom of 7 Eccles Street (730:23-25).

Molly is left with a powerful and poetic remembrance of things past:

> I wouldnt answer first [Bloom has just proposed to her on the Hill of Howth in May of 1888] only looked out over the sea and the sky I was thinking of so many things he didnt know of Mulvey and Mr Stanhope and Hester and father and old captain Groves and the sailors playing all birds fly and I say stoop and washing up dishes they called it on the pier and the sentry in front of the governors house with the thing round his white helmet poor devil half roasted and the Spanish girls laughing in their shawls and their tall combs and the auctions in the morning the Greeks and the jews and the Arabs and the devil knows who else from all the ends of Europe and Duke street and the fowl market all clucking outside Larby Sharons and the poor donkeys slipping half asleep and the vague fellows in the cloaks asleep in the shade on the steps and the big wheels of the carts of the bulls and the old castle thousands of years old yes and those handsome Moors all in white and turbans like kings asking you to sit down in their little bit of a shop and Ronda with the old windows of the posadas glancing eyes a lattice hid for her lover to kiss the iron and the wineshops half open at night and the castanets and the night we missed the boat at Algeciras the watchman going about serene with his lamp and O that awful deepdown torrent O and the sea the sea crimson sometimes like fire and the glorious sunsets and the figtrees in the Alameda gardens yes and all the queer little streets and pink and blue and yellow houses and the rosegardens and the jessamine and geraniums and cactuses and Gibraltar as a girl where I was a Flower of the mountain yes when I put the rose in my hair like the Andalusian girls used or shall I wear a red yes and how he kissed me under the Moorish wall (782-783)

[Joyce's picture of Gibraltar is purely imaginative; he never visited the Rock. A. (pp. 231-32) discusses his use of sources, the main ones being the *Gibraltar Directory and Guide Book,* issued annually after 1873. There were other sources as well which are most fully discussed by James Van Dyck Card in "A Gibraltar Sourcebook for 'Penelope,'" *James Joyce Quarterly* 8 (Winter 1971), pp. 163-73, and by H. (pp. 69-73).]

EARLY AND MIDDLE   1880s UP TO 1886

The last terrible years and the sad end of Rudolph Bloom.

1. During the earlier 1880s he sells imitation diamonds and other trinkets. Leopold goes to work for him after graduating from high school in 1881.(See pp. 41-42 above.)

2. Goes on to other things (as reported by the Nameless One, a Dublin gossip):

> Mr. Bloom with his argol bargol. And his old fellow before him perpetrating frauds, old Methusalem Bloom, the robbing bagman, that poisoned himself with the prussic acid after he swamping the country with his baubles and his penny diamonds. Loans by post on easy terms. Any amount of money advanced on note of hand. Distance no object. No security. Gob he's like Lanty MacHale's goat that'd go a piece of the road with every one. (336)

3. Returns to his ancestral faith:

> Poor papa with his hagadah book, reading backwards with his finger to me. Pessach. Next year in Jerusalem. Dear, O Dear! All that long business about that brought us out of the land of Egypt and into the house of bondage *alleluia. Shema Israel Adonai Elohenu.* No, that's the other. Then the twelve brothers, Jacob's sons. And then the lamb and the cat and the dog and the stick and the water and the butcher and then the angel of death kills the butcher

and he kills the ox and the dog kills the cat. Sounds a bit silly till you come to look into it well. Justice it means but it's everybody eating everyone else. That's what life is after all. (122)

[The *Haggada* or *Haggadah,* Jewish rabbinical literature of the non-legal genus, consists of exegesis or exposition of Scriptures, usually imaginative developments of thoughts suggested by the text; or a didactic or homiletic exposition. G. has detailed explanations for the train of allusions running through Bloom's memory.]

4. Leopold scoffs at his father's observance of ancient rituals and rites, and for the rest of his life feels guilty about it (724:8-20).

5. Becomes the proprietor of the Queen's Hotel in Ennis, Clare (723:31-32). [How the impoverished Rudolph Bloom could have acquired this hotel, a quite respectable one, is another of the many factual puzzles or mysteries of the book.]

6. An infirm, elderly widower who sleeps with his dog:

I have felt this instant a twinge of sciatica in my left glutear muscle. It runs in our family. Poor dear papa, a widower, was a regular barometer from it. He believed in animal heat. A skin of tabby lined his winter waistcoat. Near the end, remembering king David and the Sunamite, he shared his bed with Athos, faithful after death. A dog's spittle, as you probably . . . (*He winces.*) Ah! (528)

7. Senile:

An old man widower, unkempt hair, in bed, with head covered, sighing: an infirm dog, Athos: aconite, resorted to by increasing doses of grains and scruples as a palliative of recrudescent neuralgia: the face in death of a septuagenarian suicide by poison. (724)

Occasionally he ate without having previously removed his hat. Occasionally he drank voraciously the juice of gooseberry fool from an inclined plate. Occasionally he removed from his lips the traces of food by means of a lacerated envelope or other accessible fragment of paper.

What two phenomena of senescence were more frequent?

The myopic digital calculation of coins, eructation consequent upon repletion. (725)

8. Makes love to Molly's old clothes (?). Molly: "his father must have been a bit queer to go and poison himself after her still poor old man I suppose he felt lost always making love to my things too the few old rags I have" (767) [This statement offers some dating problems which are discussed below, p. 76.]

9. Ruined financially. Molly: "go and ruin himself altogether the way his father did down in Ennis" (765)

10. June 21. Rudolph receives the news of Ellen Bloom's death. This must be conjecture, but the circumstantial evidence is fairly convincing. Molly above (No. 8) had asserted: "to go and poison himself after her [death] still poor old man I suppose he felt lost" (767). And in his suicide note for Leopold Rudolph wrote: "Tomorrow [June 28] will be a week that I received . . . it is no use Leopold to be . . . with your dear mother . . . that is not more to stand . . . to her . . . all for me is out . . ." (723). [As pointed out above (p. 00), Joyce had once contemplated in a chronology having Ellen Bloom die in 1890. Having her die before her husband, of course, increases the pathos of the end of the poor old man.]

Bloom never thinks of his mother's death and rarely of his mother, although when he does it is with obvious sorrow. In the graveyard at Glasnevin he does give her a brief thought: "Mine [his own grave plot which he has purchased] over there toward Finglas, the plot I bought. Mamma poor mamma, and little Rudy [his dead son]." (111) And when her apparition appears in an hallucination in Bella Cohen's, he cries out: "Mamma!" (438). More important are mementos of her: a potato talisman and a cameo brooch. The potato, always carried by Bloom, is referred to throughout the day and evening of June 16. More importantly, it is Bloom's good luck charm, and on at least two occasions it appears, to him at least, that it works. On approaching the red-light district near midnight he is almost run over by a sandstrewer, but manages to jump out of the way in time. He attributes his good luck to "Poor mamma's panacea" (435:9-27). In Bella Cohen's Bloom surrenders his charm to Zoe (476:7-19), after which he undergoes his worst experience (hallucinatory once more), his degradation at the hands of Bella or Bello Cohen. He finally retrieves the potato (555:12-24): "(*With feeling.*) It is nothing, but still a relic of poor mamma." (555) After this retrieval his fortunes, with one exception, turn for the better. Ellen Bloom's brooch appears on her person when she puts in her apparitional appearance at Bella Cohen's (438:24), and is now in Bloom's desk at 7 Eccles Street (721:9-10).

11. The events of June 27, 1886:

What suggested scene was then reconstructed by Bloom?
The Queen's Hotel, Ennis, County Clare, where Rudolph Bloom (Rudolf Virag) died on the evening of the 27 June 1886, at some hour unstated, in consequence of an overdose of monkshood (aconite) selfadministered in the form of a neuralgic liniment, composed of 2 parts of aconite liniment to 1 of chloroform liniment (purchased by him at 10.20 a.m. on the morning of 27 June 1886 at the medical hall of Francis Dennehy, 17 Church street, Ennis) after having, though not in consequence of having, purchased at 3.15 p.m.

on the afternoon of 27 June 1886 a new boater straw hat,
extra smart (after having, though not in consequence of
having, purchased at the hour and in the place aforesaid,
the toxin aforesaid), at the general drapery store of James
Cullen, 4 Main street, Ennis. (684-685)

12. His suicide note:

Dogs' home over there. [Bloom has just observed one.]
Poor old Athos! Be good to Athos, Leopold, is my last wish.
Thy will be done. We obey them in the grave. A dying
scrawl. He took it to heart, pined away. Quiet brute. Old
men's dogs usually are. (90) In sloping, upright and back-
hands: Queen's hotel, Queen's hotel, Queen's Ho . . . (684)

an envelope addressed *To My Dear Son Leopold.*
    What fractions of phrases did the lecture of those five
whole words evoke?
    Tomorrow will be a week that I received . . . it is no use
Leopold to be . . . with your dear mother . . . that is not
more to stand . . . to her . . . all for me is out . . . be kind to
Athos, Leopold . . . my dear son . . . always . . . of me . . . *das
Herz . . . Gott . . . dein . . .* (723)

13. June 28. Bloom arrives at the Hotel:

    Poor papa! Poor man! I'm glad I didn't go into the room
to look at his face. That day! O dear! O dear! Ffoo! Well,
perhaps it was the best for him.
    Mr. Bloom went round the corner and passed the droop-
ping nags of the hazard. No use thinking of it any more.
(76)

14. The coroner's inquest:

    That afternoon of the inquest. The redlabelled bottle on
the table. The room in the hotel with hunting pictures.
Stuffy it was. Sunlight through the slats of the Venetian
blinds. The coroner's ears, big and hairy. Boots giving evidence. Thought he was asleep first. Then saw like yellow

streaks on his face. Had slipped down to the foot of the bed. Verdict: overdose. Death by misadventure. The letter. For my son Leopold.

No more pain. Wake no more. Nobody owns. (97)

15. The Burial. As Dignan's coffin sinks out of sight on the morning of June 16, 1904, Bloom thinks back:

Far away a donkey brayed. Rain. No such ass. Never see a dead one, they say. Shame of death. They hide. Also poor papa went away. (110) Last time I was here was Mrs Sinico's funeral [October, 1903]. Poor papa too. The love that kills. (114)

16. After thinking of his father's last days, Bloom wonders if the same fate awaits him, but concludes that his prudent financial accumulations will save him. The endowment policy, the bank passbook, the certificate of the possession of scrip (725:15-16).

17. The memory of the suicide lives on. In the cab on the way to Dignam's funeral at Glasnevin cemetery, the conversation of the four occupants, Martin Cunningham, Jack Power, Simon Dedalus, and Leopold Bloom, turns to suicide and its attendant disgrace. Only Martin Cunningham knows or remembers that Bloom's father had killed himself and, being a kindly man, tries to ease the pain which he knows the subject is giving Bloom (96:15-32). Later Cunningham explains the matter to Jack Power (101:27-37). Once again, and this time with much less charity, Cunningham explains the Bloom change of name and the suicide to the denizens of Barney Kiernan's (337:32-38).

1886

Bloom.

1. Now a door-to-door salesman, he discusses his "favorite topics" occasionally with casual acquaintances and prospective purchasers on doorsteps, front parlors and in third-class suburban railway carriages (667:22-25).

2. Takes a plunge into infinity while trying to square the circle (699:19-32). [Joyce has Bloom involved twice in attempts to square the circle: 1882 and 1886.]

3. Engages in political prophecy; he writes a prophecy about the possible consequences of William Gladstone's proposed Irish Home Rule Bill of 1886, which was never passed into law. Nor was Bloom's sealed prophecy ever unsealed (721:1-4).

4. Has in his possession, as of 1904, Thom's *Dublin Post Office Directory* of 1886 (708:16).

1886 OR 1887
MOLLY ON REHOBOTH TERRACE IN DUBLIN

It is not clear from the text when the Tweedys turned up in Dublin, except that it has to be after May 1886, when Molly had her experience with Mulvey in Gibraltar. Bloom thinks they met in 1887; but Molly appears to remember old Rudolph Bloom making love to her old clothes (767:38-39), and Rudolph Bloom died on June 27, 1886. It seems highly unlikely that between May and June of 1886, the Tweedys could have moved to Dublin, and Molly and Bloom could have met and achieved the degree of intimacy indicated by the old clothes incident (771:12).

1886, 1887, 1888

Bloom is involved in politics in some way and is connected with Alderman John Hooper who is to give the

Blooms a wedding present of a stuffed owl (113:28-29; 694:17-18; 707:26-27). The entry on the Doyles for 1887 (p. 00 below) has further evidence of Bloom in politics. It is also suggested that Bloom once worked for Valentine Dillon, lawyer, politician, and Lord Mayor of Dublin in 1894-1895 (465:13-14).

1887

1. Leopold and Molly meet at the home of Mat Dillon. Molly: "he excited me I dont know how the first night ever we met when I was living in Rehoboth terrace we stood staring at one another for about 10 minutes as if we met somewhere I suppose on account of my being jewess looking after my mother" (771) Leopold:

> First night when first I saw her at Mat Dillon's in Terenure. Yellow, black lace she wore. Musical chairs. We two the last. Fate. After her. Fate. Round and round slow. Quick round. We too. All looked. Halt. Down she sat. All ousted looked. Lips laughing. Yellow knees.
> —*Charmed my eye* . . .
> Singing. *Waiting* she sang. I turned her music. Full voice of perfume of what perfume does your lilactrees. Bosom I saw, both full, throat warbling. First I saw. She thanked me. Why did she me? Fate. Spanishy eyes. Under a peartree alone patio this hour in old Madrid one side in shadow Dolores shedolores. At me. Luring. Ah, alluring. (275)
> —I see her! It's she! The first night at Mat Dillon's! (542)

2. Bloom meets Major Tweedy and thereafter remembers him quite often: A hard bargainer (56:32). Mustaschioed (57:19). A member of the Royal Dublin Fusiliers (72:35-38). A drinker (377:19). There are three apparitions of Major Tweedy in fantasies at Bella Cohen's; as a

major general in the Zulu War (1879), in which he is said to have obtained his majority in the defense of Rorke's Drift (457:11-15); as a major, confronting the Citizen in mutual hostility to indicate the enmity between an Irish nationalist and an Irishman who fought in the British Army (596:4-8); and as a major in action in the battle of Rorke's Drift (596:20-28). Just before Bloom retires he thinks of the Major twice (710:1-11; 730:1-5).

Molly's memories provide a few more details about Tweedy. A pipe smoker: "I wish hed [Bloom] even smoke a pipe like father to get the smell of a man" (752) A brogue-speaker: "my accent [an Irish brogue] ... all father left me in spite of his stamps" (762-763) [From this we learn that Tweedy's venture in stamps did not eventuate in any legacy for Molly.] A non-Stoic. Molly complains that Bloom, when ill [the specific occasion she refers to happened in the summer of 1893] is also the opposite of stoical: "O tragic and that dyinglooking ... father was the same" (738)

The exact rank of Major Tweedy is one of Joyce's many games with the reader. As E. explains, Tweedy was based on an old ex-soldier named Powell living in Dublin in Joyce's day, who called himself "Major" though he had been in actuality a sergeant major. He had served many years in the army and took part in the Crimean War. After retiring from the service he bought a farm in Cork. He finally turned up in Dublin, after having drunk up his Cork property, and married a woman of some means by whom he had several handsome daughters, two of whom are mentioned in *Ulysses,* Mrs. Gallaher and Mrs. Clinch (E., p. 46).

On October 14, 1921, Joyce wrote to his favorite aunt, Mrs. Josephine Murray, asking for information about certain Dubliners:

"I want all the information, gossip or anything you remember about the Powells—chiefly the mother and daughters. Were any of them born abroad? When did Mrs. Powell die? I never heard of a 3rd brother, only Gus and Charley. The women were Mrs. Gallaher, Mrs. Clinch, Mrs. Russell. Where did they live before marriage? When did the major, if that was his rank, die?" (L. I, p. 174.)

In the Ormond Hotel bar on June 16, 1904, three Dublin stalwarts, Simon Dedalus, Ben Dollard, and "Father" Cowley, gossip and reminisce about the Blooms; Dedalus here remembers Tweedy as a "drummajor": "—Yes, begad [says Dedalus]. I remember the old drummajor." (269) To complicate matters further Molly remembers her father on Gibraltar as a drill instructor, hardly an occupation for a major: "while father was up at the drill instructing" (759)

Further, according to Molly, she (Molly) has undergone some social slights and snubs in Dublin because she is the daughter of a "soldier," i.e., not an officer. Thus when she is fulminating against the young Dublin singers of the day, Kathleen Kearney and other such "sparrowfarts," she silently exclaims: "soldiers daughter am I ay and whose are you bootmakers and publicans" (762)

However, to complicate matters still further, Molly's train of association here continues on to remember how splendid it was for her on band night in Gibraltar to walk down the Alameda on an officer's arm (762:36-39). Further, Tweedy's best friend and drinking companion on Gibraltar was, so we are told, an officer, Captain Groves (if he in fact was a captain). Perhaps they were two old enlisted men and drinking companions who in private addressed one another as "Major" and "Captain."

What then was Tweedy? Major? Sergeant major? drum major? Historically—although I do not think this would have bothered Joyce—he could not have been a drum major since that ancient title was abolished in 1881, although it was reintroduced in 1928. My guess is that Joyce intended Tweedy to be, like Powell, an ex-sergeant major posing in retirement as a major, just as the jingling bed shipped from Gibraltar was supposed to have belonged to General Napier but was in reality purchased secondhand from old Cohen.

Finally, although rising from the ranks to become a major would have been an exceedingly rare occurrence in the British Army at this time, the assumed title of "major" appears to have had a particular appeal. Richard Pigott, the unsavory character who forged the letters designed to incriminate Parnell in the Phoenix Park murders, always insisted on being called "Major" when on visits to seaside resorts.

3. May 1887. Bowling at Mat Dillon's. [This constitutes the most extensive multiple memory in the book, in that it involves both Blooms and John Henry Menton.] Molly and Leopold often met at the home of Mat Dillon in Roundtown, a suburb of Dublin. Dillon was an extremely hospitable man who had eight daughters. He had a lilac garden and close to it a lawn upon which his guests played at bowls. One evening in May 1887 there was a game of bowls in which Bloom bested a young lawyer named John Henry Menton, who was also interested in Molly at the time. Stephen Dedalus and his mother were also at Mat Dillon's on that day and were witnesses of the game. It was the first occasion upon which Bloom, Molly, and Stephen came together. Years later Bloom, Molly, and Menton each remember these times very vividly:

Bloom:

A scene disengages itself in the observer's [Bloom's] memory, evoked, it would seem, by a word of so natural a homeliness as if those days were really present there (as some thought) with their immediate pleasures. A shaven space of lawn one soft May evening, the wellremembered grove of lilacs at Roundtown, purple and white, fragrant slender spectators of the game but with much real interest in the pellets as they run slowly forward over the sward or collide and stop, one by its fellow, with a brief alert shock. And yonder about that grey urn where the water moves at times in thoughtful irrigation you saw another as fragrant sisterhood, Floey, Atty, Tiny and their darker friend with I know not what of arresting in her pose then, Our Lady of the Cherries, a comely brace of them pendent from an ear, bringing out the foreign warmth of the skin so daintily against the cool ardent fruit. A lad of four or five in linseywoolsey (blossomtime but there will be cheer in the kindly hearth when ere long the bowls are gathered and hutched) is standing on the urn secured by that circle of girlish fond hands. He frowns a little just as this young man does now [the Stephen Dedalus of June 16, 1904] with a perhaps too conscious enjoyment of danger but must needs glance at whiles towards where his mother watches from the *piazzetta* giving upon the flower-close with a faint shadow of remoteness or of reproach (*alles Vergangliche*) ["all that is transitory"] in her glad look. (422) [Floey, Atty, Tiny are Mat Dillon's daughters; "their darker friend," "Our Lady of the Cherries," is Molly; the lad of "four or five" is Stephen; "his mother" is May Dedalus. Joyce's style here is meant to be imitative of Walter Pater.]

Bloom elsewhere remembers that this was one of two meetings he had with Stephen as a boy. In the lilac garden meeting, Stephen, then five, was reluctant to shake Bloom's hand (680:6-9).

Menton at Dignam's funeral on June 16, 1904, well remembers the event:

—Who is that chap behind with Tom Kernan? John
Henry Menton asked. I know his face.

Ned Lambert glanced back.

—Bloom, he said, Madam Marion Tweedy that was, is,
I mean, the soprano. She's his wife.

—O, to be sure, John Henry Menton said. I haven't seen
her for some time. She was a finelooking woman. I danced
with her, wait, fifteen seventeen golden years ago, at Mat
Dillon's, in Roundtown. And a good armful she was.

He looked behind through the others.

—What is he? he asked. What does he do? Wasn't he
in the stationery line? I fell foul of him one evening, I
remember, at bowls.

Ned Lambert smiled.

—Yes, he was, he said, in Wisdom Hely's. A traveller
for blottingpaper.

—In God's name, John Henry Menton said, what did she
marry a coon like that for? She had plenty of game in her
then.

—Has still, Ned Lambert said. He does some canvassing
for ads.

John Henry Menton's large eyes stared ahead. (106)

And finally gets his revenge:

> Solicitor, I think [thinks Bloom]. I know his face. Menton.
> John Henry, solicitor, commissioner for oaths and affi-
> davits. Dignam used to be in his office. Mat Dillon's long
> ago. Jolly Mat convivial evenings. Cold fowl, cigars, the
> Tantalus glasses. Heart of gold really. Yes, Menton. Got his
> rag out that evening on the bowling green because I sailed
> inside him. Pure fluke of mine: the bias. Why he took such
> a rooted dislike to me. Hate at first sight. Molly and
> Floey Dillon linked under the lilactree, laughing. Fellow
> always like that, mortified if women are by.
>
> Got a dinge in the side of his hat. Carriage probably.
>
> —Excuse me, sir, Mr Bloom said beside them.

They stopped.

—Your hat is a little crushed, Mr Bloom said, pointing.

John Henry Menton stared at him for an instant without moving.

—There, Martin Cunningham helped, pointing also.

John Henry Menton took off his hat, bulged out the dinge and smoothed the nap with care on his coatsleeve. He clapped the hat on his head again.

—It's all right now, Martin Cunningham said.

John Henry Menton jerked his head down in acknowledgment.

—Thank you, he said shortly.

They walked on towards the gates. Mr Bloom, chapfallen, drew behind a few paces so as not to overhear. (115)

When Bloom returns to 7 Eccles Street on June 17, 1904, he tells Molly that he has seen Menton at Dignam's funeral. Molly then gives him a thought:

meet ah yes I met do you remember Menton and who else who let me see that big babbyface I saw him and he not long married flirting with a young girl at Pooles Myriorama and turned my back on him when he slinked out looking quite conscious what harm but he had the impudence to make up to me one time well done to him mouth almighty and his boiled eyes of all the big stupoes I ever met and thats called a solicitor (739) [Poole's Myriorama, a traveling picture show, appeared in Dublin once a year in the 1890s (G.). Thus Menton must have been married sometime in the 1890s.]

And since Bloom had brought Stephen home she remembers him on that day of seventeen years ago: "I suppose hes a man now by this time he was an innocent boy then and a darling little fellow in his lord Fauntleroy suit and curly hair like a prince on the stage when I saw him at Mat Dillons he liked me too I remember they all do" (774)

Other memories of Mat Dillon and his family. Molly: "her [Floey Dillon's] father was an awfully nice man he was near seventy always good humour well now Miss Tweedy or Miss Gillespie theres the pyannyer that was a solid silver coffee service he had too on the mahogany side-board" (758) Floey Dillon, who was Molly's special friend: "because he [Bloom] used to be a bit on the jealous side whenever he asked who are you going to and I said over to Floey" (743) Floey now married: "Floey Dillon since she wrote to say she was married to a very rich architect if Im to believe all I hear with a villa and eight rooms" (758) Mamy Dillon: "who knows whod be the 1st man Id meet [Molly is thinking of going out to the market on the morning of June 17] theyre out looking for it in the morning Mamy Dillon used to say they are and the night too that was her massgoing" (780) Molly tries to help Atty Dillon write answers to the love letters and a proposal of marriage from a lawyer who later jilted her:

> just a few words not those long crossed letters Atty Dil-
> lon used to write to the fellow that was something in the
> four courts that jilted her after out of the ladies letter-
> writer when I told her to say a few simple words he could
> twist how he liked not acting with precipit precipitancy
> with equal candour the greatest earthly happiness answer
> to a gentlemans proposal affirmatively my goodness
> theres nothing else its all very fine for them but as for
> being a woman as soon as youre old they might as well
> throw you out in the bottom of the ash pit. (758-759)
> [There is a period in the text at the end of Molly's
> fourth sentence.]

Bloom: "Mat Dillon and his bevy of daughters: Tiny, Atty, Floey, Maimy, Louy, Hetty. Molly too. Eightyseven that was. Year before we [married]." (377) [In the same letter of October 14, 1921 to Mrs. Murray, in which he had asked about the Powells, Joyce also asked about the Dillons: "Also any information you have about the Dillons (Mat Dillon and his bevy of daughters, Tiny, Floey, Atty, Sara, Nannie and *Mamie,* especially the last, the cigarette smoker and Spanish type). Get an ordinary sheet of foolscap and a pencil and scribble any God damn drivel you may remember about these people." (L. I, p. 174.)

In a letter of November 2, 1921 to Mrs. Murray Joyce pursued the Dillons further: "Do you know anything of Mat Dillon's daughter Mamy who was in Spain? If so, please let me know." (L. I, p. 175.)]

4. Another home that Leopold and Molly frequent is that of Luke and Caroline Doyle who lived in Kimmage (705:9). H. & K. say there was a real Luke Doyle, a building surveyor, who lived at Camac Place, more properly described as being in Dolphin's Barn, rather than in Kimmage.

Henry Doyle, evidently a son of Luke and Caroline, is neither intelligent nor graceful. Molly: "he [Bloom] had a few brains not like that other fool Henry Doyle he was always breaking or tearing something in the charades I hate an unlucky man" (747) Bloom: "Rip: tear in Henny Doyle's overcoat." (377) The Doyles prophecy great things for Bloom, now a political aspirant and very voluble in his beliefs. Molly:

> he used to amuse me the things he said with that half slooth-
> ering smile on him and all the Doyles said he was going
> to stand for a member of Parliament O wasnt I the born
> fool to believe all his blather about home rule and the land
> league sending me that long strool of a song out of the
> Huguenots to sing in French to be more classy O beau
> pays de la Touraine that I never even sang once explaining
> and rigmaroling about religion and persecution he wont let
> you enjoy anything naturally (771)

A climactic evening of charades at the Doyles with Bloom playing Rip van Winkle. Bloom: "In Luke Doyle's long ago, Dolphin's Barn, the charades." (158) [This memory is set off by Bloom meeting on the street on June 16, 1904, Mrs. Breen, née Josie Powell (discussed below—see p. 88). So we know that Josie Powell was also a guest at the Doyles.]:

> At Dolphin's barn charades in Luke Doyle's house. (377) Rip van Winkle we played. Rip: [. . . .] Van: breadvan delivering. Winkle: cockles and periwinkles. Then I did Rip Van Winkle coming back. She leaned on the sideboard watching. Moorish eyes. Twenty years asleep in Sleepy Hollow. All changed. Forgotten. The young are old. (377)
>
> BELLO
>
> (*Ruthlessly.*) No, Leopold Bloom, all is changed by woman's will since you slept horizontal in Sleepy Hollow your night of twenty years. Return and see.
>
> (*Old Sleepy Hollow calls over the wold.*)
>
> SLEEPY HOLLOW
>
> Rip Van Winkle! Rip Van Winkle!
>
> BLOOM
>
> (*In tattered moccasins with a rusty fowlingpiece, tiptoeing, fingertipping, his haggard bony bearded face peering through the diamond panes, cries out.*) I see her! It's she! The first night at Mat Dillon's! But that dress, the green! And her hair is dyed gold and he . . .
>
> BELLO
>
> (*Laughs mockingly.*) That's your daughter, you owl, with a Mullingar student. (542)
>
> [A fused memory on Bloom's part; he puts together the first night at Mat Dillon's and the night of the charades at the Doyles.]

Bloom is unable to sleep that night and stays up to watch the coming of the dawn:

What prospect of what phenomena inclined him to remain? [Bloom is standing alone outside his home in the early morning of June 17, 1904.]

The disparition of three final stars, the diffusion of daybreak, the apparition of a new solar disk.

Had he ever been a spectator of those phenomena?

Once, in 1887 after a protracted performance of charades in the house of Luke Doyle, Kimmage, he had awaited with patience the apparition of the diurnal phenomenon, seated on a wall, his gaze turned in the direction of Mizrach, the east.

He remembered the initial paraphenomena?

More active air, a matutinal distant cock, ecclesiastical clocks at various points, avine music, the isolated tread of an early wayfarer, the visible diffusion of the light of an invisible luminous body, the first golden limb of the resurgent sun perceptible low on the horizon. (705)

The first kiss on the night after the charades. Molly: "the night he kissed my heart at Dolphins barn I couldnt describe it simply it makes you feel like nothing on earth but he never knew how to embrace well" (747) Bloom:

He smiled, glancing askance at her mocking eye [on the morning of June 16, 1904.] The same young eyes. The first night after the charades. Dolphin's Barn. (64) June. A kiss on the shoulder: Nightstock in Mat Dillon's garden where I kissed her shoulder. Wish I had a full length oil-painting of her then. June that was too I wooed. (376-377)

1888

Leopold Bloom and Marion Tweedy, having fallen in love, become engaged, copulate and conceive, marry, and settle down to wedded bliss. Molly—some general impressions. His voice: "I could always hear his voice talking when the room was crowded and watch him" (743) His teeth: "splendid set of teeth he had made me hungry to look at them" (746) His politeness: "then still I like that in him polite to old women like that and waiters and beggars too hes not proud out of nothing" (738) His intelligence: "he had a few brains" (747) His handsome looks: "he was very handsome at that time trying to look like lord Byron I said I liked though he was too beautiful for a man and he was a little before we got engaged" (743) His pose of being a poet: "first I thought he was a poet like Byron and not an ounce of it in his composition" (775) Love at first sight: "it was he excited me I dont know how the first night" (771)

January 6, "Old Christmas night"—a housewarming at Georgina Simpson's. Another friend is Georgina Simpson who has a housewarming at her home to which are invited Leopold, Molly, and other friends, among them Josie Powell, the prettiest deb in Dublin— although she has buckteeth: *"herbivorous buck-teeth,"* (442)—Molly's best friend, and an admirer herself of Leopold, a feeling he reciprocates. Their flirtation at Georgina Simpson's party sets off the first lovers' quarrel between Molly and Leopold. (Here the games played are "Irving Bishop" [telepathy], finding-the-pin blindfolded, and thought-reading).

Molly:

> I know they were spooning a bit when I came on the scene he was dancing and sitting out with her the night of Georgina Simpsons housewarming and then he wanted to ram it down my neck on account of not liking to see her a wallflower that was why we had the standup row over politics he began it not me when he said about Our Lord being a carpenter at last he made me cry of course a woman is so sensitive about everything I was fuming with myself after for giving in only for I knew he was gone on me and

the first socialist he said He was he annoyed me so much I couldnt put him into a temper . . . after that I pretended I had on a coolness with her over him (742-743)

Bloom [Bloom reenacts his memory of the Christmas party in an hallucination in Bella Cohen's, set off by meeting Josie, now Mrs. Breen, on the morning of June 16]:

BLOOM

(*Seizes her wrist with his free hand.*) Josie Powell that was, prettiest deb in Dublin. How time flies by! Do you remember, harking back in a retrospective arrangement, Old Christmas night Georgina Simpson's housewarming while they were playing the Irving Bishop game, finding the pin blindfold and thoughtreading? Subject, what is in this snuffbox?

MRS. BREEN

You were the lion of the night with your seriocomic recitation and you looked the part. You were always a favourite with the ladies.

BLOOM

(*Squire of dames, in dinner jacket, with watered-silk facings, blue masonic badge in his buttonhole, black bow and mother-of-pearl studs, a prismatic champagne glass tilted in his hand.*) Ladies and gentlemen, I give you Ireland, home and beauty.

MRS. BREEN

The dear dead days beyond recall. Love's old sweet song.

BLOOM

(*Meaningfully dropping his voice.*) I confess I'm teapot with curiosity to find out whether some person's something is a little teapot at present.

MRS. BREEN

(*Gushingly.*) Tremendously teapot! London's teapot and I'm simply teapot all over me. (*She rubs sides with him.*)

After the parlour mystery games and the crackers from the tree we sat on the staircase ottoman. Under the mistletoe. Two is company.

BLOOM

(*Wearing a purple Napoleon hat with an amber halfmoon, his fingers and thumbs passing slowly down to her soft moist meaty palm which she surrenders gently.*) The witching hour of night. I took the splinter out of this hand, carefully, slowly. (*Tenderly, as he slips on her finger a ruby ring.*) Là ci darem la mano.

MRS. BREEN

(*In a onepiece evening frock executed in moonlight blue, a tinsel sylph's diadem on her brow with her dancecard fallen beside her moonblue satin slipper, curves her palm softly, breathing quickly.*) Voglio e non. You're hot! You're scalding! The left hand nearest the heart.

BLOOM

When you made your present choice [of Denis Breen] they said it was beauty and the beast. I can never forgive you for that. (*His clenched fist at his brow.*) Think what it means. All you meant to me then. (*Hoarsely.*) Woman, it's breaking me! (444-446)

MRS. BREEN

(*To Bloom.*) High jinks below stairs. (*She gives him the glad eye.*) Why didn't you kiss the spot to make it well? You wanted to.

BLOOM

(*Shocked.*) Molly's best friend! Could you? (446)

It was in fact only a matter of months and he [Bloom] could easily foresee him [Stephen] participating in their musical and artistic *conversaziones* during the festivities of the Christmas season, for choice, causing a slight flutter in the dovecotes of the fair sex and being made a lot of by ladies out for sensation, cases of which, as he happened to know, were on record, in fact, without giving the show away, he himself once upon a time, if he cared to, could easily have . . . (663-664)

February 2. Bloom has not completely abandoned his political interests. That evening he climbed a tree on Northumberland Road in order to watch a torchlight procession escorting into Dublin the Marquis of Ripon and John Morley, English politicians who, at this time, favored Home Rule for Ireland (716:42-717:5).

February 14, Valentine's Day. But he has other interests as well, and on this day he sends Miss Marion Tweedy the following acrostic:

P*oets oft have sung in rhyme*
O*f music sweet their praise divine.*
L*et them hymn it nine times nine.*
D*earer far than song or wine,*
Y*ou are mine. The world is mine.* (678)

Bloom, however, also appears to have sent, anonymously, a valentine, a representation of a gazelle, to Josie Powell (444:13-14).

Things get warm. Molly lends him a book with an ulterior purpose in doing so: "I read and the shadow of Ashlydyat Mrs. Henry Wood Henry Dunbar by that other woman I lent him afterwards with Mulveys photo in it so as he see I wasnt without" (756) He makes her a present: "and he made me the present of lord Byrons poems and the three pairs of gloves" (743)

He expresses intense interest in her gloves, bedroom and drawers:

begging me to give him a tiny bit cut off my drawers that was the evening coming along Kenilworth square he kissed me in the eye of my glove and I had to take it off asking me questions is it permitted to inquire the shape of my bedroom so I let him keep it as if I forgot it to think

of me when I saw him slip it into his pocket of course hes
mad on the subject of drawers thats plain to be seen (746)

The Tweedys move to Brighton Square and Bloom is
able to see Molly's bedroom there:

the very 1st opportunity he got a chance in Brighton
square running into my bedroom pretending the ink got on
his hands to wash it off with the Albion milk and sulphur
soap I used to use and the gelatin still round it O I
laughed myself sick at him that day (771)

Bloom thinks things are getting too hot and tries to
stay away, but he cannot:

when he saw me from behind following in the rain I saw
him before he saw me however standing at the corner of
the Harolds cross road with a new raincoat on him with
the muffler in the Zingari colours to show off his complex-
ion and the brown hat looking slyboots as usual what was
he doing there where hed no business they can go and get
whatever they like from anything at all with a skirt on it
and were not to ask any questions but they want to know
where were you where are you going I could feel him coming
along skulking after me his eyes on my neck he had been
keeping away from the house he felt it was getting too
warm for him so I half turned and stopped then he pestered
me to say yes till I took my glove off slowly watching him
he said my openwork sleeves were too cold for the rain
anything for an excuse to put his hand anear me drawers
drawers the whole blessed time till I promised to give him
the pair off my doll to carry about in his waistcoat pocket
O Maria Santissima he did look a big fool dreeping in
the rain splendid set of teeth he had made me hungry to
look at them and beseeched of me to lift the orange petticoat I had on with sunray pleats that there was nobody he
said hed kneel down in the wet if I didnt so persevering he
would too and ruin his new raincoat you never know what

freak theyd take alone with you theyre so savage for it if
anyone was passing so I lifted them a bit and touched his
trousers outside (746)

One night Molly is afraid she's told Bloom too much
about herself in talking of her dreams: "I let out too much
the night before talking of dreams so I didnt want to let
him know more than was good for him" (743)

The next night Bloom almost proposes:

it showed he could hold in and wasnt to be got for the
asking he was on the pop of asking me too the night in the
kitchen I was rolling the potato cake theres something I want
to say to you only for I put him off letting on I was in a
temper with my hands and arms full of pastry flour (743)

He writes letters constantly: "then writing a letter
every morning sometimes twice a day I liked the way he
made love then he knew the way to take a woman" (747)

Molly begins to practice writing her new name (per-
haps-to-be): "I never thought that would be my name
Bloom when I used to write it in print to see how it looked
on a visiting card or practising for the butcher and oblige
M Bloom" (761)

Molly lets Josie Powell in on some of what is going on:

though she didnt like it so much the day I was in fits of
laughing with the giggles I couldnt stop about all my hair-
pins falling one after another with the mass of hair I had
youre always in great humour she said yes because it grigged
her because she knew what it meant because I used to tell
her a good bit of what went on between us not all but just
enough to make her mouth water (743-744)

Josie, Molly, and Leopold have a three-way relationship:

she used to be always embracing me Josie whenever he was
there meaning him of course glauming me over and when I

> said I washed up and down as far as possible asking me did
> you wash possible the women are always egging on to that
> putting it on thick when hes there they know by his sly eye
> blinking a bit putting on the indifferent when they come out
> with something the kind he is what spoils him (743)

May 1888. A question is asked and an answer is given.
Leopold and Molly take the train to Howth: "that was an
exceptional man that common workman that left us alone
in the carriage that day going to Howth" (748)

Lion's Head, Howth, on a beautiful day. Molly: "though
I had the devils own job to get it out of him though I liked
him for that it showed he could hold in and wasnt to be got
for the asking" (743)

Molly has two recollections of the proposal, a short
prosaic one and a lengthy romantic one: Prosaism: "make
a declaration [to Josie Powell Breen] with his plabbery
kind of a manner to her like he did to me" (743) Romance:

> the sun shines for you he said the day we were lying
> among the rhododendrons on Howth head in the grey
> tweed suit and his straw hat the day I got him to propose
> to me yes first I gave him the bit of seedcake out of my
> mouth and it was leapyear like now yes 16 years ago My
> God after that long kiss I near lost my breath yes he said
> I was a flower of the mountain yes so we are flowers all
> a womans body yes that was one true thing he said in his
> life and the sun shines for you today yes that was why I
> liked him because I saw he understood or felt what a
> woman is and I knew I could always get round him and I
> gave him all the pleasure I could leading him on till he
> asked me to say yes and I wouldnt answer first only looked
> out over the sea and the sky I was thinking of so many
> things he didnt know (782) and I thought well as well him
> as another [this refers to Mulvey's kiss in 1886 and Bloom's
> kiss and proposal in 1888] and then I asked him with my

eyes to ask again yes and then he asked me would I yes to say yes my mountain flower and first I put my arms around him yes and drew him down to me so he could feel my breasts all perfume yes and his heart was going like mad and yes I said yes I will Yes. (783)

Bloom [At Davy Byrnes's pub on the afternoon of June 16, Bloom has a glass of wine and sees two flies copulating.]:

Stuck on the pane two flies buzzed, stuck.

Glowing wine on his palate lingered swallowed. Crushing in the winepress grapes of Burgundy. Sun's heat it is. Seems to a secret touch telling me memory. Touched his sense moistened remembered. Hidden under wild ferns on Howth. Below us bay sleeping sky. No sound. The sky. The bay purple by the Lion's head. Green by Drumleck. Yellow-green towards Sutton. Fields of undersea, the lines faint brown in grass, buried cities. Pillowed on my coat she had her hair, earwigs in the heather scrub my hand under her nape, you'll toss me all. O wonder! Coolsoft with ointments her hand touched me, caressed: her eyes upon me did not turn away. Ravished over her I lay, full lips full open, kissed her mouth. Yum. Softly she gave me in my mouth the seedcake warm and chewed. Mawkish pulp her mouth had mumbled sweet and sour with spittle. Joy: I ate it: joy. Young life, her lips that gave me pouting. Soft, warm, sticky gumjelly lips. Flowers her eyes were, take me, willing eyes. Pebbles fell. She lay still. A goat. No-one. High on Ben Howth rhododendrons a nannygoat walking sure-footed, dropping currants. Screened under ferns she laughed warmfolded. Wildly I lay on her, kissed her; eyes, her lips, her stretched neck, beating, woman's breasts full in her blouse of nun's veiling, fat nipples upright. Hot I tongued her. She kissed me. I was kissed. All yielding she tossed my hair. Kissed, she kissed me. (175-176)

This constellation of images—Howth, rhododendrons, and a nannygoat—constitute the primary memory-mechanism by which Bloom recalls the greatest moment of his life. These images appear and reappear throughout the day and night of June 16, 1904 (271:20-21; 288:13-14; 377:6-9; 379:18-20; 550:4-16; 628:11-18).

Bloom ponders the mysteries of sexual attraction, sameness and uniqueness:

> Curious she an only child, I an only child. So it returns. Think you're escaping and run into yourself. Longest way round is the shortest way home. And just when he and she. Circus horse walking in a ring. (377) Why me? [he asks Molly]. Because you were so foreign from the others. (380)

That Molly fell in love with him gives Bloom a life-long assurance that he is not ugly: "Ought to attend to my appearance my age. Didn't let her [Gerty MacDowell] see me in profile. Still, you never know. Pretty girls and ugly men marrying. Beauty and the beast. Besides I can't be so if Molly." (369) [The exact month of the proposal is never given in the text. It has to be in the spring or summer of 1888 because of all kinds of indications. I chose the month of May for the following reasons. First, Molly's initial experience with a man, Mulvey, took place on a lovely day high on a mount, Gibraltar, overlooking the sea in the month of May. We also know that the bowling incident at Mat Dillon's took place in May 1887. Joyce enjoyed employing such parallels and no doubt would have done so for the Bloom-Molly plighting of troth. Second, Bloom had to become a Catholic in order to marry Molly. To find out how long he would have had to take instruction before being baptized as a Catholic I have consulted Father Stephen Kuder, S.J. of the Graduate Theological Union, Berkeley. Father Kuder says it would be impossible to tell precisely unless one had access to the directives of local bishops of the time. However, an educated guess would put the time as about six months or perhaps less. The Blooms marry in October and Bloom would have had to become a Catholic before the actual ceremony. Strictly speaking, then, he should have begun his instruction six months before, in April of 1888. Balancing probabilities, however, I assume that Joyce would have preserved his "May" parallelism, no matter what, and for all one knows, five months of instruction may have sufficed in certain dioceses at that time. Third, in a general way May rather than June was Joyce's favorite month. John Joyce married Mary Jane Murray on May 5, 1880, and, in the words of Joyce's biographer, ". . . the month of May, when his parents were married, always seemed a lucky month to James Joyce" (E., p. 17). Joyce himself, born in February 1882, had to have been conceived in May of the preceding year, as was the fictional Stephen Dedalus. Bloom was born in May, around the sixth day of the month, and it would not have been at all unlikely for Joyce to have had Bloom propose to Molly on his (Bloom's) birthday. At least Joyce set great store on his own birthdays and arranged to have both *Ulysses* and *Finnegans Wake* published on his name day (February 2). Blazes Boylan makes his first pass at Molly (see the entry for May 29, 1903) in the month of May. Bloom was stung by the bee and borrowed the book from the Capel Street library in May. Molly, in a year unspecified, mentions: "the candle I lit that evening in Whitefriars street chapel for the month of May see it brought its luck" (741). What the luck was is never specified, unless Molly is referring to Boylan in which case the year would be 1904.

Although *Ulysses* itself takes place in June, there are more references to the word "May" than to any of the other names of the months of the year, according to the Hanley *Word Index*: "May," twenty references (sixteen are to the month of May); "June," seventeen; "February," six; "September," six; "March," five; "December," five; "January," four (plus one "Januarys"); "October," four; "August," three; "November," two; "July," one; "April," none. As indicated above, not all the "Mays" refer to the month of the year. Four of them constitute other meanings of the word, and two of them refer to Stephen Dedalus's mother, which brings me to my last point. The nickname or familiar name of Joyce's own mother, to whom he was deeply attached, and vice versa, despite doctrinal differences, was "May." Thus in Bella Cohen's she appears from the grave: "I was once the beautiful May Goulding. I am dead." (580)]

Affianced. Molly tells Bloom something—exactly what is not clear—about her mother: "he hadnt an idea about my mother till we were engaged otherwise hed never have got me so cheap as he did he was ten times worse himself" (745-746)

Molly confesses to Father Corrigan certain premarital intimacies:

I hate that confession when I used to go to Father Corrigan he touched me father and what harm if he did where and I said on the canal bank like a fool but whereabouts on your person my child on the leg behind high up was it yes rather high up was it where you sit down yes O Lord couldnt he say bottom right out and have done with it what has that got to do with it and did you whatever way he put it I forget no father and I always think of the real father what did he want to know for when I already confessed it to God he had a nice fat hand the palm moist always I wouldnt mind feeling it neither would he Id say by the bullneck in his horsecollar I wonder did he know me in the

box I could see his face he couldnt see mine of course hed
never turn or let on (741)

Visits a gynecologist, Dr. Collins:

I ought to go to the doctor only it would be like before
I married him when I had that white thing coming from me
and Floey made me go to that dry old stick Dr Collins for
womens diseases on Pembroke road your vagina he called it
I suppose thats how he got all the gilt mirrors and carpets
getting round those rich ones off Stephens green running
up to him for every little fiddlefaddle her vagina and her
cochinchina theyve money of course so theyre all right I
wouldnt marry him not if he was the last man in the world
besides there something queer about their children always
smelling around those filthy bitches all sides asking me if
what I did had an offensive odour what did he want me to
do but the one thing gold maybe what a question if I
smathered it all over his wrinkly old face for him with all
my compriment I suppose hed know then and could you
pass it easily pass what I thought he was talking about
the rock of Gibraltar the way he puts it . . . still all the
same paying him for that how much is that doctor one
guinea please and asking me had I frequent omissions
where do those old fellows get all the words they have
omissions with his shortsighted eyes on me cocked sideways
I wouldnt trust him too far to give me chloroform or God
knows what else still I liked him when he sat down to write
the thing out frowning so severe his nose intelligent like
that you be damned you lying strap O anything no matter
who except an idiot he was clever enough to spot that of
course (770-771)

Bloom tells Major Tweedy and Marion of the romantic
honeymoon that awaits and of a great future for Leopold
and Molly Bloom:

all the things he told father he was going to do and me
but I saw through him telling me all the lovely places we

could go for the honeymoon Venice by moonlight with the
gondolas and the lake of Como he had a picture cut out
of some paper of and mandolines and lanterns O how nice I
said whatever I liked he was going to do immediately if
not sooner will you be my man will you carry my can he
ought to get a leather medal with a putty rim for all the
plans he invents (765)

Bloom discusses his favorite topics with the Major and
his daughter, both together and separately, in Mat Dillon's parlor (667:25-28).

September 1. Mrs. Riordan comes to live with the
Dedaluses (680:20-21).

September 8. Leopold sends Molly eight poppies for
her birthday: "he knew the way to take a woman when he
sent me the 8 big poppies because mine was the 8th"
(747)

September 10. Sexual intercourse between Leopold and
Molly; Milly conceived. Molly:

I was dying to find out was he circumcised [Bloom was
not circumcised] he was shaking like a jelly all over they
want to do everything too quick take all the pleasure out
of it and father waiting all the time for his dinner he told
me to say I left my purse in the butchers and had to go
back for it what a Deceiver (746) with female issue born
15 June 1889, having been anticipatorily consummated
[before the marriage of Leopold and Molly] on the 10
September of the same year and complete carnal intercourse, with ejaculation of semen within the natural female
organ, (736) [Bloom never thinks of this moment.]

Bloom's letters become explicit:

then he wrote me that letter with all those words in it
how could he have the face to any woman after his company
manners making it so awkward after when we met asking

me have I offended you with my eyelids down of course he saw I wasnt (746-747) all thinking of him and his mad crazy letters my Precious one everything connected with your glorious Body everything underlined that comes from it is a thing of beauty and of joy for ever something he got out of some nonsensical book (771) [The aphorism "A thing of beauty is a joy forever," has been put to strange uses, but never so grotesque as this, for what Bloom is talking about is Molly's urine, menstrual blood, vaginal discharges, and, especially, feces.]

October. Bloom baptized a Catholic by the reverend Charles Malone, C.C., in the church of the Three Patrons, Rathgar (682:22-23; 716:27-29).

Molly has not had her menstrual and the lovers wonder if she is pregnant (which she is): "that he had me always at myself 4 or 5 times a day sometimes and I said I hadnt are you sure O yes I said I am quite sure in a way that shut him up I knew what was coming next" (771)

October 8. The marriage of Leopold (age twenty-two) and Molly (age eighteen). Molly: "I was married 88" (775) "I could have been a prima donna only I married him" (763) Bloom: "marriage had been celebrated 1 calendar month after the 18th anniversary of her birth (8 September 1870), viz. 8 October," (736) "Eh! I have sixteen years of black slave labour behind me." (554)

The Doyles, Dillons, and Alderman John Hooper give them wedding presents: a stuffed owl from Hooper (113:28-29; 694:17-18; 707:26-27); a clock of connemara marble from the Dillons (694:17-18; 707:22-24); a dwarf tree from the Doyles (707:24-26).

Molly and Josie's friendship dwindles:

youre looking blooming Josie used to say after I married him (761) but that wasnt my fault she didnt darken the door

> much after we were married (744) Be sure now and write to
> me [Bloom has been thinking of the fragility of female
> friendships.] And I'll write to you. Now won't you? Molly
> and Josie Powell. Till Mr. Right comes along then meet
> once in a blue moon. *Tableau!* O, look who it is for the
> love of God! How are you at all? What have you been
> doing with yourself? Kiss and delighted to, kiss, to see
> you. Picking holes in each other's appearance. You're look-
> ing splendid. Sister souls showing their teeth at one an-
> other. How many have you left? Wouldn't lend each other a
> pinch of salt. (369)

Bloom acquires a new job with Wisdom Hely (155:20-21).

[Bloom appears to have worked for Hely twice. The first
time was in his early married years. It is impossible from
the text to ascertain when he quit or was fired, but by 1893
Bloom was working for Joe Cuffe, who discharged him in
1894. The second time with Hely was 1894 to 1895; this
time he was fired, as Molly explicitly says (753:20-21).
(Two chronologies also place him in Hely's in 1895.) The
problems involved in dating these matters, and others,
are discussed in the entry for 1894.]

He appears to have been still working for Hely in 1889
because on June 16, 1904, he thinks of a co-worker in
Hely's who died fifteen years ago (114:8-9).

1888-1893

The early years of the Blooms' married life were happy
ones. They changed residences several times but were
always within the radius of the old Jewish section of
Dublin, where Leopold had been born. They therefore
had a circle of Jewish friends and a social life, no longer
one of their felicities in 1904. One of Bloom's reminis-

cences provides a picture of the general ambience of these golden years:

> Citrons too [Bloom is thinking of the fruit]. Wonder is poor Citron still alive in Saint Kevin's parade. And Mastiansky with the old cither. Pleasant evenings we had then. Molly in Citron's basketchair [. . . .] They [citrons] fetched high prices too Moisel told me. Arbutus place: Pleasants street: pleasant old times. Must be without a flaw, he said. Coming all that way: Spain, Gibraltar, Mediterranean, the Levant. Crates lined up on the quayside at Jaffa, chap ticking them off in a book, navvies handling them in soiled dungarees. (60-61)

[Citron, Mastiansky, a grocer, and Moisel were all friends of the Blooms. Pleasants Street is one of the places the Blooms lived in their early years. They may or may not have lived on Arbutus Place, which is in the same general neighborhood. H. & K. have full glosses on the proper names and the street names.] Their circle of Jewish friends is mentioned elsewhere: Shulumowitz, Goldwater, Rosenberg, Moisel, Citron, Watchman, Mastiansky, Abramovitz, Chazen (544:19-26); Mastiansky and Citron (497:17-20; 586:40).

1889

The Blooms are living on Pleasants Street and Molly is pregnant with Milly.

1. Mrs. Moisel is pregnant at the same time: "Funny sight two of them together, their bellies out. Molly and Mrs. Moisel. Mothers' meeting." (162) [Moisel himself, who lived on Heytesbury Street, was to die—date unspecified but sometime before June 16, 1904—of pyemia (705:1-2).]

2. A husband commits his "ultimate obscenity" with a wife. (I'm assuming this peculiar and exotic act was performed during Molly's pregnancy):

BELLO

(*Whistles loudly.*) Say! What was the most revolting piece of obscenity in all your career of crime? Go the whole hog. Puke it out. Be candid for once. (538)

BLOOM

Don't ask me. Our mutual faith. Pleasants street. I only thought the half of the . . . I swear on my sacred oath . . .

BELLO

(*Peremptorily.*) Answer. Repugnant wretch! I insist on knowing. Tell me something to amuse me, smut or a bloody goodghoststory or a line of poetry, quick, quick, quick! Where? How? What time? With how many? I give you just three seconds. One! Two! Thr . . .!

BLOOM

(*Docile, gurgles.*) I rererepugnosed in rerererepugnant . . . (538)

3. June 15, 1889. The birth of Milly, with Mrs. Thornton the midwife and Dr. Murren the physician:

Remember the summer morning she was born, running to knock up Mrs Thornton in Denzille street. Jolly old woman. Lots of babies she must have helped into the world. (66) Old Mrs Thornton was a jolly old soul. All my babies, she said. The spoon of pap in her mouth before she fed them. O, that's nyumyum. Got her hand crushed by old Tom Wall's son. (162) Snuffy Dr Murren. People knocking them up at all hours. For God'sake doctor. Wife in her throes. Then keep them waiting months for their fee. To attendance on your wife. No gratitude in people. Humane doctors, most of them. (162)

Milly arrives: "15 June 1889. A querulous newborn female infant crying to cause and lessen congestion." (693) (See also 736:6-7.)

4. Molly recovers quickly: "Lucky Molly got over hers lightly." (161) "Phthisis retires for the time being, then returns. How flat they look after all of a sudden! Peaceful eyes. Weight off their minds." (162)

5. Molly breast-feeds Milly (and Leopold) and is almost observed undraped by a student named Penrose who lives at the Citrons':

> I had a great breast of milk with Milly enough for two what was the reason of that he said I could have got a pound a week as a wet nurse all swelled out the morning that delicate looking student that stopped in No 28 with the Citrons Penrose nearly caught me washing through the window only for I snapped up the towel to my face that was his studenting hurt me they used to weaning her till he got doctor Brady to give me the Belladonna prescription I had to get him to suck them they were so hard he said it was sweeter and thicker than cows then he wanted to milk me into the tea well hes beyond everything I declare (754) [Joyce's original intention was to have Bloom suck Molly's breasts after the death of Rudy, for in Notesheet I for Penelope he says "L B sucked her after Rudy" (H., p. 490).]

6. Penrose also remains in Bloom's memory, in a fitful way:

> What was the name of that priestylooking chap was always squinting in when he passed? Weak eyes, woman. Stopped in Citron's saint Kevin's parade. Pen something. Pendennis? My memory is getting. Pen . . .? Of course it's years ago. (155-156) Could he walk in a beeline if he hadn't that cane? [Bloom has just helped a young blind man cross the street] Bloodless pious face like a fellow going in to be a priest.
>
>   Penrose! That was that chap's name. (181)

The name Penrose occurs three other times: uttered by Grandfather Virag (519:27), in the exhaustive list of Ulyssean proper names (586:40-41), and in the list of Molly's supposed lovers (731:25).

7. Sometime during the early married years (I place it here because Bloom remembers it by way of association with Penrose) Molly is singing in a church choir and is escorted home from choir practice by the tenor Bartell d'Arcy—after he kisses her in the church:

> Bartell dArcy too that he [Bloom] used to make fun of when he commenced kissing me on the choir stairs after I sang Gounods *Ave Maria* what are we waiting for O my heart kiss me straight on the brow and part which is my brown part he was pretty hot for all his tinny voice too my low notes he was always raving about if you can believe him I liked the way he used his mouth singing then he said wasnt it terrible to do that there in a place like that I dont see anything so terrible about it Ill tell him [Bloom] about that some day not now and surprise him ay and Ill take him there and show him the very place too we did it so now there you are like it or lump it he thinks nothing can happen without him knowing (745)

Molly remembers d'Arcy's verbal technique: "he [Simon Dedalus] had a delicious glorious voice Phoebe dearest goodbye *sweet*heart he always sang it not like Bartell dArcy sweet *tart* goodbye" (774) Bloom: "Bartell d'Arcy was the tenor, just coming out then. Seeing her home after practice. Conceited fellow with his waxedup moustache. Gave her that song *Winds that blow from the south*." (156)

8. Other matters. A notorious murder, Mrs. Maybrick's poisoning of her husband, occurs in 1889. Molly:

> take that Mrs Maybrick that poisoned her husband for what I wonder in love with some other man yet it was found out

on her wasnt she the downright villain to go and do a thing
like that of course some men can be dreadfully aggravating
drive you mad and always the worst word in the world what
do they ask us to marry them for if were so bad as all that
comes to yes because they cant get on without us white
Arsenic she put in his tea off flypaper wasnt it I wonder
why they call it that if I asked him hed say its from the
Greek leave us as wise as we were before she must have
been madly in love with the other fellow to run the chance
of being hanged O she didnt care if that was her nature
what could she do besides theyre not brutes enough to go
and hang a woman surely are they (744)

[G. and T. have full accounts of *l'affaire* Maybrick. Florence Maybrick poisoned her husband James, who died on
May 11, 1889. Mrs. Maybrick had had a lover, one Mr.
Brierly. Mrs. Maybrick was found guilty and convicted.
However, it was ascertained that James Maybrick had
long been taking drugs and patent medicines, including
strychnine and arsenic, and these facts led to Mrs. Maybrick's sentence being commuted to life imprisonment.
She was released in 1904 and wrote a book about her
experiences, *My Fifteen Lost Years.*]

Molly sees Kitty O'Shea combing her hair:

magnificent head of hair on her [a Mrs. Galbraith Molly
has seen recently] down to her waist tossing it back like
that like Kitty OShea in Grantham street 1st thing I did
every morning to look across see her combing it as if she
loved it and was full of it pity I only got to know her the day
before we left (751)

[Needless to say, this was not Parnell's Kitty O'Shea. I
date this incident as occurring in the Blooms' Pleasants
Street days because Grantham Street is quite near Pleasants Street. Synge Street ends at Pleasants Street, approximately bisecting it. One block to the south Grantham Street runs off Synge. See map, p. 138 below.]

1890

Milly cuts her teeth. Molly: "but if someone gave them [men] a touch of it themselves [pregnancy] theyd know what I went through with Milly nobody would believe cutting her teeth too" (742)

Bloom.

1. The matter of Molly's weight: "She scaled just eleven stone nine. She put on nine pounds after weaning." (547) [Since a stone is fourteen pounds, Molly weighed 154 pounds before weaning and 163 pounds afterwards. It is possible that both "nines" constitute the same nine, in which case Molly weighed 154. She has added considerable weight since then.]

2. After Milly was weaned the Blooms went with Josie Powell to the races at Leopardstown, a race track in south Dublin which opened in 1888 and is still, recently modernized, in operation. Bloom was nattily attired, and Josie was dressed to the nines, eliciting thereby great admiration from Bloom. At the races Molly won seven shillings. On the way home she ate a sandwich of spiced beef from Mrs. Joe Gallaher's lunch basket. There were two other passengers in the carriage, Rogers and Maggot O'Reilly, who mimicked a cock when they passed a farm house, making Molly laugh. They were passed by a gig driven by Marcus Tertius Moses, the tea merchant, who had his daughter with him. All indications are that Bloom and Josie were still attracted to one another at this time (448:12-449:26).

3. The Fall of Parnell. The greatest Irish political catastrophe in Bloom's lifetime (and in Joyce's mind) was the fall from power of Charles Stewart Parnell, beginning in 1890, and the subsequent early death of Parnell in 1891.

First elected to a seat in Parliament in 1875, Parnell had soon gained ascendency over his Irish colleagues (Parnell was Anglo-Irish on his paternal side and American on his maternal side), and by 1880 he was elected head of the Irish delegation at Westminster. Under his leadership and pursuing an obstructionist policy (that is, using parliamentary methods to obstruct the workings of Parliament), the Irish M.P.'s came to hold the balance of power between the English Liberal and Conservative parties, and Parnell became the greatest leader the Irish had known. He also came closer to forcing the English to grant Home Rule to Ireland than had any other Irish leader.

Parnell in his prime had charismatic powers over his colleagues and the Irish people: "You must [thinks Bloom] have a certain fascination: Parnell. Arthur Griffith [an Irish political leader in 1904] is a squareheaded fellow but he has no go in him for the mob." (163-164)

The sight on a Dublin street of Parnell's surviving brother, John Howard Parnell, now city marshal of Dublin, causes Bloom to ruminate on Charles Stewart Parnell and his family:

> There he is: the brother. Image of him. Haunting face. Now that's a coincidence. Course hundreds cf times you think of a person and don't meet him. Like a man walking in his sleep. No-one knows him. Must be a corporation meeting today. They say he never put on the city marshal's uniform since he [John Howard] got the job. Charley Boulger used to come out on his high horse, cocked hat, puffed, powdered and shaved. Look at the woebegone walk of him. Eaten a bad egg. Poached eyes on ghost. I have a pain. Great man's brother: his brother's brother. He'd look nice on the city charger. Drop into the D.B.C. probably for his coffee, play chess there. His brother used men as pawns.

Let them all go to pot. Afraid to pass a remark on him.
Freeze them up with that eye of his. That's the fascination: the name. All a bit touched. Mad Fanny and his other
sister Mrs Dickinson driving about with scarlet harness.
Bolt upright like surgeon M'Ardle. Still David Sheehy beat
him [John Howard] for south Meath. Apply for the Chiltern Hundreds and retire into public life. The patriot's
banquet. Eating orangepeels in the park. Simon Dedalus
said when they put him [John Howard Parnell or David
Sheehy] in parliament that Parnell would come back from
the grave and lead him out of the House of Commons by
the arm. (165)

Bloom (Joyce) has packed in here many Parnell memories. The first is the difference between the two brothers
despite their similar appearance. John Howard, who
should be going in his city marshal's uniform to a meeting
of the City of Dublin Corporation is going instead in
civilian dress to the D.B.C., an eatery where chess was
played, to play chess. This leads to a few thoughts on the
ruthless strength, control over men, and steely eye of
Charles Stewart. "All a bit touched" refers to the Parnell
family as a whole. Not only was there a strain of mental
instability in the past generations of the family, but
Charles Stewart Parnell, his mother, and the two sisters
mentioned here were a decidedly eccentric lot, as everyone
who knew them said. The anecdotes are legion. Suffice it
to say that Charles Stewart was subject to fits of depres-
sion, was a somnambulist and a victim of nightmares, and
was incredibly, "invincibly," as one commentator said,
superstitious. Charles Stewart Parnell once spoke to Michael Davitt of his fear of going mad and remarked that
madness was not a subject "treated lightly" in his family.
    "Mad Fanny" was Frances Parnell (1854-1882), a vig-
orous Irish nationalist herself. She finally left Ireland to

join her mother in America, where she wrote Irish
patriotic verse. Parnell was very close to Fanny, and he
was devastated by her early and rather mysterious death
in America in 1882. Timothy Healy in his memoirs said
she died of an overdose of sleeping draught. "Mrs Dickinson" was Emily Parnell (1841-1918), who wrote an odd
book, *A Patriot's Mistake,* about her brother after his
death. The *Irish Times* called it "A Patriot's Sister's
Mistake."

In 1903 David Sheehy and John Howard Parnell con-
tested the seat from South Meath and Sheehy won. "The
Chiltern Hundreds" was the name given to a method by
which an English M.P. could retire from Parliament,
usually ingloriously, and take a sinecure. Hence John
Howard Parnell's city marshalship is a sinecure.

As the Eumaeus section (pp. 613-665), in Skin-the-
Goat's cab shelter, has the most references to and discus-
sions of the Phoenix Park murders and the Invincibles, so
too does it contain the fullest discussion of Parnell and his
downfall. Most of the ruminations are by Bloom, and
reach their climax when Bloom remembers, twice, his
actual meeting with Parnell. The bulk of the Parnell
references are jammed into pages 649 to 652. They are,
however, impossible to paraphrase as Joyce presents
them here. First, the Eumaeus style is so cunningly
wrought as almost to defy any attempt to set forth the real
meaning of its serpentine and booby-trap laden sentences
in any other kind of prose conveyance than that of the
original. Or, to put it another way, any full explanation or
explication would require a small volume in itself. Second,
Joyce is playing an elaborate game with his facts in this
section. At times they are correct; most often they are
wrong; sometimes there is an admixture of truth and
error in an assertion. For example, there is a wildly

improbable interchange between Stephen and Bloom (652:9-18), where it is said that Mrs. O'Shea, Parnell's mistress, was Spanish, like Molly. Actually, Mrs. O'Shea, née Wood, was English and had married one William O'Shea, a retired Captain from the Eighteenth Hussars. However, she did have two connections to the Iberian peninsula. First, her maternal grandfather, whose name was Michell, was Admiral of the Portuguese Navy. Second, Captain O'Shea had relatives who had gone to Madrid, entered banking and intermarried with Spaniards. After their marriage in 1867 William O'Shea and his new bride went to Madrid where Willie, as he was called, worked in a bank. However, things did not work out, as was typical of anything O'Shea tried, and the O'Sheas returned to England after a year. Mrs. O'Shea did say in her memoirs that she thought, apropos of the Spanish O'Sheas, "the admixture of Irish and Spanish blood [the mixture of Molly Bloom] is most charming in result." [Katherine O'Shea (Mrs. Charles Stewart Parnell), *Charles Stewart Parnell* (London, 1914), Vol. 1, p. 70.] Joyce had, of course, read Kitty O'Shea's memoirs.

It would require much too much space, as the above remarks indicate, to separate out all the correct facts and the incorrect ones, the truths and the fantasies in the Parnell story as narrated in this section. Also the Parnell story in Eumaeus is not told chronologically but loops back and forth in time.

Nevertheless, Eumaeus manages, in its own peculiar fashion, to convey many—not all—of the essentials of the career and fate of Ireland's greatest leader and Joyce's own political hero, his "idol with feet of clay" (649).

The following account will cover the points that Joyce makes about the Parnell affair but with the facts presented correctly and with minimal attempt to tie them into the actual text, for reasons given.

The first mention of Parnell is by Skin-the-Goat, the proprietor of the cab shelter, who concludes a patriotic outburst by quoting, correctly, one of Parnell's most famous dictums: "Ireland, Parnell said, could not spare a single one of her sons." (640)

By 1880 Parnell's physical height, handsome looks, commanding presence, superb political intelligence, steely will, and charismatic powers (649:33-35; 651:23-24) had made him the undisputed leader of the Irish Parliamentary Party. The Irish people kept talismans of him, as did Mrs. Riordan, who lived with the Dedaluses from September 1, 1888 to December 29, 1891: a green brush for Parnell and a maroon one for Michael Davitt (681:16-18). In 1880 Parnell met Katherine O'Shea, now virtually separated from her husband, who had none of the power or charisma or the position in the world of Parnell. The initially platonic relationship between Parnell and Mrs. O'Shea soon turned into a love affair which later became known to people close to Parnell and to the British government, although the lovers tried to be as secretive as possible. Finally, almost a decade later, O'Shea filed a divorce suit against his wife, naming Parnell as the corespondent, and the trial was held in November 1890. The newspapers had a field day with the trial and broadcast to the world at large the juicier details of the love affair, including an account (which Joyce describes erroneously) of one of the rather ignominious ways in which Parnell tried to avoid detection by O'Shea by scrambling out of an upstairs window (651:9-10). Part of Parnell's own party then turned against him, and a famous series of meetings was held by the Irish M.P.'s in Committee

Room 15 at Westminster. At its conclusion a majority voted against Parnell's continuing as chairman of the Irish delegation. Joyce twice says that seventy-two Irish M.P.'s voted against Parnell (649:39; 660:42-43). Actually the vote against him was forty-four to twenty-nine. Parnell, however, refused to accept the verdict and returned to Ireland to carry on the fight by appealing to the Irish voters.

Bloom meets Parnell.

On December 10 Parnell arrives in Dublin to carry his fight to the people of Dublin and Ireland. One of his first acts was to recapture the *United Ireland,* a newspaper he had set up in 1881, under the editorship of William O'Brien, to express his own views. In the absence of O'Brien, who was in America, an acting editor, Matthew Bodkin, had turned the newspaper against Parnell. Upon his arrival in Dublin, Parnell and his followers took over the editorial offices of the *United Ireland* and turned out Bodkin. That evening Parnell made a speech to a large and enthusiastic crowd in the Dublin Rotunda. While this was going on, Bodkin and his followers recaptured the *United Ireland.* The next day, December 11, Parnell was to set out for Cork, but he decided first to recapture the *United Ireland.* That morning Parnell and a large crowd appeared before the locked doors of the newspaper, Parnell and some others armed with crowbars. Parnell had wanted to climb over the railings and drop into the basement area, as Bloom does at 7 Eccles Street when he finally returns home near the end of *Ulysses.* He was dissuaded from this by his followers, some of whom did drop into the basement area to attack that entrance. Parnell thundered at the front door with his crowbar and effected an entrance, as did the group of his followers from the basement entrance. After an interval Parnell, victorious, appeared at the second story window of the newspaper and spoke briefly to the large and excited crowd outside. His hat was off and his hair dishevelled.

There is an eye-witness account of this singular incident published by R. Barry O'Brien in his *The Life of Charles Stewart Parnell* (New York, 1898), Vol. II, pp. 294-297. What the account underlines is the incredible intensity of passion and commitment that Parnell could generate amongst his Dublin followers—and also what a passionate and quick-acting man he could be, once aroused. He could make men quail and did so.

Mrs. O'Shea who, of course, was not a witness, was much taken by the whole incident both at the time when she first heard of it and later, when she read O'Brien's eye-witness account. In her memoirs she wrote:

> A witness's account of the incident contained in Mr. Barry O'Brien's 'Life of Charles Stewart Parnell' appealed to me immensely, because this little affair was of intense interest to me, and all, or nearly all, I could get out of Parnell himself on the subject was a soft laugh and, "It was splendid fun. I wish I could burgle my own premises every day." [O'Shea, *Parnell,* p. 179.]

Similarly, the incident appealed immensely to Joyce, especially the missing-hat part. Of the great number of ways in which he could have involved his fictional hero, Bloom, with his political hero, Parnell, Joyce chose the *United Ireland* episode, having Bloom pick up and return the fallen hat to the failing leader. To have done this Bloom would have had to have gone into the building with Parnell's invading forces. Here then is Bloom's brush (twice-told) with greatness:

He [Bloom] saw him [Parnell] once on the auspicious occasion when they broke up the type in the *Insupressible* [the usual Eumaeus error] or was it *United Ireland,* a privilege he keenly appreciated, and, in point of fact, handed him his silk hat when it was knocked off and he said *Thank you,* excited as he undoubtedly was under his frigid expression notwithstanding the little misadventure mentioned between the cup and the lip—what's bred in the bone. (649-650) He, Bloom, enjoyed the distinction of being close to Erin's uncrowned king in the flesh when the thing occurred in the historic *fracas* when the fallen leader's— who notoriously stuck to his guns to the last drop even when clothed in the mantle of adultery—(leader's) trusty henchmen to the number of ten or a dozen or possibly even more than that penetrated into the printing works of the *Insuppressible* or no it was *United Ireland* (a by no means, by the by, appropriate appellative) and broke up the typecases with hammers [untrue] or something like that all on account of some scurrilous effusions from the facile pens of the O'Brienite scribes [untrue] at the usual mudslinging occupation, reflecting on the erstwhile tribune's private morals. Though palpably a radically altered man, he was still a commanding figure, though carelessly garbed as usual [Untrue. Parnell had always been a conspicuously careful dresser; only in his very last days did he become careless about apparel.], with that look of settled purpose which went a long way with the shillyshallyers till they discovered to their vast discomfiture that their idol had feet of clay, after placing him upon a pedestal, which she [Mrs. O'Shea], however, was the first to perceive. As those were particularly hot times in the general hullaballoo Bloom sustained a minor injury from a nasty prod of some chap's elbow in the crowd that of course congregated lodging some place about the pit of the stomach, fortunately not of a grave character. His hat (Parnell's) was inadvertently knocked off and, as a matter of strict history, Bloom was the

man who picked it up in the crush after witnessing the
occurrence meaning to return it to him (and return it to
him he did with the utmost celerity) who, panting and hat-
less and whose thoughts were miles away from his hat at
the time, being a gentleman born with a stake in the
country, he, as a matter of fact, having gone into it more
for the kudos of the thing than anything else, what's bred
in the bone, instilled into him in infancy at his mother's
knee [Parnell's mother, although American, was a passionate partisan of Irish nationalism] in the shape of
knowing what good form was came out at once because he
turned round to the donor and thanked him with perfect
aplomb, saying: *Thank you, sir* though in a very different
tone of voice from the ornament of the legal profession
[Menton] whose headgear Bloom also set to rights earlier
in the course of the day, history repeating itself with a
difference; after the burial of a mutual friend when they
had left him alone in his glory after the grim task of having
committed his remains to the grave. (654-655)

1891. THE DEFEAT AND DEATH OF PARNELL

Throughout the whole first part of 1891 Parnell continued to fight to regain his lost leadership, supporting
candidates of his choice (who usually lost) and making
political speeches in Ireland. But it was a losing game. The
Church and the farmers turned against him (651:31-38;
661:1-2). "He made a mistake to fight the priests." (649)

October 6, 1891. Parnell dies. Parnell's health had
always been precarious and it gave way completely in late
September 1891 under the stress of his exertions. He
returned home to Katherine, now Mrs. Parnell and living
at Brighton on the English coast. He was by now fatally ill
from a complex of complaints, including a weak heart,
rheumatic fever, and pneumonia. He died on Tuesday,

October 6, his last words to Mrs. Parnell being, "Kiss me, sweet wife, and I will try to sleep a little.":

> Something evidently riled them [his enemies] in his death. Either he petered out too tamely of acute pneumonia just when his various different political arrangements were nearing completion or whether it transpired he owed his death to his having neglected to change his boots and clothes after a wetting when a cold resulted and failing to consult a specialist he being confined to his room till he eventually died of it amid widespread regret before a fortnight was at an end or quite possibly they were distressed to find the job was taken out of their hands. (649)

[The sense of the sentences in Eumaeus is not always readily apparent, but the sense of this one is. Joyce was never gentle with Parnell's enemies, and here he has Bloom think that Parnell's foes had really wished to kill him and were thus sorry that pneumonia had taken him out of their hands.

The sentence is also the usual Eumaeus admixture of fantasy, or mistake, and fact. It was true that, upon the advice of a London doctor, Sir Henry Thompson, and with the insistence of Mrs. O'Shea, Parnell, because of his poor blood circulation, took precautions against wet or even cold feet: he carried around a little black bag with fresh shoes, socks, and clothing. On September 27, 1891, he made a speech in Galway, uncovered in the rain. The bag with the dry clothing, which Mrs. Parnell had prepared for him, was mislaid and for several hours Parnell had to sit in damp clothing. This began the onslaught of his finally fatal illness. It was true too that upon his arrival in Brighton Parnell would not allow his wife to call in his London specialist, Sir Henry Thompson.

However, the idea that his political arrangements were nearing completion is the reverse of the truth.]

The aftermath of Parnell's death.

The leadership of the Irish M.P.'s falls into lesser hands (649:35-37). These people would be, among others, Timothy Healy, Justin McCarthy, and John Redmond, all capable men but with little or none of the mythic powers of Parnell. A myth forms; Parnell will return:

> One morning you would open the paper, the cabman affirmed, and read, *Return of Parnell.* He bet them what they liked. A Dublin fusilier was in that shelter one night and said he saw him in South Africa. (648-649) Dead he wasn't. Simply absconded somewhere. The coffin they brought over was full of stones. He changed his name to De Wet, the Boer general [The cabman once more]. (649)

[Parnell was only forty-five when he died, thus the rumors that he was still alive. At the time of his death Parnell's body temperature was so high that no death mask was made, and the corpse was immediately placed in a lead coffin. The fact that the body was brought to Ireland for burial at Glasnevin in a sealed coffin led to the speculation that there was no body in it, only stones.]

The Parnell funeral procession followed roughly the same route as does the Dignam funeral procession in the Hades section of *Ulysses.*

The rise and fall of Parnell became in the Irish mind the classical instance of the pattern of a public tragedy. Thus in an hallucination at Bella Cohen's (478-492) Bloom reenacts Parnell's career in a political fantasy, climbing to the top amidst cries of ecstatic admiration from his constituency only to fall with that same constituency heaping execrations upon him.

The Rise:

JOHN HOWARD PARNELL

(*Raises the royal standard.*) Illustrious Bloom! Successor to my famous brother!

BLOOM

(*Embraces John Howard Parnell.*) We thank you from our heart, John, for this right royal welcome to green Erin, the promised land of our common ancestors.

(*The freedom of the city is presented to him embodied in a charter. The keys of Dublin, crossed on a crimson cushion, are given to him. He shows all that he is wearing green socks.*) (483) [There is an irony here. Among the host of superstitions that Parnell carried around with him was the idea that the color green was ominous. Thus he would have nothing green on or about his person.]

The Fall:

FATHER FARLEY

He is an episcopalian, an agnostic, an anythingarian seeking to overthrow our holy faith. (490)

[Parnell was a Protestant, a fact that the Catholic Church in Ireland never forgot, even, or especially, when his career was at its height. Furthermore, in 1880 there was a famous controversy in Parliament about Charles Bradlaugh, elected M.P. from Northampton, who was a social reformer and an atheist. Accordingly, Bradlaugh refused to take the Parliamentary oath because it contained the words "in the name of God." He was then refused his seat in the house. Bradlaugh had declared his willingness to "affirm." When a vote, which was defeated, was taken on this matter, Parnell was one of those who voted in favor of Bradlaugh, and the Church did not forget this either. (Bradlaugh finally got seated in 1886.)

Though nominally a Protestant, Parnell had no interest in religion and attended no church at all. Timothy Healy said that Parnell's only religion was that Friday was an unlucky day. If Parnell had any "belief," it was that the workings of chance ruled human affairs. Thus when the

Irish Catholic Church finally and publicly turned on Parnell it had plenty of reasons, from its point of view, for so doing.]

The people turn on him too:

THE MOB

Lynch him! Roast him! He is as bad as Parnell was. Mr. Fox! (*Mother Grogan throws her boot at Bloom. Several shop-keepers from upper and lower Dorset street throw objects of little or no commercial value, hambones, condensed milk tins, unsaleable cabbage, stale bread, sheeps' tails, odd pieces of fat.*) (492)

[In a speech in Kilkenny in 1891, Parnell had attacked Michael Davitt (who gave as well as he got in his own speeches against Parnell). When Parnell was leaving the meeting, he was struck on or about the eye by something thrown at him—either flour or lime (it was never proved to be one or the other). Joyce himself had no doubt it was quick-lime:

It was Irish humour quick and dry
That flung quick-lime in Parnell's eye

("Gas from a Burner")

On December 29, 1891, Mrs. Riordan leaves the Deda-luses' home (680:21-22). The departure was subsequent to the violent argument about Parnell that occurred at the Dedaluses' dining-room table on Christmas day and is described in the first part of *A Portrait of the Artist*. Mrs. Riordan exemplifies the hatred of Parnell that was gener-ated among his former followers subsequent to the reve-lations of the divorce trial.]

1892

The Blooms are living on Lombard Street West, in the old Jewish part of Dublin. Molly, sometime after September 8, 1892, when she turned twenty-two, has a new experience: "yet I never came properly till I was what 22 or so it went into the wrong place always" (767)

Bloom.

1. January 1. Has a second meeting with young Stephen Dedalus, now ten years of age, in the coffee room of Breslin's hotel on a rainy Sunday, Stephen being accompanied by his father and granduncle. Stephen invites Bloom to dine with them, and is seconded by his father. But Bloom gracefully declines (680:9-17).

2. January. Mrs. Riordan moves into the City Arms Hotel (680:23-25).

3. Discusses his "favorite topics" with Mastiansky in the front parlor of Lombard Street West (667:28-30).

4. December. A yuletide card arrives from Mr. and Mrs. M. Comerford (720:31-35). [This is one of the two mentions of the Comerfords (the other is by Molly in 1893) in the book. This Anglo, somewhat toffish name, is meant to suggest, I believe, that the Blooms had some friends rather higher on the social scale than previous or subsequent to their Lombard Street West days.]

1892-1893

1892-1893. LIFE ON LOMBARD STREET WEST

Molly.

1. Mastiansky's sex habits:

> better for him [Boylan] to put it into me from behind the way Mrs Mastiansky told me her husband made her like the dogs do it and stick out her tongue as far as ever she could and he so quiet and mild with his tingating either can you ever be up to men the way it takes them (749)

2. A mental list of some of the places the Blooms have lived, Lombard Street West being one (772:11).

3. The wallpaper in the house and an apron: "what kind of flowers are those they invented like the stars the wallpaper in Lombard street was much nicer the apron he gave me was like that something only I only wore it twice" (781)

Bloom.

1. Possesses a decent suit with a purple tinge to it (110:14-15).

2. "Molly in her shift in Lombard street west, hair down." (289)

3. When the painters are there, Molly scrapes her slipper on the floor while tinkling in the pot:

> And when the painters were in Lombard street west. Fine voice that fellow had. How Giuglini began. Smell that I did, like flowers. It was too. Violets. Came from the turpentine probably in the paint. Make their own use of everything. Same time doing it scraped her slipper on the floor so they wouldn't hear. (374) ["(Woman scrapes slipper when pissing)" (H., p. 154).]

4. Mastiansky imparts information to Bloom: "Chinese cemeteries with giant poppies growing produce the best opium Mastiansky told me." (108)

5. Sunspots: "There was a lot of talk about those sunspots when we were in Lombard street west." (166) [A. (p. 187) says that sunspots occurred in the summer of 1895. T. and G., however, say that the greatest sunspot activity since 1870 occurred in the summer (August) of 1893. In any case there is a misremembrance on Bloom's part since the Blooms had left Lombard Street before that summer.]

6. Milly, now three years old, holds a service: "Silly-Milly burying the little dead bird in the kitchen matchbox, a daisychain and bits of broken chainies on the grave." (113)

7. Bloom helps a blind stripling cross the street on June 16, 1904, and has a memory: "Like a child's hand his hand. Like Milly's was. Sensitive." (181)

8. Milly as a child: "A child renamed Padney Socks she shook with shocks her moneybox: counted his three free moneypenny buttons one, tloo, tlee:" (693)

1893

Molly.

1. In the cold of winter the Blooms came home from a party at the Comerfords, and Molly has to relieve herself at a male comfort station:

> and the stink of those rotten places the night coming home with Poldy after the Comerfords party oranges and lemonade to make you feel nice and watery I went into 1 of them it was so biting cold I couldnt keep it when was that 93 the canal was frozen yes it was a few months after a pity a couple of the Camerons [who displayed themselves to her on Gibraltar] werent there to see me squatting in the mens place meadero ["urinal" in Spanish] I tried to draw a picture of it before I tore it up like a sausage or something (753)

[On November 2, 1921, Joyce wrote from Paris to Mrs. William Murray, his favorite aunt and his most valued reference for Dubliana, asking some questions: "Thirdly and last. Do you remember the cold February of 1893. I think you were in Clanbrassil street. I want to know whether the canal was frozen and if there was any skating." (L. I, p. 175).]

2. Old Goodwin, a pianist of sorts who was Molly's accompanist for concerts during these years, calls about a concert and Molly is unready for a caller:

> the day old frosty face Goodwin called about the concert in Lombard street and I just after dinner all flushed and tossed with boiling old stew dont look at me professor I had to say Im a fright yes but he was a real old gent in his way it was impossible to be more respectful nobody to say youre out you have to peep out through the blind (747)

3. The night of the concert is cold and windy; Goodwin is drunk at the piano; and the Blooms return home for some unusual sex:

> I dont like my foot so much still I made him spend once with my foot the night after Goodwins botchup of a concert so cold and windy it was well we had that rum in the house to mull and the fire wasnt black out when he asked to take off my stockings lying on the hearthrug in Lombard street (745) [See Bloom's remembrance of the same occasion below in No. 3 of his memories for 1893.]

4. Sometime before or during March of 1893 the Blooms moved to Raymond Terrace, in the same general neighborhood as their other residences, where Rudy Bloom was conceived; they were living in an upstairs flat: "those that have a fine son like that [Stephen Dedalus] theyre not satisfied and I none was he not able to make one it wasnt my fault we came together when I was watching the two dogs up in her behind in the middle of the naked street" (778) [See Bloom's remembrance of the same occasion below in No. 7 of his memories for 1893.]

5. The memory of leaving Lombard Street for Raymond Terrace sticks in Molly's mind as the beginning of the Blooms' Odyssey around Dublin: "God here we are as bad as ever after 16 years how many houses were we in at

all Raymond Terrace [Spring of 1893] and Ontario terrace [1897] and Lombard street [1892-1893] and Holles
street [1895] . . . and then the City Arms hotel [1893-
1894] worse and worse" (772) And her husband's behavior on such occasions: "and he goes about whistling
every time were on the run again his huguenots or the
frogs march pretending to help the men with our 4 sticks
of furniture" (772)

6. c. May 6. Milly gives her father a birthday present:
"the moustachecup she [Milly] gave him [for his twenty-
seventh birthday]" (780) [See Bloom's remembrance
below, No. 8 for 1893.]

7. Summer. A choir picnic at Sugarloaf Mountain;
Bloom sprains his foot: "tragic and that dyinglooking one
off the south circular when he sprained his foot at the
choir party at the sugarloaf Mountain the day I wore that
dress" (738) [See Bloom's remembrance below, No. 10
for 1893.]

8. Bloom takes to bed, is visited by Miss Stack, and
grows a beard:

> Miss Stack bringing him flowers the worst old ones she
> could find at the bottom of the basket anything at all to
> get into a mans bedroom with her old maids voice trying
> to imagine he was dying on account of her to never see
> thy face again though he looked more like a man with his
> beard a bit grown in the bed (738)

Bloom.

1. January 30. Bloom "commissioned," so it is said, by
Michael Gunn to write, but did not write, "If Brian Boru"
for *Sinbad the Sailor* (678:26-33). [This farrago is discussed in some detail by A. (pp. 78-80).]

2. February. Closes a carriage door for Mrs. Bellingham
on a very cold day (465:33-466:6). [Subsequent to this it is

suggested that Bloom sent an obscene letter to Mrs. Bellingham. See below, No. 11, p. 157, in "The Secret Life of Leopold Bloom."]

3. The windy night of the concert and coming home to Lombard Street:

> Windy night that was I went to fetch her there was that lodge meeting on about those lottery tickets after Goodwin's concert in the supper room or oakroom of the mansion house. He and I behind. Sheet of her music blew out of my hand against the high school railings. Lucky it didn't. Thing like that spoils the effect of a night for her. Professor Goodwin linking her in front. Shaky on his pins, poor old sot. His farewell concerts. Positively last appearance on any stage. May be for months and may be for never. Remember her laughing at the wind, her blizzard collar up. Corner of Harcourt road remember that gust? Brrfoo! Blew up all her skirts and her boa nearly smothered old Goodwin. She did get flushed in the wind. Remember when we got home raking up the fire and frying up those pieces of lap of mutton for her supper with the Chutney sauce she liked. And the mulled rum. Could see her in the bedroom from the hearth unclamping the busk of her stays. White.
>
> Swish and soft flop her stays made on the bed. Always warm from her. Always liked to let herself out. Sitting there after till near two, taking out her hairpins. Milly tucked up in beddyhouse. Happy. Happy. That was the night . . . (156)

4. Bloom and the Royal Hungarian Lottery. In the previous reminiscence Bloom referred to "that lodge meeting on about those lottery tickets." This is a reference to his promoting the Royal Hungarian Lottery, getting in trouble for it, and being rescued from his difficulties by his fellow Masons. Molly: "either hes going

to be run into prison over his old lottery tickets that was to be all our salvations or" (772) The Nameless One, an anonymous gossip, in Barney Kiernan's pub:

> He was bloody safe he wasn't run in himself under the act that time as a rogue and vagabond only he had a friend in court. Selling bazaar tickets or what do you call it royal Hungarian privileged lottery. True as you're there. O, commend me to an israelite! Royal and privileged Hungarian robbery. (313)

In Bloom's drawer at Eccles Street are two coupons of the Royal and Privileged Hungarian Lottery (721:24-25).

[When Bloom became a Mason is never exactly specified although he appears to have been one as far back as January 6, 1888 when at Georgina Simpson's housewarming he gives a toast and is described as wearing a "blue masonic badge" (445:3). Jews had been admissable to the Masonic order since 1723. There is evidence in the text that Bloom is still a Mason on June 16, 1904.]

5. Milly finds a mirror in professor Goodwin's hat:

> Poor old professor Goodwin. Dreadful old case. Still he was a courteous old chap. Old fashioned way he used to bow Molly off the platform. And the little mirror in his silk hat. The night Milly brought it into the parlour. O, look what I found in professor Goodwin's hat! All we laughed. Sex breaking out even then. Pert little piece she was. (63)

6. The Blooms leave Lombard Street West: "Three years old she [Milly] was in front of Molly's dressingtable just before we left Lombard street west. Me have a nice face." (372) [Milly was three from June 15, 1892 to June 15, 1893.]

7. March. Rudy conceived on Raymond Terrace:

Must have been that morning in Raymond Terrace she was at the window, watching the two dogs at it by the wall of the cease to do evil. And the sergeant grinning up. She had that cream gown on with the rip she never stitched. Give us a touch, Poldy. God, I'm dying for it. How life begins.

Got big then. Had to refuse the Greystones concert. My son inside her. (89)

Molly wanting to do it at the window. (108)

8. c. May 6. Milly gives Bloom a birthday present, a moustache cup of imitation crown Derby (694:31-33). On the morning of June 16, 1904, Bloom uses the cup and thinks: "Silly Milly's birthday gift. Only five she was then. No wait: four." (62) The cup now rests in the Blooms' cupboard (675:7), and Stephen is served his libation in it by Bloom (677:1-3).

9. June 15. Bloom gives Milly a birthday present: "I gave her the amberoid necklace she broke. Putting pieces of folded brown paper in the letterbox for her." (62)

10. Summer. The choir picnic on Sugarloaf Mountain:

Milly was a kiddy then. Molly had that elephantgrey dress with the braided frogs. Mantailored with self-covered buttons. She didn't like it because I sprained my ankle first day she wore choir picnic at the Sugarloaf. As if that. Old Goodwin's tall hat done up with some sticky stuff. Flies' picnic too. Never put a dress on her back like it. Fitted her like a glove, shoulder and hips. Just beginning to plump it out well [Molly's pregnancy was beginning to show]. Rabbit pie we had that day. People looking after her. (155)

11. A summer drought makes it necessary to take water from the Grand and Royal canals (671:16-18).

12. A Raymond Terrace idyl: "Happy. Happier then. Snug little room that was with the red wallpaper, Dockrell's, one and ninepence a dozen. Milly's tubbing night.

American soap I bought: elderflower. Cosy smell of her bathwater. Funny she looked soaped all over. Shapely too." (155)

13. A retrospective on the happy years:

> I was happier then. Or was that I? Or am I now I? Twentyeight I was. She twentythree when we left Lombard street west something changed. Could never like it again after Rudy. Can't bring back time. Like holding water in your hand. Would you go back to then? Just beginning then. Would you? (168) [Bloom, or Joyce, makes a mistake here. Bloom (born around May 6, 1866) and Molly (born on September 8, 1870) could only have been twenty-eight and twenty-three together from May 6 to September 8, 1894. Also, strictly speaking, the last happy days were on Raymond Terrace.]

The happiest times for the Blooms were the years of their courtship and the early married years, roughly 1887 to 1893. This was their Eden. The Fall was to come in late 1893 and early 1894, as will be explained below. There was a geographical dimension to the years of happiness. Bloom was born at 52 Clanbrassil Street—a major artery running south in an unstraight line from the Liffey—in the old Jewish section of Dublin. At the present day, as one walks south on Clanbrassil Street and approaches the neighborhood where Bloom was born, one begins to see Jewish names appearing on shops: "Gross," "Cohen," "Goldwater," "Fine," "Rubenstein," "Erlich." Dubliners have told me that many Jews have now moved farther south to Terenure, but in Bloom's day this was the area in which most Jews would have lived, although, it should be added, it was by no means a ghetto, and there would have been plenty of gentiles living there as well. For a description of the Blooms' various residences see my "Afoot in

Dublin in Search of the Habitations of Some Shades,"
James Joyce Quarterly 8 (Winter, 1971), pp. 129-141.

Clanbrassil Street had deep personal reverberations for
Joyce. When John Joyce was courting Mary Jane Murray,
to the unease of her father, the Murrays were living at 7
Clanbrassil Street. John Joyce moved into No. 15 in order
to be close to the object of his affections. James's favorite
aunt, Josephine Murray, also lived on Clanbrassil Street,
and his letters to her asking information on Dublin
matters when he was composing *Ulysses* were sent to her
there.

At the present day there is a No. 52 Clanbrassil, a brick,
attached, two-story dwelling, just south of South Circular
Road, in which, presumably, our hero was born and
through whose window he looked out on the activities of
the busy street. Moreover, all the early residences of Mr.
and Mrs. Leopold Bloom were in the old Jewish neighborhood, as the map below (p. 138) indicates. "Raymond
Terrace," as a name, no longer exists; but it once was that
portion of what is now South Circular Road between St.
Albans Place and Raymond Street. The Blooms lived
there briefly in 1893 in a second story flat.

Thus when the Blooms left Raymond Terrace in 1893
to go to the City Arms Hotel (in the cattle district in
northwest Dublin), where Bloom worked for Joe Cuffe,
Bloom, quite literally, left the home of his father and his
last, and only, years of domestic felicity: "First we feel.
Then we fall," as it is put in *Finnegans Wake.*]

14. The Blooms are now living at the City Arms Hotel,
knowing Mrs. Riordan; Bloom is working for Joe Cuffe,
the cattleman (680:20-29).

15. Bloom goes down to the kitchen at night to get
raisins for Molly: "Night I went down to the pantry in the

kitchen. Don't like all the smells in it waiting to rush out. What was it she wanted? The Malaga raisins. Thinking of Spain. Before Rudy was born." (151)

16. November 1893 to January 1894. The crucial months in the personal life of the Blooms, involving their last normal copulation and the birth and early death of their only son, Rudy.

November.

> —O, by God, says Ned [Lambert to the Citizen and the others in Barney Kiernan's pub], you should have seen Bloom before that son of his that died was born. I met him one day in the south city markets buying a tin of Neave's food six weeks before the wife was delivered. (338)

November 27. The last occasion for the Blooms of complete carnal intercourse (736:8-10). [In earlier versions of the Cyclops episode in Barney Kiernan's pub, where there is so much gossip about the Blooms in their City Arms days, Joyce has it said by his gossipers that Bloom had become impotent (he was not doing "the trick of the loop at all"), that Molly was given to fits of hysteria about this, and that the Blooms were considering a divorce. See Myron Schwartzman, "The V.A.8 Copybook: An Early Draft of the 'Cyclops' Chapter of *Ulysses* with Notes on its Development." *James Joyce Quarterly,* 12 (Fall 1974/Winter 1975), pp. 64-122; Michael Groden, " 'Cyclops' in Progress, 1919," *James Joyce Quarterly,* ibid. p. 153. In the final version of *Ulysses* there is no suggestion that Bloom had become impotent.]

17. The birth, short life, early death, and memory of little Rudy.

December 29. Born (736:11-12) with a dwarf's face, mauve and wrinkled, and a dwarf's body, weak as putty (96:4-5): "She [Mrs. Thornton, the midwife] knew from the first poor little Rudy wouldn't live. Well, God is good, sir. She knew at once. He would be eleven now if he had lived." (66)

January 9, 1894. Dies, aged eleven days (736:12; 390: 30-32): "Mistake of nature. If it's healthy it's from the mother. If not the man. Better luck next time." (96).

The burial. Molly, who was "wondrous stricken," had been knitting for him a "corselet of lamb's wool," and he was buried in it (390:31-40):

> I told him [Bloom] about some Dean or Bishop was sitting beside me in the jews Temples gardens when I was knitting that woollen thing (740) I suppose I oughtnt to have buried him in that little woolly jacket I knitted crying as I was but give it to some poor child but I knew well Id never have another our 1st death too it was we were never the same since O Im not going to think myself into the glooms about that any more (778) I saw him [Stephen] driving down to the Kingsbridge station with his father and mother I was in mourning thats 11 years ago now yes hed be 11 though what was the good in going into mourning for what was neither one thing nor the other of course he insisted (774) [Molly makes an understandable mistake here; it was ten years ago—January of 1894 while in mourning for Rudy— that she saw the Dedaluses. At the same time it is true that by June 16, 1904, Rudy would have been eleven, since he was born on December 29, 1893.]

The memory:

> Noisy selfwilled man [Simon Dedalus]. Full of his son. He is right. Something to hand on. If little Rudy had lived. See him grow up. Hear his voice in the house. Walking beside Molly in an Eton suit. My son. Me in his eyes. Strange feeling it would be. From me. Just a chance. (89) I could have helped him on in life. I could. Make him independent. Learn German too. (89) Does he ever think

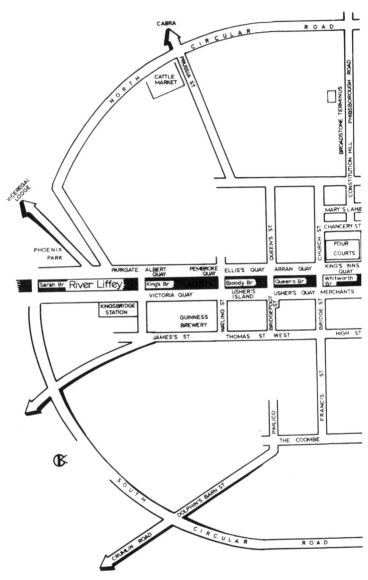

A schematic map of Dublin which shows on its upper part, right, Eccles Street and, left, the cattle market on Prussia Street, where Bloom worked in 1893-1894. In front of

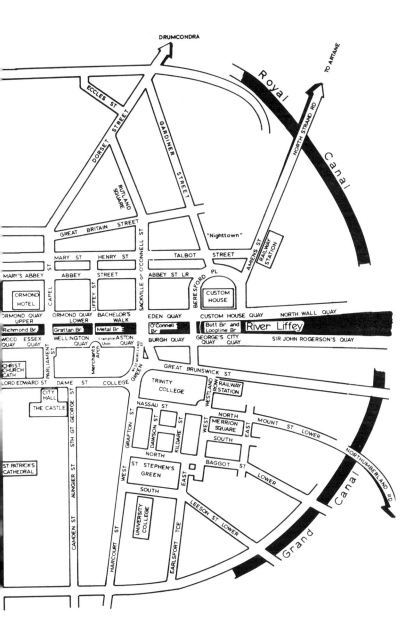

the cattle market is the City Arms Hotel, where the Blooms lived during these years. On the lower half, center, is Clanbrassil Street, in the old Jewish area, where Bloom was born.

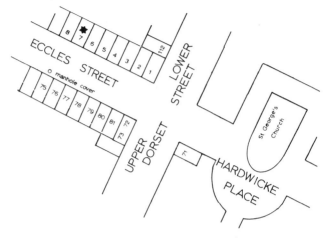

7 Eccles Street and vicinity, where
the Blooms lived after 1903.

of the hole waiting for himself [the priest at Paddy Dignam's interment]? They say you do when you shiver in the
sun. Someone walking over it. Callboy's warning. Near you.
Mine over there toward Finglas, the plot I bought. Mamma
poor mamma, and little Rudy. (111) All gone. All fallen.
[. . . .] I too, last my race. Milly young student. Well,
my fault perhaps. No son. Rudy. [. . . .] Soon I am old.
(285)

Bloom seeing Stephen, the talented young man who is
wasting his substance on whores and drink, is reminded
again of his own loss (390:37-391:2).

A vision:

(*Silent, thoughtful, alert, he* [Bloom] *stands on guard, his
fingers at his lips in the attitude of a secret master. Against
the dark wall a figure appears slowly, a fairy boy of eleven,
a changeling, kidnapped, dressed in an Eton suit with glass
shoes and a little bronze helmet, holding a book in his hand.
He reads from right to left inaudibly, smiling, kissing the
page.*)

BLOOM

(*Wonderstruck, calls inaudibly.*) Rudy!

RUDY

(*Gazes unseeing into Bloom's eyes and goes on reading, kissing, smiling. He has a delicate mauve face. On his suit he has diamond and ruby buttons. In his free left hand he holds a slim ivory cane with a violet bowknot. A white lambkin peeps out of his waistcoat pocket.*) (609)

1893-1894. LIFE AT THE CITY ARMS HOTEL

Molly.

1. The W.C. at the City Arms:

> then the City Arms hotel worse and worse says Warden Daly [some kind of proverbial expression or a fragment from a popular song] that charming place [the water-closet] on the landing always somebody inside praying then leaving all their stinks after them always know who was in there last (772)

2. Molly gets Bloom's breakfast in bed because he says he is ill:

> YES BECAUSE HE NEVER DID A THING LIKE THAT BEFORE AS ASK [this is the first line of Molly's monologue] to get his breakfast in bed [before Bloom goes to sleep on June 17, he asks Molly to get him breakfast in bed] with a couple of eggs since the *City Arms* hotel when he used to be pretending to be laid up with a sick voice (738)

3. Bloom is trying to get into the good graces of Mrs. Riordan: "doing his highness to make himself interesting to that old faggot Mrs Riordan that he thought he had a great leg of" (738)

4. Mrs. Riordan, piety and talk:

> greatest miser ever was actually afraid to lay out 4d for her methylated spirit telling me all her ailments she had

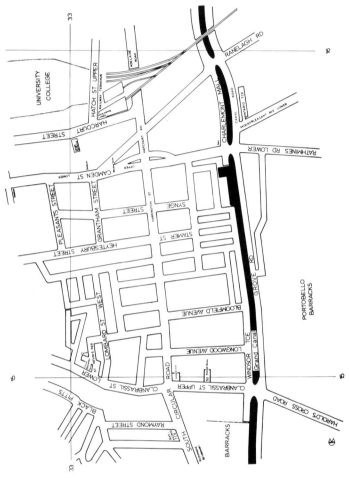

This shows the house, 52 Clanbrassil Street, of Bloom's birth; the high school he attended from 1877 to 1880; Pleasants Street, where the newly married Blooms lived from 1888 to c. 1892; Lombard Street West, where they lived from 1892 to 1893; Raymond Terrace where Rudy was conceived in the spring of 1893; and Ontario Terrace where the Blooms lived in 1897-1898.

too much old chat in her about politics and earthquakes
and the end of the world let us have a bit of fun first
God help the world if all the women were her sort down
on bathingsuits and lownecks of course nobody wanted her
to wear I suppose she was pious because no man would
look at her twice I hope Ill never be like her a wonder
she didnt want us to cover our faces but she was a welleducated woman certainly and her gabby talk about Mr
Riordan here and Mr Riordan there I suppose he was glad
to get shut of her (738)

5. Mrs. Riordan's dog: "and her dog smelling my fur
and always edging to get up under my petticoats" (738) "I
loved rousing that dog in the hotel rrrsssst awokwok-
awok" (760)

6. The stupidity of cattlemen: "where does their great
intelligence come in Id like to know grey matter they have
it all in their tail if you ask me those country gougers up in
the City Arms intelligence they had a damn sight less than
the bulls and cows they were selling the meat" (757-758)

Bloom.

1. Memories of Mrs. Riordan include her bezique cards
and counters, her Skye terrier, her supposititious wealth,
her lapses of responsiveness and incipient catarrhal deaf-
ness (681:13-18).

2. Sometimes on summer evenings Bloom propels Mrs.
Riordan in her bathchair from the City Arms to the
corner of the North Circular Road, where through her
binoculars she observes the traffic passing back and forth
between the city and Phoenix Park (680:30-681:2).

3. Mrs. Riordan's rumbling stomach and Molly fondling her dog: "Dog's cold noses. Old Mrs Riordan with the
rumbling stomach's Skye terrier in the City Arms hotel.
Molly fondling him in her lap. O the big doggy-bow-
wowsy-wowsy!" (174)

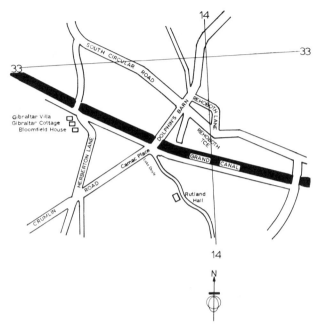

Reheboth Terrace, where Molly and her father first lived when they came to Dublin.

4. The infelicities of eating at the City Arms: "Hate people all round you. City Arms hotel *table d'hote* she called it. Soup, joint and sweet. Never know whose thoughts you're chewing. Then who'd wash up all the plates and forks?" (170-171)

5. Mrs. Duggan and her drunken husband: "Worst of all at night Mrs Duggan told me in the City Arms. Husband rolling in drunk, stink of pub off him like a polecat. Have that in your nose in the dark, whiff of stale boose. Then ask in the morning: was I drunk last night?" (373)

6. Bloom thinks of a cat: "That half tabbywhite tortoiseshell in the *City Arms* with the letter em on her forehead. Body fifty different colours." (378)

7. Bloom, an actuary for Joe Cuffe, the cattle dealer: "Because [says the Nameless One] he was up one time in a knacker's yard. Walking about with his book and pencil here's my head and my heels are coming." (315) (See also 399:16-20; 680:26-29.)

8. Mornings in the cattle market:

> Those mornings in the cattlemarket the beasts lowing in their pens, branded sheep, flop and fall of dung, the breeders in hobnailed boots trudging through the litter, slapping a palm on a ripemeated hindquarter, there's a prime one, unpeeled switches in their hands. (59) Wretched brutes there at the cattlemarket waiting for the poleaxe to split their skulls open. Moo. Poor trembling calves. Meh. Staggering bob. Bubble and squeak. Butchers' buckets wobble lights. Give us that brisket off the hook. Plup. Rawhead and bloody bones. Flayed glasseyed sheep hung from their haunches, sheepsnouts bloodypapered snivelling nosejam on sawdust. Top and lashers going out. Don't maul them pieces, young one. (171) cows lowing, the cattle market, (282:8-9)

9. Cuffe's prices: "Thursday of course. Tomorrow is killing day. Springers. Cuffe sold them about twentyseven quid each. For Liverpool probably. Roast beef for old England." (97)

10. Cuffe's name surfaces elsewhere: in Bloom's list of people he has worked for (465:13); as number nineteen of Molly's supposed lovers (731:32); Cuffe's prime springers mentioned (294:39); and in a list of Bloom's employers by Molly (772:19).

Pisser Burke and the Nameless One.

At this same period, 1893-1894, there is living at the City Arms Hotel one Andrew Burke with the euphonious nickname of "Pisser." Pisser Burke's sole occupation in

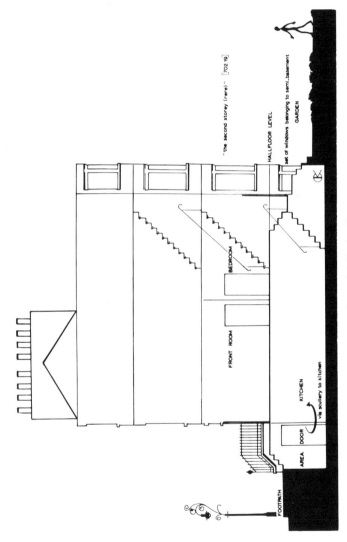

"the second storey (rere)" [702 19]

HALLFLOOR LEVEL

set of windows belonging to semi-basement

GARDEN

BEDROOM

FRONT ROOM

KITCHEN

via scullery to kitchen

DOOR

AREA

FOOTPATH

Plan of 7 Eccles Street

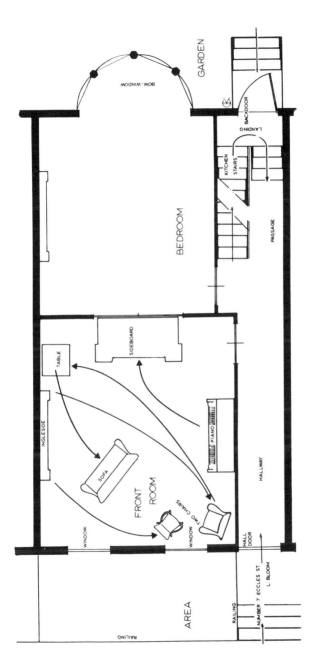

The half-floor level of 7 Eccles Street, with probable arrangement(s) of the furniture.

life is spying upon other people and gossiping about them; and he appears to have kept an especially close watch on the Blooms. Pisser has one friend, never named in *Ulysses* and therefore known as the Nameless One, who is the supreme Dublin gossip and who tells the story of the Cyclops episode, which takes place in Barney Kiernan's pub in the late afternoon of June 16, 1904. Pisser kept Nameless fully informed on the Blooms, and Nameless himself must also have been hanging around the City Arms, since he is described by Molly as that: "long-nosed chap" (765). The Nameless One is a walking encyclopedia of Dublin malice—never a charitable word for anyone, and the keeper of the keys for all the closets that have skeletons (and they all do). He disgorges his Bloomiana, mostly to himself, in Barney Kiernan's pub on the afternoon of June 16, 1904. Although the dirt he dishes up is by now ten or more years old, the time lag matters not at all to him or, presumably, to his auditors (it is not always clear when Nameless is thinking to himself and when he is talking to others); which is Joyce's way of saying that in Dublin gossip never dies and is ever-fresh. And the Nameless One is, you might say, the very voice of Dublin itself, as was his creator.

The Nameless One reports some of Pisser Burke's findings on the Blooms at the City Arms:

1. Bloom and Mrs. Riordan's nephew [Bloom and the Citizen are having an argument about a point in Irish history]·

> And Bloom, of course, with his knockmedown cigar putting on swank with his lardy face. Phenomenon! The fat heap he married is a nice old phenomenon with a back on her like a ballalley. Time they were stopping up in the *City Arms* Pisser Burke told me there was an old one [Mrs. Riordan]

there with a cracked loodheramaun of a nephew and Bloom trying to get the soft side of her doing the mollycoddle playing bézique to come in for a bit of the wampum in her will and not eating meat of a Friday because the old one was always thumping her craw and taking the lout out for a walk. And one time he led him the rounds of Dublin and, by the holy farmer, he never cried crack till he brought him home as drunk as a boiled owl and he said he did it to teach him the evils of alcohol and by herrings if the three women didn't near roast him it's a queer story, the old one, Bloom's wife and Mrs O'Dowd that kept the hotel. Jesus, I had to laugh at Pisser Burke taking them off chewing the fat and Bloom with his *but don't you see?* and *but on the other hand.* And sure, more be token, the lout I'm told was in Power's after, the blender's, round in Cope street going home footless in a cab five times in the week after drinking his way through all the samples in the bloody establishment. Phenomenon! (305-306)

2. Molly weeps to Mrs. O'Dowd, the owner of the hotel, about her indefatigable husband:

Pisser Burke was telling me in the hotel the wife used to be in rivers of tears sometimes with Mrs O'Dowd crying her eyes out with her eight inches of fat all over her. Couldn't loosen her farting strings but old cod's eye was waltzing around her showing her how to do it. What's your programme today? (315)

Molly provides some imitations of her husband's interrogations:

would you do this that and the other with the coalman yes with a bishop yes I would because I told him some Dean or Bishop was sitting beside me in the jews Temples gardens when I was knitting that woollen thing (740) who is in your mind now tell me who are you thinking of who is it tell me his name who tell me who the German Emperor is it yes imagine Im him (740)

3. Bloom gets sick once a month:

> One of those mixed middlings he is. Lying up in the hotel
> Pisser was telling me once a month with headache like a
> totty with her courses. Do you know what I'm telling you?
> It'd be an act of God to take a hold of a fellow the like
> of that and throw him in the bloody sea. Justifiable homi-
> cide, so it would. (338)

4. Bloom, who can swim, takes Molly, who cannot,
rowing off Bray, with almost disastrous results, while
Pisser Burke and the Nameless One look on:

> but Id never again in this life get into a boat with him
> after him at Bray telling the boatmen he knew how to row
> if anyone asked could he ride the steeplechase for the gold
> cup hed say yes then it came on to get rough the old thing
> crookeding about and the weight all down my side telling
> me to pull the right reins now pull the left and the tide
> all swamping in floods in through through the bottom and
> his oar slipping out of the stirrup its a mercy we werent
> all drowned he can swim of course me no theres no danger
> whatsoever keep yourself calm in his flannel trousers Id
> like to have tattered them down off him before all the
> people and give him what that one calls flagellate till he
> was black and blue do him all the good in the world only
> for that longnosed chap I dont know who he is with that
> other beauty Burke out of the City Arms hotel was there
> spying around as usual on the slip always where he wasnt
> wanted if there was a row on you vomit a better face there
> was no love lost between us thats 1 consolation . . . I
> couldnt even change my new white shoes all ruined with
> the saltwater and the hat I had with that feather all blowy
> and tossed on me how annoying and provoking (764-765)
> [Pisser is listed as one of Molly's "lovers" (731:32)].

All the evidence about Bloom in the years 1893-1894
indicate that he was, as the above quotations demon-

strate, most un-Bloomlike. The Bloom of 1904 is temperate, courteous, retiring, prudent, calm, and benevolent. The Bloom of 1893-1894 is diametrically different: a sharper and a conniver; a busybody; a nonstop talker; inconsiderate, aggressive, and outspoken; and, above all, stubborn and pigheaded. It is the exhibition of these two latter qualities that enable one to date two other of Molly's memories, which would otherwise be undatable, as taking place during these years: the first, when the Blooms go to the Mallow Concert at Maryborough by train and Leopold almost causes a disaster:

> besides something always happens with him the time going to the Mallow Concert at Maryborough ordering boiling soup for the two of us then the bell rang out he walks down the platform with the soup splashing about taking spoonfuls of it hadnt he the nerve and the waiter after him making a holy show of us screeching and confusion for the engine to start but he wouldnt pay till he finished it the two gentlemen in the 3rd class carriage said he was quite right so he was too hes so pigheaded sometimes when he gets a thing into his head a good job he was able to open the carriage door with his knife or theyd have taken us on to Cork I suppose that was done out of revenge on him (748)

And the second, when the Blooms encounter an insolent shop girl in a rich shop on Grafton Street:

> I hate those rich shops get on your nerves nothing kills me altogether . . . about the shop girl in that place in Grafton street I had the misfortune to bring him into and she as insolent as ever she could be with her smirk saying Im afraid were giving you too much trouble whats she there for but I stared it out of her yes he was awfully stiff and no wonder but he changed the second time he looked Poldy pigheaded as usual like the soup (752)

[This appears to be a fused memory on Molly's part. It is enclosed in a more important memory, that of Molly going to see Joe Cuffe in 1894, after Cuffe has fired Bloom, in order to try to see if she can get her husband rehired (see p. 152) below). But she also appears to have spoken on another occasion to the manager of a Grafton Street department store, Poldy in attendance. The tie between the two memories is, evidently, the fact that both men stared at her chest.]

1894

Bloom.

In the Lestrygonian section (pp. 151-183) on June 16, 1904, Bloom in searching for the year, which turns out to be 1894, of an event in the past, has his lengthiest and most complicated memory chain:

> How long ago is that? Year Phil Gilligan died. We were in Lombard street west. Wait, was in Thom's. Got the job in Wisdom Hely's year we married. Six years. Ten years ago: ninetyfour he died, yes, that's right, the big fire at Arnott's. Val Dillon was lord mayor. The Glencree dinner. (155)

[This memory chain continues on for a long paragraph involving events of 1894 and finally an event of the summer of 1893, the choir picnic at Sugarloaf. It is set off by Bloom trying to remember the year—"How long ago is that?"—he visited the Tranquilla Convent, which he has just thought of, when he was collecting accounts for Hely, the second time he worked for him (the visit itself will be set forth below). There are two ambiguities at the beginning of this train of association: "We were in Lombard street west," which they were not in 1894, and "Wait, was in Thom's." When Bloom actually worked at Thom's is a mystery, although several different periods are suggested in the book. The way I interpret the memory mechanism of the first part of the paragraph is that Bloom is rather uncertainly searching around for his year and finally hits it when he recalls the year of Phil Gilligan's death: "Ten years ago: ninetyfour he died, yes that's right." After that he, and the reader, are on solid ground. Historically, there was a fire at Arnott's, a large Dublin department store, in 1894; Valentine B. Dillon was Mayor of Dublin in 1894-1895. Phil Gilligan is fictional, but we are told in Ithaca (704:35) that he died of tuberculosis.

The most mysterious matter then is when Bloom worked for Thom's.

Bloom most often dates events and locates years by the places in which the Blooms were living at the time; to a lesser degree by his job at the time. In searching for 1894 he first thinks of Lombard Street West and then thinks, "wait," he was in Thom's, both of which associations appear to be wrong.

There are several choices for the year or years Bloom worked for Thom's.

1. If he is attaching it to Lombard Street West days while his memory is looking for 1894, then there is a presumption that he worked for Thom's at some time between 1892 and 1894, although it should be added that the "wait" looks as if it is meant to separate the time at Thom's from the Lombard Street West days.

2. At another place in *Ulysses,* in an hallucination at Bella Cohen's, it is suggested that Bloom was working for Thom's at the time he proposed to Molly in 1888 (550:12-13).

3. On June 16, 1904, it is suggested that Bloom rather recently worked for Thom's. When he flees from the enraged Citizen at the end of the Barney Kiernan episode,

he is apotheosized as, among other things, "late of Messrs Alexander Thom's," (342).

4. At the same time we know that the Thom's *Directory* in Bloom's possession is dated 1886; surely the prudent member would have picked up a directory when working there. Chronology VI.C.7 (1) also places him at Thom's in 1886.

Take your choice: (1) 1886, (2) 1888, (3) 1892-93-94, (4) sometime previous to June 16, 1904. It is somehow fitting that Joyce should have started the most false hares about the firm that produced the reference book that probably meant more to him than any other, *The Post Office Directory and Calendar for 1886,* put out by Thom, Ltd., Dublin and therefore known as "Thom's." In any event Bloom did in fact once work for Thom's: "Lukewarm glue in Thom's next door when I was there." (123) He also made a mistake at Thom's and was very likely fired for it: "Remember about the mistake in the valuation when I was in Thom's. Twentyeight it is." (377)

Winter. Molly and Lenehan and the Glencree banquet. The Glencree (a reformatory south of Dublin) banquet:

> the lord Mayor looking at me with his dirty eyes Val Dillon that big heathen I first noticed him at dessert when I was cracking the nuts with my teeth I wished I could have picked every morsel of that chicken out of my fingers it was so tasty and browned and as tender as anything only for I didn't want to eat everything on my plate those forks and fishslicers were hallmarked silver too I wish I had some I could easily have slipped a couple into my muff when I was playing with them then always hanging out of them for money in a restaurant for the bit you put down your throat we have to be thankful for our mangy cup of tea (750)

After the Glencree banquet the Blooms returned by horsecart in the early morning hours of a beautiful winter's night by way of Featherbed Mountain, along with Chris Callinan and Lenehan, a Dublin drifter first introduced to Joyce's fictional world in "Two Gallants" in *Dubliners*. Lenehan sat next to Molly on one side of the car, with Callinan and Bloom on the other. While Bloom explained the names of stars and constellations to Callinan and the driver, Lenehan busied himself with getting as close as he could to Molly's amplitudes.

Molly: "[Lenehan] that sponger he was making free with me after the Glencree dinner coming back that long joult over the featherbed mountain after" (750) On the afternoon of June 16, 1904, Lenehan tells the story in some detail to M'Coy (234:3-235:17).

Bloom:

> The Glencree dinner. Alderman Robert O'Reilly emptying the port into his soup before the flag fell, Bobbob lapping it for the inner alderman. Couldn't hear what the band played. For what we have already received may the Lord make us. Milly was a kiddy then. Molly had that elephant-grey dress with the braided frogs. Mantailored with self-covered buttons. (155)

Molly tells him about Mulvey after they arrive home, then falls asleep: "Fell asleep then. After Glencree dinner that was when we drove home the featherbed mountain. Gnashing her teeth in sleep. Lord mayor had his eye on her too. Val Dillon. Apoplectic." (371)

Bloom.

1. Fired by Cuffe for insulting a cattleman: "till Joe Cuffe [says the Nameless One] gave him the order of the boot for giving lip to a grazier. Mister Knowall. Teach

your grandmother how to milk ducks." (315) (See also
409:29-32.) Molly tries to get him rehired:

> when he could have been in Mr Cuffes still only for what
> he did then sending me to try and patch it up I could
> have got him promoted there to be the manager he gave
> me a great mirada ["look," Spanish] once or twice first
> he was as stiff as the mischief really and truly Mrs Bloom
> only I felt rotten simply with the old rubbishy dress that
> I lost the leads out of the tails with no cut in it but
> theyre coming into fashion again I bought it simply to
> please him I knew it was no good (752) he was awfully
> stiff and no wonder but he changed the second time he
> looked Poldy pigheaded as usual like the soup but I could
> see him looking very hard at my chest when he stood up
> to open the door for me it was nice of him to show me
> out in any case Im extremely sorry Mrs Bloom believe me
> without making it too marked the first time after him being
> insulted and me being supposed to be his wife I just half
> smiled I know my chest was out that way at the door when
> he said Im extremely sorry and Im sure you were (752-753)

2. Reduced to some kind of elaborate ploy involving a
card party, reported by the Nameless One [In a book
marked by a urinary and cloacal obsession the following
piece of exposition is quite extraordinary; it is delivered
by Nameless in the W.C. of Barney Kiernan's pub while
the speaker, who has gonorrhea, is urinating.]:

> Goodbye Ireland I'm going to Gort. So I just went round
> to the back of the yard to pumpship and begob (hundred
> shillings to five) while I was letting off my (*Throwaway*
> twenty to) letting off my load gob says I to myself I knew
> he was uneasy in his (two pints off of Joe and one in
> Slattery's off) in his mind to get off the mark to (hundred
> shillings is five quid) and when they were in the (dark
> horse) Pisser Burke was telling me card party and letting

on the child was sick (gob, must have done about a gallon)
flabbyarse of a wife speaking down the tube *she's* [Milly]
better or *she's* (ow!) all a plan so he could vamoose with
the pool if he won or (Jesus, full up I was) trading without
a licence (ow!) Ireland my nation says he (hoik! phthook!)
never be up to those bloody (there's the last of it) Jeru-
salem (ah!) cuckoos. (335)

[Nameless first thinks of the Gold Cup horserace, run
that day and won by Throwaway, a long shot. Dubliners
believe, quite mistakenly, that Bloom had some money
on Throwaway and is thus at this point flush. His not
standing treat for drinks for the denizens of Barney
Kiernan's, which he never does anyway, is therefore
doubly heinous. Nameless also reckons up some of the
drinks that he had cadged this day: two from Joe in
Kiernan's and one from someone else in Slattery's, another pub.]

[For Milly's illnesses see the section on Milly as a child,
pp. 159-160.]

3. Evidently rehired by Hely. Hely was both a stationer
and an accountant; one of Bloom's jobs was to collect the
accounts of convents; one such collection at the Tranquilla
convent in 1894 stays alive in his memory for years:

Devil of a job it was collecting accounts of those convents.
Tranquilla convent. That was a nice nun there, really sweet
face. Wimple suited her small head. Sister? Sister? I am sure
she was crossed in love by her eyes. Very hard to bargain
with that sort of woman. I disturbed her at her devotions
that morning. But glad to communicate with the outside
world. Our great day, she said. Feast of Our Lady of Mount
Carmel [either July 16 or the Sunday following]. Sweet
name too: caramel. She knew, I think she knew by the way
she. If she had married she would have changed. I suppose
they really were short of money. Fried everything in the

best butter all the same. No lard for them. My heart's broke eating dripping. They like buttering themselves in and out. (155) All kinds of crazy longings [Bloom is thinking of women's tastes during their menstruals]. Licking pennies. Girl in Tranquilla convent that nun told me liked to smell rock oil. Virgins go mad in the end I suppose. Sister? (368)

The nun appears as the nymph in an hallucination in Bella Cohen's (552:18-23).

Bloom also deals in stationery and is called a traveller for blotting paper by Ned Lambert (106:26-27). Bloom remembers Hely's stationery on June 16 (263:32-33).

1893-1894 TO 1904
"THE SECRET LIFE OF LEOPOLD BLOOM"

The Blooms' normal sexual life ended on Tuesday, November 27, 1893, as noted above. After the death of Rudy they must have feared another pregnancy and have practised some forms of birth control. A variety of birth control methods were available to them, and on June 16, 1904, Bloom is carrying a prophylactic in his pocketbook: "Ill see if he has that French letter still in his pocketbook I suppose he thinks I dont know deceitful men all their 20 pockets arent enough for their lies" (772) But there is no evidence that the Blooms have employed such a device in their sexual intercourse. They appear to have practised *coitus interruptus*: "no satisfaction in it pretending to like it till he comes and then finish it off myself" (740) And when Joyce described their last complete sexual intercourse, he spelled out the definition: "complete carnal intercourse, with ejaculation of semen within the natural female organ." (736) They also, beginning in 1895 while living in Holles Street, practice cunnilingus (773:2-10).

At some time in the past he had tried to get Molly to enter into his coprophiliac fantasies and urges: "and another time it was my muddy boots hed like me to walk in all the horses dung I could find" (745) Bloom also ejaculates on her bottom, and he also masturbates although she does not know this.

In any event Bloom's innate voyeuristic and fetishistic proclivities were greatly increased, and it must have been from 1894 down to 1904 that he began to live his "secret life"—a "secret life," it should be added, without sexual intercourse. Most of these memories are not more specifically datable within this ten-year span (corresponding, of course, to the ten-year period during which Homer's Ulysses struggled to get home to Ithaca and Penelope).

1. One dark night he almost accosts Mrs. Clinch, a respectable acquaintance (370:26-28). [For Mrs. Clinch, see pp. 78-79 above.]

2. He pays a girl to say dirty words:

> Girl in Meath street that night. All the dirty things I made her say all wrong of course. My arks she called it. It's so hard to find one who. Aho! If you don't answer when they solicit must be horrible for them till they harden. And kissed my hand when I gave her the extra two shillings. Parrots. Press the button and the bird will squeak. Wish she hadn't called me sir. Oh, her mouth in the dark! And you a married man with a single girl! (370)

3. Ogles a high-class whore in Jammet's restaurant (371:24-25).

4. The frowzy whore of Ormand Quay, whom Bloom sees twice on "Ulysses"-day: once in the afternoon, (290:5-17), once after midnight on June 17 (632:12-26, 32-41). Bloom once makes an assignation with her but does not keep it; the whore knows Molly is Bloom's wife;

she would like to do Bloom's wash (290:7-17; 632:22-26).

5. Some rather bizarre and arcane activities:

THE SINS OF THE PAST

(*In a medley of voices.*) He went through a form of clandestine marriage with at least one woman in the shadow of the Black Church. Unspeakable messages he telephoned mentally to Miss Dunn at an address in d'Olier Street while he presented himself indecently to the instrument in the callbox. By word and deed he encouraged a nocturnal strumpet to deposit fecal and other matter in an unsanitary outhouse attached to empty premises. In five public conveniences he wrote pencilled messages offering his nuptial partner to all strongmembered males. And by the offensively smelling vitriol works did he not pass night after night by loving courting couples to see if and what and how much he could see? Did he not lie in bed, the gross boar, gloating over a nauseous fragment of wellused toilet paper presented to him by a nasty harlot, stimulated by gingerbread and a postal order? (537)

[Since this list is recorded in an hallucination at Bella Cohen's, it is doubtful whether all these estimable activities were actually performed by Bloom. Certainly he "wanted" to perform them. He did not go through a form of clandestine marriage; on the other hand he undoubtedly did telephone, mentally, unspeakable messages to Miss Dunn. We can assume that he would have liked to do them all, and did some, such as spying on lovers.]

6. Trails whores on the streets, maybe; at least Bella Cohen so charges (542:27-28).

7. Visits the "for men only" Mutoscope pictures in Capel Street (368:25-29).

8. Watches a girl who blushes as she watches a monkey at the zoo (471:29-31).

9. Sees two sluts singing a smutty song on a rainy night

in the Coombe, a street in a run-down section of Dublin. (78:36-79:10; 552:27-553:5).

10. Stares at the full bosom of Mrs. Yelverton Barry in the Theatre Royal (Bloom is in the gods; Mrs. Barry in a box); and writes her an anonymous and obscene letter, perhaps (465:25-32).

11. Having closed the carriage door for Mrs. Bellingham during the cold snap of February 1893, as noted above, Bloom pursues other activities with Mrs. Bellingham in his imagination (465:30-466:10; 466:19-33).

12. Sees the Honourable Mrs. Mervyn Talboys at a polo match, and his mind is stirred once more to erotic fantasies (467:1-20).

13. A furtive act: *"handsomemarriedwomanrubbed againstwidebehindinClonskeatram,"* (586)

14. Actually does converse with and is alone in a hotel room with Mrs. Miriam Dandrade, a high-class Spanish-American whore, from whom he buys some of her wraps and her black underclothes:

> That one at the Grosvenor this morning [an upper-class woman whose silk-clad ankle Bloom wished to see as she stepped up into her carriage across the street. He was frustrated in this desire, as usual, when a tram came between them (73:32-74:31).] [. . . .] Who is this she was like? O yes? Mrs Miriam Dandrade that sold me her old wraps and black underclothes in the Shelbourne hotel. Divorced Spanish American. Didn't take a feather out of her my handling them. As if I was her clotheshorse. Saw her in the viceregal party when Stubbs the park ranger got me in with Whelan of the *Express.* Scavenging what the quality left. High tea. Mayonnaise I poured on the plums thinking it was custard. Her ears ought to have tingled for a few weeks after. Want to be a bull for her. Born courtesan. No nursery work for her, thanks. (160-161)

Puts on Mrs. Dandrade's clothes, lies down in bed and imagines that he is about to be violated by a series of men, at least so Bella Cohen charges (536:10-30).

15. The bulk of Bloom's secret life appears to have consisted of three activities:

Voyeurism: "Typist going up Roger Greene's stairs two at a time to show her understandings." (372)

Masturbation (409:14-23, 32-36).

And "collecting": "a nun maybe like the smutty photo he has shes as much a nun as Im not" (738); in the drawer at 7 Eccles Street are two erotic photographs (721:25-31) and a press clipping from an English periodical about corporal punishment in girls' schools (721:16-18).

Other events of the early and middle 1890s.

1. Josie Powell, who was a year or so older than Molly (158:24), marries the unfortunate Mr. Denis Breen. Nameless sums it all up:

> And she with her nose cockahoop after she married him because a cousin of his old fellow's was pew opener to the pope. Picture of him on the wall with his smashall sweeney's moustaches. The signor Brini from Summerhill, the eyetallyano, papal zouave to the Holy Father, has left the quay and gone to Moss street. And who was he, tell us? A nobody, two pair back and passages, at seven shillings a week, and he covered with all kinds of breastplates bidding defiance to the world. (321)

Bloom says it was a mating of the beauty and the beast (446:1-5).

2. Tom Kernan falls down in the W.C. of a pub and bites his tongue: "and Tom Kernan that drunken little barrelly man that bit his tongue off falling down the mens W C drunk in some place or other" (773) [Mr. Kernan's

fall is the efficient cause for the plot of "Grace" in *Dubliners*. The actual fall was taken by John Joyce in the middle 1890s (E., p. 43).]

3. Bloom sees Hengler's Circus, probably in 1894, and remembers: his horror at the trapeze act (64:29-31); that a clown came up to where Bloom was sitting alone in the stands and, to the delight of the crowd, announced that Bloom was his father (696:19-25). [I am assigning this memory to c. 1894 because in Skin-the-Goat's cab shelter the mysterious sailor Murphy relates a wildly impossible anecdote of having seen Simon Dedalus, performing in Hengler's circus, shoot two eggs off two bottles at fifty yards with his left hand and over his shoulder. The bewildered, but always intrepid, Bloom asks how long ago this was. Murphy explains that Simon Dedalus had toured the world with Hengler's circus and that he (Murphy) saw the performers in Stockholm; as to how long ago, he says: "it might be a matter of ten years." (624) Bloom responds: "—Curious coincidence, Mr. Bloom confided to Stephen unobtrusively." (624)]

4. Milly's illnesses as a child. The mumps: "well I hope shell get someone [Milly is now in Mullingar] to dance attendance on her the way I did when she was down with the mumps her glands swollen wheres this and wheres that of course she cant feel anything deep yet" (767) Worms: "only I like letting myself down after in the hole [of the toilet] as far as I can squeeze and pull the chain then to flush it nice cool pins and needles still theres something in it I suppose I always used to know by Millys [stool] when she was a child whether she had worms or not" (770) The Blooms' memories do not agree on what Milly's childhood illnesses were, nor is Bloom himself consistent in his remembrances. At one point he thinks she had only measles:

> Gasworks. [The cab going to Glasnevin cemetery for Dig-
> nam's funeral passes by the Grand Canal and the gasworks.]
> Whooping cough they say it cures. Good job Milly never
> got it. Poor children! Doubles them up black and blue in
> convulsions. Shame really. Got off lightly with illness com-
> pared. Only measles. Flaxseed tea. (90)

But she has also had wildfire [erysipilas] and nettlerash:
"Poor kids. Only troubles wildfire and nettlerash. Calomel
purge I got her for that. After getting better asleep with
Molly." (379) He takes her pulse: "I felt her pulse.
Ticking. Little hand it was: now big. Dearest Papli. All
that the hand says when you touch. Loved to count my
waistcoat buttons." (380)

5. Other memories of Milly's childhood. Her father ties
a ribbon around her blonde hair; she spits in the lake in
Stephen's green; Bloom tells her about Plevna and she
pulls a plait of her hair to make herself remember it; she
dreams of having a conversation with a horse named
Joseph and offers Joseph a tumbler full of lemonade
(694:2-16).

And mementos. Bloom has in his drawer: a Vere
Foster handwriting copy book with Milly's drawings, one
of which is of him (720:25-29); an infantile epistle
addressed to him (721:6-9). Bloom as pedagogue; he
used the matrimonial gifts of the owl and the clock to
explain to her the respective physical properties, both
particular and general, of each (694:17-29).

Milly reciprocates by being attentive to his necessities,
anticipating his desires, and admiring his scientific
knowledge (694:33-39).

Sometime during this period Bloom takes Milly on a
memorable excursion by water around the Kish lighthouse on the "Erin's King" in rough weather. Milly, the
girl-child, is unafraid:

On the *Erin's King* that day around the Kish. Damned old tub pitching about. Not a bit funky. Her pale blue scarf loose in the wind with her hair. (67) Not such damn fools [seagulls]. Also the day I threw that stale cake out of the Erin's King picked it up in the wake fifty yards astern. Live by their wits. (152) Day we went out for the pleasure cruise in the Erin's King, throwing them the sack of old papers. Bears in the zoo. Filthy trip. Drunkards out to shake up their livers. Puking overboard to feed the herrings. Nausea. And the women, fear of God in their faces. Milly, no sign of funk. Her blue scarf loose, laughing. Don't know what death is at that age. And then their stomachs clean. (379) (*Far out in the bay between Bailey and Kish Lights the* Erin's King *sails, sending a broadening plume of coal-smoke from her funnel towards the land.*) (550) not forgetting the Irish lights, Kish and others, liable to capsize at any moment rounding which he once with his daughter had experienced some remarkably choppy, not to say stormy, weather. (630)

But once her parents frightened her: "But being lost they fear. When we hid behind the tree at Crumlin. I didn't want to. Mamma! Mamma! Babes in the woods. Frightening them with masks too. Throwing them up in the air to catch them. I'll murder you. Is it only half fun?" (379)

1895. "ON THE ROCKS" IN HOLLES STREET

Molly.

1. Lost habitations: "how many houses were we in at all Raymond Terrace and Ontario terrace and Lombard street and Holles street" (772)

2. Lost jobs for Bloom: "every time were just getting on right something happens or he puts his big foot in it Thoms and Helys and Mr Cuffes and Drimmies" (772)

3. Bloom gives her permission to pose in the nude: "the woman is beauty of course thats admitted when he said I could pose for a picture naked to some rich fellow in Holles street when he lost the job in Helys" (753)

4. Sells her clothes: "and I was selling the clothes" (753)

5. Plays the piano in a temperance hall: "and strumming in the coffee palace" (753)

6. Takes an interest in a young doctor:

> looking out of the window if there was a nice fellow even in the opposite house [that is, across from 7 Eccles Street] that medical [Dr. O'Hare] in Holles street the nurse [Miss Callan] was after when I put on my gloves and hat at the window to show I was going out not a notion what I meant arent they thick never understand what you say even youd want to print it up on a big poster for them not even if you shake hands twice with the left he didnt recognize me either when I half frowned at him outside Westland row chapel where does their great intelligence come in Id like to know grey matter they have it all in their tail if you ask me (757-758)

[The Dublin Maternity Hospital, much larger now than it was in 1895, is on Holles Street. Sometime early in 1920 Joyce wrote to his aunt Mrs. Murray asking for various facts about Dublin, among them: "I also want all the information you can give, tittletattle, facts, etc. about Holles Street maternity hospital." (L. p. 136).]

7. Bloom wants some arcane sex, which she first refuses to assent to but finally capitulates:

> I suppose Im nothing any more when I wouldnt let him lick me in Holles street one night man man tyrant as ever for the one thing he slept on the floor half the night naked the way the jews used when somebody dies belonged to them and wouldnt eat any breakfast or speak a word wanting to be petted so I thought I stood out enough for

one time and let him he does it all wrong too thinking only of his own pleasure his tongue is too flat or I dont know what he forgets that we then I dont Ill make him do it again if he doesnt mind himself and lock him down to sleep in the coalcellar with the blackbeetles (773)

8. A man in the pit of the Gaiety Theatre tries to get close to her:

a lot of that touching must go on in theatres in the crush in the dark theyre always trying to wiggle up to you that fellow in the pit at the pit at the Gaiety for Beerbohm Tree in Trilby the last time Ill ever go there to be squashed like that for any Trilby or her barebum every two minutes tipping me there and looking away hes a bit daft I think I saw him after trying to get near two stylish dressed ladies outside Switzers window at the same little game I recognized him on the moment the face and everything but he didnt remember me (767) [Beerbohm Tree's *Trilby* played at the Gaiety on October 10 and 11, 1895 (G. and T.).]

Bloom.

1. Makes "progressive" suggestions to Hely which are ignored; the proposer is finally dismissed:

I suggested to him about a transparent show cart with two smart girls sitting inside writing letters, copybooks, envelopes, blotting paper. I bet that would have caught on. Smart girls writing something catch the eye at once. Everyone dying to know what she's writing. Get twenty of them round you if you stare at nothing. Have a finger in the pie. Women too. Curiosity. Pillar of salt. Wouldn't have it of course because he didn't think of it himself first. Or the inkbottle I suggested with a false stain of black celluloid. His ideas for ads like Plumtree's potted under the obituaries, cold meat department. You can't lick 'em. What? Our envelopes. Hello! Jones, where are you going? Can't

stop, Robinson, I am hastening to purchase the only reliable
inkeraser *Kansell,* sold by Hely's Ltd, 85 Dame Street. Well
out of that ruck I am. (154-155)

2. The *Palme,* a ship, goes down (638:4-12). [The facts
as given here are wrong. The *Palme* was Finnish, not
Norwegian. It did not go down but ran aground on
December 24, 1895. An Irish lifeboat capsized drowning
fifteen men, in an attempt to rescue the crew of the
Palme. On December 26 the *Palme's* crew was rescued.
Albert William Quill did write "The Storm of Christmas
Eve, 1895" (G.).]

3. Milly (age six) has a nightmare, and her father and
mother come to her room (692:32-36).

4. Bloom sells Molly's combings: "Ten bob I got for
Molly's combings when we were on the rocks in Holles
street. Why not?" (369)

5. Washes Molly's undergarments: "Still, candour com-
pelled him to admit that he had washed his wife's undergarments when soiled in Holles Street [...] initialled with
Bewley and Draper's marking ink (hers were, that is)"
(632)

6. Molly does not make much money at the Coffee
Palace (634:35-635:4).

7. Tries on Molly's clothes and washes them:

BLOOM

(*A charming soubrette with dauby cheeks, mustard hair
and large male hands and nose, leering mouth.*) I tried her
things on only once, a small prank, in Holles street. When
we were hardup I washed them to save the laundry bill.
My own shirts I turned. It was the purest thrift. (536)

8. The Blooms live in a tenement owned by Nurse
Callan of the Maternity Hospital (385:22-25).

Nurse Callan looks in on Bloom when he is alone:

"Must call to the hospital. Wonder is nurse Callan there still. She used to look over some nights when Molly was in the Coffee Palace." (373) Nurse Callan loves Dr. O'Hare (who is now dead; see entry for 1901 below): "That young Dr. O'Hare I noticed her brushing his coat." (373)

Nurse Callan is young-looking and a virgin, and still is nine years later in 1904 (385:25-29; 386:17-22).

9. Ben Dollard's concert. Ben Dollard borrows a dress suit (which proves to be rather tight around his capacious scrotum) from the Blooms for a concert in which he is to sing. Molly:

> and Ben Dollard base barreltone the night he borrowed the swallowtail to sing out of in Holles street squeezed and squashed into them and grinning all over his big Dolly face like a wellwhipped childs botty didnt he look a balmy ballocks sure enough that must have been a spectacle on the stage imagine paying 5/- in the preserved seats for that to see him and Simon Dedalus too (774)

Bloom:

> Ben Dollard's famous. Night he ran round to us to borrow a dress suit for that concert. Trousers tight as a drum on him. Musical porkers. Molly did laugh when he went out. Threw herself back across the bed, screaming, kicking. With all his belongings on show. O, saints above, I'm drenched! O, the women in the front row! O, I never laughed so many! Well, of course, that's what gives him the base barreltone. For instance eunuchs. (270)

On June 16, 1904, at the Ormond Bar, Ben Dollard, "Father" Bob Cowley and Simon Dedalus reminisce about the same occasion. Dollard needed some trousers in a hurry for a concert in which he was to sing. Cowley thought of borrowing a pair from Bloom whom he knew was "on the rocks" in Holles Street. Dollard, Cowley, and

Dedalus, after some difficulty, succeeded in locating the Blooms' tenement on Holles Street. Dollard borrowed the trousers, and the three noticed, and were surprised by, the large numbers of luxurious clothing belonging to Molly, leading to some suspicion on their part that she might at this time have another occupation besides playing in the Coffee Palace. The reminiscences of the three concludes with Simon Dedalus impugning Molly's virtue (268:4-269:28). The concert itself was a great success, even though Professor Goodwin at the piano was drunk (268:14-20; 575:1-6, 34-35). Ben Dollard sang "Love and War" with "all his belongings on show" and evidently to great acclaim (521:26-522:12).

[There is a strong presumption that in these dire days Molly was practising the oldest profession of all. The evidence is all circumstantial but nevertheless revealing. We are told explicitly that Bloom was willing to let her be photographed in the nude by a rich man; Father Cowley says: "who was it gave me the wheeze she was doing the other business?" (268:38-39); Dedalus, Cowley, and Dollard, as noted above, saw that Molly had many expensive (Merrion Square Style) clothes despite the Blooms' extreme poverty; Simon Dedalus remarks that she has often taken off her clothes (269:7-8) and that she is the Daughter of the Regiment (269:19-20).

On June 16, 1904, Bloom contemplates, with complete equanimity, the possibility that Boylan may pay his wife for her services; furthermore this thought occurs in connection with a Holles Street memory:

> Hair strong in rut. Ten bob I got for Molly's combings when we were on the rocks in Holles street. Why not? Suppose he gave her money. Why not? All a prejudice. She's worth ten, fifteen, more a pound. All that [sexual intercourse] for nothing. Bold hand [Boylan's]. Mrs Mar-

ion. [Boylan's letter in the morning was not addressed to "Mrs. Leopold Bloom" but to "Mrs. Marion Bloom."] (369)

If Molly was in fact a prostitute at this time, then there is some sense to one of her own observations, puzzling on the face of it, about the size of Boylan's erect member: "like iron or some kind of crowbar standing all the time . . . no I never in all my life felt anyone had one the size of that to make you feel full up" (742) This observation is puzzling because, according to the overt (as opposed to the covert) facts of the book, Molly has only experienced the thrust of three male penises, Bloom's, Boylan's and Gardner's. [For Molly and Gardner see pp. 173-174.] This is hardly enough experience to say about such matters: "no I never in all my life"

The usual contradictory evidence is contained in one of Molly's observations about her husband on June 17, 1904: "can you feel him trying to make a whore of me what he never will" (740)]

1896

1. Mrs. Riordan's last days and demise. Mrs. Riordan goes into a rest home: "Our Lady's Hospice for the dying. Deadhouse handy underneath. Where old Mrs. Riordan died. They look terrible the women. Her feeding cup and rubbing her mouth with the spoon. Then the screen round her bed for her to die." (97) Tears up her will: "I'm disappointed in you! You bad man!" (490) Dies (681:11-12). Leaves nothing to the Blooms: "and she never left us a farthing all for masses for herself and her soul" (738)

2. The Blooms are probably still on Holles Street in 1896, since Milly at the time of her nightmare is described as being six years of age. She would have remained six until June 15, 1896.

3. Molly has her picture taken by Lafayette, a Westmoreland Street photographer. Bloom carries the picture, now somewhat soiled, in his wallet and shows it to Stephen on June 17, 1904, as an example of a "Spanish type":

> Stephen, obviously addressed, looked down on the photo showing a large sized lady, with her fleshy charms on evidence in an open fashion, as she was in the full bloom of womanhood, in evening dress cut ostentatiously low for the occasion to give a liberal display of bosom, with more than vision of breasts, her full lips parted, and some perfect teeth, standing near, ostensibly with gravity, a piano, on the rest of which was *In old Madrid,* a ballad, pretty in its way, which was then all the vogue. Her (the lady's) eyes, dark, large, looked at Stephen, about to smile about something to be admired, Lafayette of Westmoreland street, Dublin's premier photographic artist, being responsible for the esthetic execution. (652)

After observing the picture, Stephen says the right thing: "Besides he said the picture was handsome which, say what you like, it was, though at the moment she was distinctly stouter. And why not?" (653-654) "that voluptuous loveliness which the inspired pencil of Lafayette had limned for ages yet to come." (418) Bloom later tells Molly he has shown the picture to Stephen: "what is he driving at now showing him my photo its not good of me I ought to have got it taken in drapery that never looks out of fashion still I look young in it I wonder he didnt make him a present of it altogether and me too after all why not" (774)

4. On March 21, at 4:46 A.M. the clock that Mat Dillon had given the Blooms for a wedding present stops (707: 22-24).

1897

The Blooms are living on Ontario Terrace.

1. They have a servant girl, Mary Driscoll, who steals from them and continuously excites Bloom:

> not that I care two straws who he does it with or knew before that way though Id like to find out so long as I dont have the two of them under my nose all the time like that slut that Mary we had in Ontario terrace padding out her false bottom to excite him bad enough to get the smell of those painted women off him once or twice I had a suspicion by getting him to come near me when I found the long hair on his coat without that one when I went into the kitchen pretending he was drinking water 1 woman is not enough for them it was all his fault of course ruining servants then proposing that she could eat at our table on Christmas if you please O no thank you not in my house stealing my potatoes and the oysters 2/6 per doz going out to see her aunt if you please common robbery so it was but I was sure he had something on with that one it takes me to find out a thing like that he said you have no proof it was her proof O yes her aunt was very fond of oysters but I told her what I thought of her suggesting me to go out to bealone with her I wouldnt lower myself to spy on them the garters I found in her room the Friday she was out that was enough for me a little bit too much I saw too that her face swelled up on her with temper when I gave her her weeks notice better do without them altogether do out the rooms myself quicker only for the damn cooking and throwing out the dirt I gave it to him anyhow either she or me leaves the house I couldnt even touch him if I thought he was with a dirty barefaced liar and sloven like that one denying it up to my face and singing about the place in the W C too because she knew she was too well off yes (739-740)

But, as usual, Bloom does not make it:

> He says this, a censor of morals, a very pelican in his piety, who did not scruple, oblivious of the ties of nature, to attempt illicit intercourse with a female domestic drawn from the lowest strata of society. Nay, had the hussy's scouringbrush not been her tutelary angel it had gone with her as hard as with Hagar, the Egyptian! (409)

In a fantasy in Bella Cohen's the "romance" between Mary Driscoll, described as a slipshod servant girl, and Bloom is reenacted: she was with the Blooms for four months at six pounds per year and whatever else she could pick up, with Fridays off; Bloom gave her presents, in particular some smart emerald garters. He defended her against Molly's charge that she stole their oysters. One morning when Molly was out shopping Bloom, in slippers and house jacket, surprised Mary in the rear of the premises with a request for a safety pin; he attempted (for the only time in his life) a direct assault, but Mary Driscoll beat him off with her scouring brush; Bloom told her to keep quiet about it (460:6-461:19).

2. One night Bloom brings home a dog with a lame paw, causing another domestic altercation: "like the night he walked home with a dog if you please" (768) Bloom:

> Anyhow, upon weighing the pros and cons, getting on for one as it was, it was high time to be retiring for the night. The crux was it was a bit risky to bring him [Dedalus] home as eventualities might possibly ensue (somebody having a temper of her own sometimes) and spoil the hash altogether as on the night he misguidedly brought home a dog (breed unknown) with a lame paw, not that the cases were either identical or the reverse, though he [Dedalus] had hurt his hand too, to Ontario Terrace, as he very distinctly remembered, having been there, so to speak. (657)

3. Milly (age eight) has a nightmare (692:32-36).

4. A night in a box at the Gaiety Theatre for *The Wife of Scarli*. Molly:

> that night it [her menstrual] came on me like that the one and only time we were in a box that Michael Gunn [the owner of the Gaiety] gave him to see Mrs Kendal and her husband at the Gaiety something he did about insurance for him Drimmies I was fit to be tied though I wouldnt give in with that gentleman of fashion staring down at me with his glasses and him the other side of me talking about Spinoza and his soul thats dead I suppose millions of years ago I smiled the best I could all in a swamp leaning forward as if I was interested having to sit it out then to the last tag I wont forget that wife of Scarli in a hurry supposed to be a fast play about adultery that idiot in the gallery hissing the woman adulteress he shouted I suppose he went and had a woman in the next lane running round all the back ways after to make up for it I wish he had what I had then hed boo I bet the cat itself is better off than us have we too much blood up in us (769) [This places Bloom as working at Drimmies in insurance at this period, and Chronology VI.C.7(1) has an entry for 1896, "L. B. in Drimmies." *The Wife of Scarli* was performed in Dublin at the Gaiety Theatre on October 22, 1897 (T.).]

Bloom:

> Her high long snore. Night we were in the box. Trombone under blowing like a grampus, between the acts, other brass chap unscrewing, emptying spittle. Conductor's legs too, bagstrousers, jiggedy jiggedy. Do right to hide them. (271) Night Michael Gunn gave us the box. Tuning up. Shah of Persia liked that best. Remind him of home sweet home. Wiped his nose in curtain too. Custom his country perhaps. That's music too. Not as bad as it sounds. Tootling. Brasses braying asses through uptrunks. Doublebasses,

helpless, gashes in their sides. Woodwinds mooing cows.
Semigrand open crocodile music hath jaws. Woodwind like
Goodwin's name.

   She looked fine. Her crocus dress she wore, lowcut, belongings on show. Clove her breath was always in theatre
when she bent to ask a question. Told her what Spinoza
says in that book of poor papa's. Hypnotised, listening.
Eyes like that. She bent. Chap in dresscircle, staring down
into her with his operaglass for all he was worth. Beauty
of music you must hear twice. Nature woman half a look.
(284)

5. After a quarrel with Molly, Bloom goes to work at
Drimmie's not properly dressed: "And the day I went to
Drimmie's without a necktie. Wrangle with Molly it was
put me off." (370)

1898

   1. The Blooms are probably still living on Ontario
Terrace since Milly has been described in 1897 as eight
years of age, which she would have remained until June
15, 1898.

   2. Bloom sends out a coin to circulate among the human
community in order to see if it will return. He marks a
florin with three notches on the milled edge and gives it in
payment to his regular grocer, J. and T. Davy at 1
Charlemont Mall, which is just across the Grand Canal
from Ontario Terrace. The coin never does return to
Bloom (696:25-30, 33-34).

   3. Bloom and Sandow. [Eugene Sandow was a nine-
teenth-century strong man whose book *Strength and
How to Obtain It* was published in London in 1897.
Bloom has it in his library mistitled by Joyce as *Physical
Strength and How to Obtain It*. In 1898, from May 2 to
May 14, Sandow performed at the Empire Palace in

Dublin (T.). There would thus be a reasonable presumption that Bloom bought his copy of Sandow at this time and began the exercises prescribed by Sandow.]

Bloom labors for two months on Sandow's prescribed exercises and records his measurements on a chart which is still in his drawer in 1904 (721:33-38). He performs the exercises before a mirror (681:19-29).

On June 16, 1904, Bloom twice reminds himself to take up Sandow's exercises once more:

> Morning mouth bad images. Got up wrong side of the bed. Must begin again those Sandow's exercises. On the hands down. (61) Close shave that [Bloom has just jumped out of the way of a sand strewer] but cured the stitch [in his side]. Must take up Sandow's exercises again. On the hands down. Insure against street accident too. (435)

1899-1902. THE BOER WAR YEARS

During the Boer War Molly appears to have had her one other lover besides Blazes Boylan, one Lieutenant Stanley G. Gardner, Eighth Battalion, Second East Lancers Regiment. Gardner evidently first saw her at a concert: "they [the young ladies of Dublin] dont know how to sing a song like that Gardner said no man could look at my mouth and teeth smiling like that and not think of it" (762) A conversation ensues: "I was afraid he mightnt like my accent first he so English" (762-763) He is not a snob: "theyre so snotty about themselves some of those cads he wasnt a bit like that" (763) A declaration: "he was dead gone on my lips" (763) Intimacy: "he [Bloom] never knew how to embrace well like Gardner" (747) "and touched his [Bloom's in 1888] trousers outside the way I used to Gardner after with my ring hand to keep him from doing worse where it was too public" (746) Mulvey's heavy, gold Claddagh ring is passed on to Gardner:

he [Mulvey] gave me that clumsy Caddagh ring for luck
that I gave Gardner going to South Africa (762) if it brought
its bad luck with it like an opal or pearl must have been
pure 16 carat gold because it was very heavy I can still
see his face clean shaven (762)

The farewell to Gardner who is off to war:

he was a lovely fellow in khaki and just the right height
over me Im sure he was brave too he said I was lovely the
evening we kissed goodbye at the canal lock my Irish beauty
he was pale with excitement about going away or wed be
seen from the road he couldnt stand properly and I so hot
as I never felt they could have made their peace in the
beginning or old oom Paul [the Boer President Paul Kru-
ger] and the rest of the old Krugers go and fight it out
between them instead of dragging on for years killing any
finelooking men there were (749)

Gardner dies of fever in South Africa:

going to South Africa where those Boers killed him with
their war and fever (762) killing any finelooking men there
were with their fever if he was even decently shot it
wouldnt have been so bad (749) I hate the mention of politics after the war that Pretoria and Ladysmith and Bloem-
fontein [battles in South Africa] where Gardner Lieut
Stanley G 8th Bn 2nd East Lancs Rgt of enteric fever
(748-749)

[This love affair could have taken place any time from
1899 to 1901 when Molly was twenty-eight to thirty years
old. The British were continually sending out reinforce-
ments, but the peace was signed on May 31, 1902, so it is
unlikely that Gardner would have been sent out that year.]

Molly has one other constellation of Boer War memories: "the lancers O the lancers theyre grand or the
Dublins that won Tugela his [Boylan's] father made his

money over selling the horses for the cavalry" (749) [The Lancers was Gardner's regiment. The Battle of Colenso was fought at the Tugela River in December 1899. The Irish regiments, both the First and Second Royal Dublin Fusilliers, suffered heavy casualties (G. and T.). The true story of how Boylan's father, Dan Boylan, made his money out of the Boer War is told by the Nameless One: "Dirty Dan the dodger's son off Island bridge that sold the same horses twice over to the government to fight the Boers." (319) The Citizen similarly declares: "We know him [Boylan], says the citizen. The traitor's son. We know what put English gold in his pocket." (318)

1899

Bloom and the Boer War.

Bloom was pro-Boer, as befitting an Irishman, but he also was, prudently, concerned about the security of his investments in English government stocks, his: "four per cents" (409:7-13).

1. Involved in a student demonstration against Joe Chamberlain and is almost arrested:

> That horse policeman the day Joe Chamberlain was given his degree in Trinity he got a run for his money. My word he did! His horse's hoofs clattering after us down Abbey street. Luck I had the presence of mind to dive into Manning's or I was souped. He did come a wallop, by George. Must have cracked his skull on the cobblestones. I oughtn't to have got myself swept along with those medicals. And the Trinity jibs in their mortarboards. Looking for trouble. Still I got to know that young Dixon who dressed that sting for me in the Mater and now he's in Holles street where Mrs Purefoy. Wheels within wheels. Police whistle in my ears still. All skedaddled. Why he fixed on me. Give

me in charge. Right here it began [where he was almost arrested].
—Up the Boers!
—Three cheers for De Wet!
—We'll hang Joe Chamberlain on a sourapple tree. (162-163)

Among the many accusations made against Bloom in the hallucinations in Bella Cohen's is that he booed Joe Chamberlain (457:25-26). [Joe Chamberlain (1836-1914) was the British Colonial Secretary from 1895 to 1903 and was therefore blamed, probably wrongly, for the outbreak of the Boer War. He was granted an honorary degree by Trinity College, Dublin, on December 18, 1899, causing the student demonstration described by Bloom. DeWet was a Boer statesman and general, particularly effective at guerrilla warfare. Dr. Dixon, first encountered by Bloom here, was later to dress the bee sting that Bloom was to receive on May 23, 1904.]

2. His friend Percy Apjohn falls in action at Modder River (704:34). [This battle, in which British losses were heavy, was fought in November, 1899.]

3. In hallucinations in Bella Cohen's Bloom becomes Major Tweedy fighting for the English in the Boer War (although other wars and battles are woven into the fantasies) (457:27-458:3; 484:1-8; 596:12-15).

4. The last thought that Bloom gives to the Boer War surfaces at his home just before he goes to bed and when he is contemplating "Wonderworker," an enema device he had sent for from London for Molly: "What a pity the government did not supply our men with wonderworkers during the South African campaign! What a relief it would have been!" (722) [There are some characteristic cloacal jokes here. The word "relief" was often seen in the newspapers during the Boer War to indicate that a seige had

been lifted or a trapped garrison had been "relieved."
Further, this is the last thought in the book that Bloom
gives to the Boer War, and it constitutes yet another
examples of the characteristic Joycean deflation by way
of a coda. As the musical chapter, Sirens—that cacaphony
and symphony of imaginary sounds—concludes with
Bloom breaking wind, so with the Boer War we conclude
in the bowels of the British soldiers, so to speak. Ithaca
Notesheet No. 12 indicates that Joyce was basing his irony
on the actual testimony of a British soldier who had returned from South Africa (H., p. 468).]

Other events of the year.

1. Bloom has in his drawer at 7 Eccles Street a pink
ribbon which had festooned an Easter egg in the year 1899
(721:18-19).

2. A famous murder, the Childs case, occurs, and the
passengers going to Glasnevin on the morning of June 16,
1904, pass by the house where it happened; a brief
discussion of it ensues (99:42-100:17). [Thomas Childs,
age seventy-six, was murdered on September 2, 1899, at 5
Bengal Terrace, Glasnevin. His brother Samuel was ac-
cused of the murder, and was acquitted in October 1899.
His lawyer was the celebrated and eloquent Seymour
Bushe (E., p. 95). Joyce himself had attended the trial.
Seymour Bushe's forensic eloquence in the Childs case
remains in Dublin memory as an example of powerful
rhetoric. His summarizing defense speech is described,
and its peroration quoted verbatim, by J. J. O'Malloy in the
newspaper office (139:21-140:20). The Childs case is also
alluded to at 410:26-29; 412:13-14; and 456:22.]

1900

February 12. H. Rumbold, a barber, hangs Joe Gann
(303:23-24).

1901

1. Nova, a nascent star, appears (698:31-32).
2. Queen Victoria dies:

> Widowhood not the thing since the old queen died. Drawn
> on a guncarriage. Victoria and Albert. Frogmore memor-
> ial mourning. But in the end she put a few violets in
> her bonnet. Vain in her heart of hearts. All for a shadow.
> Consort not even a king. Her son was the substance. Some-
> thing new to hope for not like the past she wanted back,
> waiting. It never comes. (102)

[Queen Victoria insisted on staying in mourning for her
husband Prince Albert (d. 1861) for many years longer
than others thought sensible. The Frogmore Memorial
was a special mausoleum she had constructed for Albert,
herself, and her mother at Frogmore Lodge at Windsor
Castle. She did not allow her son, later Edward VII, to
share any power, for which she was much criticized. He
did not become monarch until her death, by which time he
was sixty years old (G.).]

In 1904 Queen Victoria is still a pervasive memory for
Dubliners. Bloom thinks of her twice more (85:1-2;
161:28-29). A scandalous story of her supposed private
life is told by Joe in Barney Kiernan's pub (330:30-36).

3. Population of Ireland: 4,386,035. Bloom is calcu-
lating how much reclaimable material there would be in
the excrement produced by this number. He figures that
each individual produces eighty pounds annually (718:19-
26). [At one time Joyce evidently had intended that
Bloom work for the census. Notesheet No. 13 for Ithaca
says: "LB & census 1891." Joyce first wrote in the year
1881 and then changed it to 1891 (H., pp. 475-476).]

4. Osmond Tearle, Shakespearean actor, dies (690:9).

5. Christmas. Dr. O'Hare, Nurse Callan's love, dies of stomach cancer on Mona Island (385:30-386:4).

1902

Bloom sees Josie Powell Breen: "Same blue serge dress she [he has just run into Josie on June 16, 1904] had on two years ago, the nap bleaching. Seen its best days." (158)

1902 OR 1903

Jack Power takes a mistress who becomes a friend:

and they [men] call that friendship killing and then bury-ing one another [Molly has been thinking of drunks and funerals] and they all with their wives and families at home more especially Jack Power keeping that barmaid he does of course his wife is always sick or going to be sick or just getting better of it and hes a goodlooking man still though hes getting a bit grey over the ears (773) His [Bloom's] eyes passed lightly over Mr Power's goodlooking face. Grey-ish over the ears. *Madame:* smiling. I smiled back. A smile goes a long way. Only politeness perhaps. Nice fellow. Who knows is that true about the woman he keeps? Not pleasant for the wife. Yet they say, who was it told me, there is no carnal. You would imagine that would get played out pretty quick. Yes, it was Crofton met him one evening bringing her a pound of rumpsteak. What is this she was? Barmaid in Jury's. Or the Moira, was it? (93) [There is no indica-tion of the date of the inception of this affair. By the manner in which both Blooms think of it, I am assuming that it is of fairly recent origin.]

1903

Molly.

1. The Blooms move to 7 Eccles Street; Molly brings no salt:

> I never brought a bit of salt in even when we moved in
> the confusion musical academy he was going to make on the
> first floor drawingroom with a brassplate or Blooms private
> hotel he suggested go and ruin himself altogether the way
> his father did down in Ennis (765)

[There is no evidence in the text itself as to when the
Blooms moved to Eccles Street, the last domicile mentioned being Ontario Terrace in 1897-1898. But given
their previous habits, constant changes and moves, sometimes synchronized with Bloom's frequent changes of
occupation and sometimes not, it is not likely that they
have been at 7 Eccles for a period of years. They are always
either just arriving or just leaving, as was John Joyce and
family when James Joyce was a boy. I chose 1903 for the
move to Eccles Street for the following reasons: (1) In the
fullest chronology, VI.C.7(1), the notes for 1903 are "L.B.
Freeman., Eccles." The chronological notations of these
manuscripts were not always followed out, but one knows
from this one that Joyce's intention, at one time anyway,
was to move the Blooms into 7 Eccles in 1903; and also to
have Bloom begin to work for the *Freeman's Journal* in
that same year or the year before. This coincidence also
makes sense since the date of a new job and a new
domicile often do coincide. In VI.C.7(2) Bloom is placed in
Freeman's for 1902-1904, as he is in V.A.8. (2) The
question of whether or not 7 Eccles Street will be turned
into a private hotel has still not been settled; such a crucial
marital wrangle could hardly have gone on for years. Thus
when on the afternoon of June 16, 1904, Molly throws a
coin to a beggar, the one-legged sailor, she knocks over a
sign which read "Unfurnished Apartments" (225:38-39),
and which is subsequently returned to its place (234:10-
11). But if Bloom had persuaded her to put up the sign,

she is by no means willing to follow out its implications: "Im sure Im not going to take in lodgers off the street for him if he takes a gesabo of a house like this" (779-780) (3) But, as usual, there is contradictory evidence. Bloom had passed Irishtown Strand, on the bay in south Dublin, on the morning of June 16, 1904, in the funeral carriage. In the cab shelter he thinks of the Strand and how different it looks, he having not seen it for "years"—since he had gone to reside in the north side at 7 Eccles Street (651:42-652:2). But it should also be said that although Bloom's old habitations, jobs, haunts were south of the Liffey, they were in the inner city and at a considerable distance from Irishtown Strand on the bay.

On balance, the Blooms have been at Eccles Street a comparatively short time.]

2. (Either 1903 or 1904.) There is, perhaps, a burglar in the house at night and the frightened Bloom goes down to the kitchen to "apprehend" him [the Bloom's bedroom is at the rear of their dwelling]:

> not that hed be much use [if she should be assaulted by an intruder] still better than nothing the night I was sure I heard burglars in the kitchen and he went down in his shirt with a candle and a poker as if he was looking for a mouse as white as a sheet frightened out of his wits making as much noise as he possibly could for the burglars benefit there isnt much to steal indeed the Lord knows still its the feeling especially now with Milly away (766)

3. Her last concert takes place over a year ago in May (?) of 1903. Bloom, she suspects, has arranged it for her, as a protective act of patriotism, since the concert was celebrating the English victory in the Boer War:

> what would they say eloped with him [Boylan] that gets you on the stage the last concert I sang at where its over a

year ago when was it St Teresas hall Clarendon St little
chits of missies they have now singing Kathleen Kearney
[a young singer described in "A Mother" in *Dubliners*]
and her like on account of father being in the army and my
singing the absentminded beggar and wearing a brooch for
lord Roberts when I had the map of it all and Poldy not
Irish enough was it him managed it this time I wouldnt
put it past him (748)

["The Absent Minded Beggar," a patriotic Boer War
poem by Kipling, was set to music by Sir Arthur Sullivan.
It was sung on fund-raising occasions. Lord Roberts was
the victorious British general of the Boer War. After the
British had suffered their initial setbacks in the war,
Roberts was appointed Commander-in-Chief late in 1899,
and arrived in South Africa on January 10, 1900. He
relieved Ladysmith on February 28 and Mafeking on May
17. In October 1900 he handed over the command to
Kitchner and returned to England.

The implication of all this is that Bloom thought he
should publicly atone for his pro-Boer sympathies during
the war.

Molly's phrase, "when I had the map of it all" (748) is
an oblique reference, I believe, to the common saying that
someone has the map of Ireland written all over his, or
her, face. This constitutes the only reference in the book
to the fact that she looks Irish as well as Spanish-Jewish.
Ithaca Notesheet No. 2: "MB has look of old Tweedy" (H.,
p. 422).]

4. Christmas. Larry O'Rourke, owner of the pub nearest
to 7 Eccles Street, sends the Blooms a rather inexpensive
Christmas present: "he makes his money easy Larry they
call him the old mangy parcel he sent at Xmas a cottage
cake and a bottle of hogwash he tried to palm off as claret

that he couldnt get anyone to drink God spare his spit for fear hed die of the drouth" (750)

Bloom.

1. A woman dies in childbirth at the Holles Street Maternity Hospital, as it is remarked in the anteroom of the hospital on June 16, 1904 (388:38-389:1).

2. The American revivalists, Torry and Alexander, visit Dublin (151:20-21). [Actually Torry and Alexander were in Dublin in 1904. Bloom's mention of "polygamy" here alludes to the fact that J. Alexander Dowie, the American revivalist who is supposed to be in Dublin on June 16, 1904, was later charged with, among other things, polygamy (G.).]

3. February. A cyclone or hurricane occurs blowing down trees (138:3-5; 396:38).

4. c. March 25, Lady Day, the Feast of the Annunciation of the Blessed Virgin, the eleventh (eighth surviving) child of Theodore and Mina Purefoy is born. One year later, March 25, 1904, the mother bites off the last of her "chick's" nails (397:36-37). [There was an Irish superstition that if a child's nails were cut off before it was a year old it would be "light-fingered and addicted to stealing" (G.).]

5. June 26. Bloom goes to Ennis for the vigil of his father. He therefore misses Mrs. Dedalus's funeral (695: 25-27). On the train he performs the good deed of returning to a farmer's daughter a bag she had left behind (166:26-28).

6. August. Bob Cowley lends a valise to M'Coy, who claims that his wife, a singer, is to give a concert at the Wicklow regatta. Cowley never again saw the valise which, presumably, disappeared into a pawn shop or a second-hand store (76:7-9).

7. September. Bloom meets Blazes Boylan at the shop of their mutual tailor, Mesias, and the two strike up a friendship. Boylan, a singer, already has an eye on Molly. The two agree on a provincial musical tour featuring Molly and Boylan, sharing the expenses and dividing the proceeds (732:31-733:2). Bloom, evidently, had gone to Mesias to have his trousers altered, at the cost of eleven shillings (497:21-24). And Mesias tell Bloom he is one-in-a-million in that his testicles hang down on the right hand side (476:1-5). Subsequent to their meeting, Bloom and Boylan have drinks together at the Bleeding Horse pub in Camden Street, so at the least Corley tells Stephen he has seen them so doing when he (Corley) encounters Stephen and Bloom after midnight on June 17 (618:18-20).

8. September. Mortimer Edward Purefoy conceived by Theodore and Mina Purefoy. He is to be born on the evening of June 16, 1904. The Purefoys are the symbol of fecundity and its consequences in *Ulysses*:

> Poor Mrs Purefoy! Methodist husband. Method in his madness. Saffron bun and milk and soda lunch in the educational dairy. Eating with a stopwatch, thirty-two chews to the minute. Still his muttonchop whiskers grew. Supposed to be well connected. Theodore's cousin in Dublin Castle. One tony relative in every family. Hardy annuals he presents her with. Saw him out at the Three Jolly Topers marching along bareheaded and his eldest boy carrying one in a marketnet. The squallers. Poor thing! Then having to give the breast year after year all hours of the night. Selfish those t.t's are. Dog in the manger. Only one lump of sugar in my tea, if you please. (161)

Molly pays a visit [date unknown but evidently fairly recently, that is, 1903-1904] to the Purefoy household:

and Mina Purefoys husband give us a swing out of your whiskers filling her up with a child or twins once a year as regular as the clock always with a smell of children off her the one they called budgers or something like a nigger with a shock of hair on it Jesusjack the child is a black the last time I was there a squad of them falling over one another and bawling you couldnt hear your ear supposed to be healthy not satisfied till they have us swollen out like elephants or I dont know what (742)

9. October 14. Mrs. Sinico is killed in an accident at Sydney Parade railroad station (695:21-22).

10. October 17. The burial of Mrs. Sinico at Glasnevin with Bloom in attendance. Paddy Dignam's funeral on June 16, 1904, is the first time he has been back to the cemetery since this time (114:41). At Mrs. Sinico's funeral he placed a shilling in the left lower pocket of his waistcoat and has kept it there ever since (711:4-8).

11. October. David Sheehy beats John Howard Parnell in the election for the M.P. from South Meath (165:19-20).

12. December 31. Bloom looks at his bank passbook and finds his savings amount to £18-14-6 (723:7-11).

1902-1904. MILLY BLOOM IN ADOLESCENCE

On June 15, 1902, Milly Bloom turned thirteen. On September 15, 1903, aged fourteen, she first menstruated. I am assuming that the emergent pattern of behavior to be described below began around 1902 when Milly was twelve to thirteen years of age.

Molly.

1. Milly appears to be omnipresent: "I couldnt turn around with her in the place lately unless I bolted the door

first gave me the fidgets coming in without knocking first when I put the chair against the door just as I was washing myself there below with the glove" (766)

2. Vain: "get on your nerves then doing the loglady [lazy, stupid] all day put her in a glasscase with two at a time to look at her" (766)

3. Careless: "if he knew [evidently Molly did not tell Bloom of this mishap] she broke off the hand off that little gimcrack statue with her roughness and carelessness before she left [but Molly covers up for her] that I got that little Italian boy to mend so that you cant see the join for 2 shillings" (766)

4. Disobedient: "wouldnt even teem [drain] the potatoes for you of course shes right not to ruin her hands" (766)

5. Will not observe proper table manners, is reprimanded and weeps: "and I told her over and over again not to leave knives crossed like that . . . that was the last time she turned on the teartap" (768)

6. Talks back and gets disciplined with some severity:

> but theres no use going to the fair with the thing answering me like a fishwoman when I asked to go for a half a stone of potatoes the day we met Mrs Joe Gallaher at the trottingmatches and she pretended not to see us in her trap with Friery the solicitor we werent grand enough till I gave her 2 damn fine cracks across the ear for herself take that now for answering me like that and that for your impudence she had me that exasperated of course contradicting I was badtempered too because how was it there was a weed in the tea or I didnt sleep the night before cheese I ate was it (767-768)

[The reference to being snubbed by Mrs. Joe Gallaher at the trotting matches is meant to be an indication, one of several, that the Blooms, over the years, have come down in the world; for in the early 1890s (see p. 108 above) the Blooms, Josie Powell, and others went together to the races at Leopardstown, and Bloom remembers that on that occasion Molly was eating a sandwich of spiced beef out of Mrs. Joe Gallaher's lunch basket.

Molly's assertions or declarations often have more than one reference in the general context, or welter, of her ruminations. Here the phrase "we werent grand enough" (768) probably applies both to Mrs. Gallaher and to Milly, who was evidently exhibiting the familiar adolescent trait of being ashamed of one's parents. Molly fuses the two snubs, but she also suggests that Milly answering her like a fishwoman and Mrs. Gallaher looking through her may have happened the same day, and that she was in a bad temper anyway on the day that she struck Milly.

E. (footnote, p. 46) explains the uses to which Joyce puts the real Gallaher family, one Joyce knew very well from his childhood days. According to E., the incident Molly refers to was at the Crosstown races, and Friery the solicitor was not driving Mrs. Gallaher but her sister, Mrs. Clinch, whose name Joyce used for the respectable woman Bloom once almost accosted as a prostitute (see pp. 78-79, 155).]

7. Bloom won't discipline her: "because she has nobody to command her as she said herself well if he doesnt correct her faith I will" (768)

8. Bloom does a lot of talking to her, but when she is in trouble she'll turn to her mother:

> I noticed he was always talking to her lately at the table explaining things in the paper and she pretending to understand sly of course that comes from his side of the house and helping her into her coat but if there was anything wrong with her its me shed tell not him (766)

9. Critical of her mother and vice versa:

> her tongue is a bit too long for my taste your blouse is open
> too low she says to me the pan calling the kettle black-
> bottom and I had to tell her not to cock her legs up like
> that on show on the windowsill before all the people pass-
> ing they all look at her like me when I was her age of
> course any old rag looks well on you (767)

10. Doesn't want to be touched: "then a great touchme-
not too in her own way at the Only Way in the Theatre
royal take your foot away out of that I hate people touching
me afraid of her life Id crush her skirt with the pleats"
(767) [*The Only Way* (1899) was a dramatic adaptation of
Dickens' *A Tale of Two Cities,* written by two Irish
clergymen, Freeman Croft Wills and Frederick Lang-
bridge (G. and T.).]

11. Is entranced by Martin-Harvey, matinee idol and
the star, as Sydney Carton, of *The Only Way,* which leads
Molly to some lucubrations on Sydney Carton and love as
self-sacrifice:

> she clapped when the curtain came down because he looked
> so handsome then we had Martin Harvey for breakfast
> dinner and supper I thought to myself afterwards it must be
> real love if a man gives up his life for her that way for
> nothing I suppose there are few men like that left its hard
> to believe in it though unless it really happened to me the
> majority of them with not a particle of love in their
> natures to find two people like that nowadays full up of
> each other that would feel the same way as you do theyre
> usually a bit foolish in the head (767)

12. Flirts, romps, and smokes, and pulls at the traces
in other ways:

> now shes well on for flirting too with Tom Devans two
> sons imitating me whistling with those romps of Murray

girls calling for her can Milly come out please shes in
great demand to pick what they can out of her round in
Nelson street riding Harry Devans bicycle at night its as
well he [Bloom] sent her where she is [in Mullingar] she
was just getting out of bounds wanting to go on the skating-
rink and smoking their cigarettes through their nose I smelt
it off her dress when I was biting off the thread of the
button I sewed on to the bottom of her jacket she couldnt
hide much from me I tell you only I oughtnt to have
stitched it and it on her it brings a parting (766-767)

13. Has matured physically: "they [Molly's breasts
when she was romping with Mulvey on Gibraltar] were
shaking and dancing about in my blouse like Millys little
ones now when she runs up the stairs" (761)

14. And red-lipped: "shes pretty with her lips so red a
pity they wont stay that way I was too" (767)

15. Corresponds: "only the usual girls nonsense and
giggling that Conny Connally writing to her in white ink
on black paper sealed with sealing wax" (767)

16. Wants to grow up too fast: "wanting to put up her
hair at 15 my powder too only ruin her skin on her shes
time enough for that all her life after of course shes
restless knowing shes pretty" (767)

17. Didn't want to kiss her mother goodbye when she
left for Mullingar: "and she didnt even want me to kiss
her at the Broadstone going away" (767)

18. Is now gone making her mother feel even more
isolated: "the Lord knows still its the feeling [fear of
burglary] especially now with Milly away" (766)

19. Molly keeps forgetting she is gone: "Im always
getting enough [food] for 3 forgetting" (764)

Bloom.
    1. Milly grows up:

> Little hand it was: now big [. . .] Her first stays I re-
> member. Made me laugh to see. Little paps to begin with.
> Left one is more sensitive, I think. Mine too. Nearer the
> heart. Padding themselves out if fat is in fashion. Her
> growing pains at night, calling, wakening me. (380)

2. Bloom's memories of her adolescence: she put away
her hoop and skipping rope; she declined to let an English
visitor take her photograph on the duke's lawn; with a
friend she went half way down Stamer Street, followed by
a sinister person, and turned abruptly back (693:13-20).

3. Milly and the womanly arts:

> Bred in the bone. Milly for example drying her handker-
> chief on the mirror to save the ironing. Best place for an
> ad to catch a woman's eye on a mirror. And when I sent her
> for Molly's Paisley shawl to Presscott's, by the way that ad
> I must, carrying home the change in her stocking. Clever
> little minx! I never told her. Neat way she carried parcels
> too. Attract men, small thing like that. Holding up her
> hand, shaking it, to let the blood flow back when it was
> red. Who did you learn that from? Nobody. Something the
> nurse taught me. O, don't they know? (372) Day I caught
> her in the street pinching her cheeks to make them red.
> Anemic a little. Was given milk too long. (67)

4. Cooks for her father: "Milly served me that cutlet
with a sprig of parsley." (172) "Milly too rock oil and
flour." (175)

5. Quarrels with him: "Coming out of her shell. Row
with her in the XL Café about the bracelet. Wouldn't eat
her cakes or speak or look. Saucebox." (66)

6. Wild and slim: "A wild piece of goods. Her slim legs
running up the staircase." (66)

7. "Wanted a dog to pass the time." (67)

8. Her first menstruation: September 15, 1903 (736:18-

20). "Frightened she was when her nature came on her first. Poor child! Strange moment for the mother too." (380)

9. After Milly's first menstrual complete mental intercourse ceases between Molly and Bloom (736:15-18).

10. At the same time Bloom's wife and daughter begin to circumscribe his actions by questioning him in detail about everything he does (736:23-29).

11. Milly and Molly. Teeth and acrimony: "Very same teeth she has. What do they love? Another themselves? But the morning she chased her with the umbrella. Perhaps so as not to hurt." (379-380) Expletives: "Molly, Milly. Same thing watered down. Her tomboy oaths. O jumping Jupiter! Ye gods and little fishes!" (89) Clothing: "Milly delighted with Molly's new blouse. At first. Put them all on to take them all off. Molly." (368) Menstruals: "But then why don't all women menstruate at the same time with the same moon, I mean? Depends on the time they were born, I suppose. Or all start scratch then get out of step. Sometimes Molly and Milly together." (368)

12. Some final thoughts on Milly at Mullingar: "Twelve and six a week. Not much. Still, she might do worse. Music hall stage." (66) "Better where she is down there: away. Occupy her." (67)

1904

Molly on conditions in Dublin.

1. Fashions: "thin ones are not so much the fashion now" (750) "the old rubbishy dress that I lost the leads out of the tails with no cut in it [that she had in 1894] but theyre coming into fashion again I bought it simply to please him" (752)

2. Inflation: "sure you cant get on in this world without

style all going in food and rent" (751) "with all the things getting dearer every day" (751)

The loneliness of Molly Bloom.
  1. The Blooms' lack of friends:

> still its a lovely hour [after two o'clock in the morning] so silent I used to love coming home after dances the air of the night they [other people] have friends they can talk to weve none either he wants what he wont get or its some woman ready to stick her knife in you I hate that in women no wonder they treat us the way they do we are a dreadful lot of bitches I suppose its all the troubles we have makes us so snappy Im not like that (778-779)

  2. Hardly any mail:

> no visitors or post ever except his cheques or some advertisement (758) only his letter [Boylan's of June 16] and the card from Milly this morning see she [Milly] wrote a letter to him [Bloom] who did I get the last letter from O Mrs Dwenn now whatever possessed her to write after so many years to know the recipe I had for pisto madrileno Floey Dillon since she wrote to say she was married to a very rich architect if Im to believe all I hear with a villa and eight rooms (758)

  3. All alone: "I dont like being alone in this big barracks of a place at night I suppose Ill have to put up with it" (765)
  4. Her fears:

> then leaving us here all day you never know what old beggar at the door for a crust with his long story might be a tramp and put his foot in the way to prevent me shutting it like that picture of that hardened criminal he was called in Lloyds Weekly News 20 years in jail then he comes out and murders an old woman for her money

imagine his poor wife or mother or whoever she is such a face youd run miles away from . . . they ought to be all shot or the cat of nine tails a big brute like that that would attack a poor old woman to murder her in her bed Id cut them off so I would (765-766)

5. Barricades herself in: "I couldnt rest easy till I bolted all the doors and windows to make sure" (765) But this makes her feel she's in jail: "but its worse again being locked up like in a prison or a madhouse" (765-766) Not that Bloom would be much help or that there is much to steal: "not that hed be much use still better than nothing . . . there isnt much to steal indeed the Lord knows still its the feeling" (766)

Leopold Bloom from Molly's point of view.

Molly's attitude toward her husband is complex, and there are three temporal dimensions to it. First, there are the memories of what he was like at the time of their courtship and marriage, and these memories are extra- ordinarily vivid, enough so to recreate for the reader the Bloom of 1887-1888, aged twenty-one to twenty-two, as set forth above in the chronology of those years. These reminiscences are very favorable, naturally, with a few exceptions. Thus a picture of Bloom—handsome, voluble, ambitious, sought-after—emerges that is quite at odds with the Bloom of 1904, both as revealed by his own thoughts and actions and by Molly's opinions about her husband of sixteen years.

Second, there are certain fundamental character traits, some of which she recognized from the start, others that were revealed by the years of marriage, some favorable, some unfavorable. Although it is impossible to make an absolute separation between this category and the third category (Molly's opinions on the Bloom of the night of June 16-17, 1904), the bulk of the following observations are based on her long-term knowledge of the subject, on which she is Dublin's leading expert, as her husband recognizes. After an enumeration of his wife's mental deficiencies (686:17-33) Bloom asks himself if there is any counterbalance for her lack of judgment regarding persons, places and things. And the answer: "The counterbalance of her proficiency of judgment regarding one person [Leopold Bloom], proved true by experiment." (686) Molly: "I know every turn in him" (781) "he cant keep a thing back" (781)

A wife on her husband—con.

1. Parsimonious about food and clothing:

> those kidfitting corsets . . . he saved the one I have but thats no good (750) when I get it [some money] Ill lash it around I tell you in fine style I always want to throw a handful of tea into the pot measuring and mincing if I buy a pair of old brogues itself do you like those new shoes yes how much were they Ive no clothes at all the brown costume and the skirt and jacket and the one at the cleaners 3 whats that for any woman cutting up this old hat and patching up the other the men wont look at you and women try to walk on you because they know youve no man (751) not to be always and ever wearing the same old hat (740)

2. Not a good patient when ill or injured:

> if ever he got anything really serious the matter with him its much better for them go into a hospital where everything is clean but I suppose Id have to dring it into him for a month yes and then wed have a hospital nurse next thing on the carpet have him staying there till they throw him out or a nun (738) O tragic and that dyinglooking . . .

when he sprained his foot (738) I hate bandaging and dosing when he cut his toe with the razor paring his corns afraid hed get blood poisoning (738)

3. Devoted to the obsequies: "hed go into mourning for the cat" (774)

4. Domestic habits. Always around the house during the day, but never providing her with proper help:

he ought to chuck that Freeman with the paltry few shillings he knocks out of it and go into an office or something where hed get regular pay or a bank where they could put him up on a throne to count the money all the day of course he prefers plottering about the house so you cant stir with him any side whats your programme today I wish hed even smoke a pipe like father to get the smell of a man or pretending to be mooching about for advertisements when he could have been in Mr Cuffes still only for what he did (752) its his fault of course having the two of us slaving here instead of getting in a woman long ago am I ever going to have a proper servant again of course then shed see him coming Id have to let her know or shed revenge it arent they a nuisance that old Mrs Fleming [the Blooms' current part-time domestic] you have to be walking round after her putting the things into her hands sneezing and farting into the pots well of course shes old she cant help it (768)

5. The monotomy of his commercial conversation:

itll be a change the Lord knows to have an intelligent person to talk to [Molly is hoping for a relationship with Stephen Dedalus] about yourself not always listening to him and Billy Prescotts ad and Keyess ad and Tom the Devils ad then if anything goes wrong in their business we have to suffer (775)

6. The discomforts of having no bath and only one bedroom and one bed:

if we had even a bath itself or my own room anyway I
wish hed sleep in some bed by himself with his cold feet
on me give us room even to let a fart God or do the least
thing better [she proceeds to break wind softly and slowly]
yes hold them like that a bit on my side piano quietly
sweeeee theres that train far away pianissimo eeeeeeee
one more song (763) that was a relief wherever you be let
your wind go free (763)

7. Political interests. Hangs around with Arthur Griffith and is therefore associated with "Sinn Fein" and will
get into trouble:

and he was going about with some of them Sinner Fein lately or whatever they call themselves talking his usual trash
and nonsense he says that little man he showed me without the neck [Arthur Griffith] is very intelligent the coming
man Griffith is he well he doesnt look it thats all I can
say still it must have been him he knew there was a boycott
(748) well have him coming home with the sack soon out of
the Freeman too like the rest on account of those Sinner
Fein or the Freemasons then well see if the little man
[Griffith] he showed me dribbling along in the wet all by
himself round by Coadys lane will give him much consolation that he says is so capable and sincerely Irish he is
indeed judging by the sincerity of the trousers I saw on
him (772) [Bloom is a Mason although he is not a member
of "Sinn Fein," whose founder, Arthur Griffith, Joyce admired. In a wild burst of improbability Joyce has Bloom give
Griffith his basic ideas for the Irish struggle against England (see pp. 208-209 below).]

8. Certain peculiar habits:

he kneels down to do it [to urinate in the chamber pot]
I suppose there isnt in all creation another man with
the habits he has look at the way hes sleeping at the foot
of the bed [the Blooms sleep reversed, his head, unpillowed,

at the foot of the bed, hers at the head] how can he without a hard bolster its well he doesnt kick or he might knock out all my teeth breathing with his hand on his nose like that Indian god he took me to show one wet Sunday in the museum in Kildare street (771)

9. He sometimes follows, to her incomprehension, certain immemorial Jewish practices: "didnt he kiss our halldoor yes he did what a madman nobody understands his cracked ideas but me" (777) [But Molly does not understand that in kissing the hall door Bloom was probably following the Jewish ceremony of the mezuzah. See p. 25 above.]

10. Is accident-prone, impudent, careless, and is always losing jobs:

besides something always happens with him (748) he goes and gives impudence (772) something happens or he puts his big foot in it (772) even that watch he gave me never seems to go properly (747) then he goes and burns the bottom out of the pan all for his Kidney (754) those old Freemans and Photo bits leaving things like that lying around hes getting very careless (754-755)

11. Sexual oddities and fetiches. Underpants: "hes mad on the subject of drawers thats plain to be seen always skeezing at those brazenfaced things on the bicycles with their skirts blowing up to their navels" (746)

His coldness and his bottom-worship:

I cant help it if Im young still can I its a wonder Im not an old shrivelled hag before my time living with him so cold never embracing me except sometimes when hes asleep the wrong end of me not knowing I suppose who he has any man thatd kiss a womans bottom Id throw my hat at him after that hed kiss anything unnatural where we havent 1 atom of any kind of expression in us all of us the

> same 2 lumps of lard before ever I do that to a man pfooh
> the dirty brutes the mere thought is enough I kiss the feet
> of you señorita theres some sense in that (777)

His incompletions: "he ought to give it up now at this age of his life simply ruination for any woman and no satisfaction in it pretending to like it till he comes and then finish it off myself anyway and it makes your lips pale" (740) Cunnilingus: "I think Ill cut all this hair off me . . . I might look like a young girl wouldnt he get the great suckin the next time he turned up my clothes on me" (769)

12. Marriage: "Id rather die 20 times over than marry another of their sex" (744)

13. Another woman would never put up with him: "of course hed never find another woman like me to put up with him the way I do know me come sleep with me yes and he knows that too at the bottom of his heart" (744)

14. His mind [Molly devotes the greatest number of observations to this mechanism]. An active, knowledgeable, stubborn, experimental, imitative, exasperating, secular, and finally unique, even mad, mentality:

> still he knows a lot of mixed up things especially about
> the body and the insides (743) if I asked him hed say its
> from the Greek (744) hes so pigheaded sometimes when he
> gets a thing into his head (748) pigheaded as usual (752)
> always with some brand new fad every other week (745)
> he thinks nothing can happen without him knowing (745)
> of course hes not natural like the rest of the world (745)
> only he thinks he knows a great lot about a womans dress
> and cooking mathering everything he can scour off the
> shelves into it (752) if I went by his advices every blessed
> hat I put on does that suit me yes take that thats alright
> the one like a wedding cake standing up miles off my head
> he said suited me or the dishcover one coming down on my

backside on pins and needles (752) hes always imitating everybody (771) they want to know where were you where are you going (746) he can never explain a thing simply the way a body can understand (754) talking his usual trash and nonsense (748) he always tells me the wrong things and no stops to say [apropos of a letter of bereavement Molly composed] like making a speech your sad bereavement sympathy (758) he ought to get a leather medal with a putty rim for all the plans he invents (765) the way he plots and plans everything out (766) slyboots as usual (746) pack of lies to hide it planning it (739) hed scoff if he heard [that she lit a candle in Whitefriars Street Chapel] because he never goes to church mass or meeting he says your soul you have no soul inside only grey matter because he doesnt know what it is to have one (741-742) hes beyond everything I declare somebody ought to put him in the budget if I only could remember the one half of the things and write a book of it the works of Master Poldy (754) what a madman nobody understands his cracked ideas but me (777)

A wife on her husband—pro.

1. Native politeness to all people: "then still I like that in him polite to old women like that and waiters and beggars too hes not proud out of nothing but not always" (738)

2. And neatness: "Poldy anyway whatever he does always wipes his feet on the mat when he comes in wet or shine and always blacks his own boots too and he always takes off his hat when he comes up in the street like that" (744)

3. Certain endearing habits: "I love to hear him falling up the stairs of a morning with the cups rattling on the tray and then play with the cat" (764)

4. Compared to Denis Breen he looks pretty good:

what was it she [Josie Powell Breen] told me O yes that sometimes he used to go to bed with his muddy boots on when the maggot takes him just imagine having to get into bed with a thing like that that might murder you any moment what a man well its not the one way everyone goes mad Poldy anyway whatever he does always (744)

5. Grateful for his prudence:

well theyre [various Dublin "characters" just thought of by Molly] not going to get my husband again into their clutches if I can help it making fun of him then behind his back I know well when he goes on with his idiotics because he has sense enough not to squander every penny piece he earns down their gullets and looks after his wife and family goodfornothings poor Paddy Dignam all the same Im sorry in a way for him what are his wife and 5 children going to do unless he was insured comical little teetotum always stuck up in some pub corner and her or her son waiting Bill Bailey wont you please come home (773-774)

6. She would not surreptitiously take money from him: "I dont want to soak it all out of him like other women do I could often have written out a fine cheque for myself and write his name on it for a couple of pounds a few times he forgot to lock it up besides he wont spend it" (780)

7. In contrast to other Dublin women, she is proud of her husband and daughter: "let them [other Dublin wives] get a husband first thats fit to be looked at and a daughter like mine" (763)

8. Finally, one must be grateful for small blessings: "well its [the name Bloom] better than Breen or Briggs does brig or those awful names with bottom in them Mrs Ramsbottom or some other kind of a bottom Mulvey I wouldnt go mad about either" (761)

Daily life for Molly.

1. Neighborhood noises, the nuns, and an alarm clock next door: "well soon have the nuns ringing the angelus

theyve nobody coming in to spoil their sleep except an odd priest or two for his night office the alarmclock next door at cockshout clattering the brains out of itself" (781)

2. Drinks stout, sent over from Larry O'Rourke's, for dinner: "my belly is a bit too big Ill have to knock off the stout at dinner or am I getting too fond of it the last they sent from ORourkes was as flat as a pancake he makes his money easy Larry they call him" (750)

3. Never knows exactly what the time is because of her faulty watch: "I never know the time even that watch he gave me never seems to go properly Id want to get it looked after" (747) [Molly tells the time by the bells of the nearby St. George's church, which ring on the hour and on each quarter hour. What she means here, I take it, is that while she is aware of the division of each hour, she is not always certain what hour it is that is being divided. Initially she thinks it is after 4:00 A.M. when Bloom returns.]

4. Spends a lot of time hanging out the window: "as bad as now [she is thinking of how bored she was on Gibraltar after the Stanhopes left] with the hands hanging off me looking out of the window if there was a nice fellow even in the opposite house" (757)

5. Molly's only sexual peccadillo, prior to her adultery with Boylan, appears to have been to display her large charms to passers-by of 7 Eccles Street. At least Dr. Dixon who used to be at the nearby Mater Misericordiae Hospital has seen them:

> Digs [Dixon is identifying Bloom for the others in Burke's pub] up near the Mater. Buckled he is. Know his dona? Yup, sartin, I do. Full of a dure. See her in her dishybilly. Peels off a credit. Lovey love-kin. None of your lean kine, not much. Pull down the blind, love. [. . . .] Got a prime pair of mincepies, no kid. And her take me to rests

> and her anker of rum. Must be seen to be believed. Your
> starving eyes and allbeplastered neck you stole my heart,
> (425)

April, May, and first week of June.

1. Post-April 3 (Easter). "The Bath of the Nymph"
[The Blooms have hanging in their bedroom a representation of "The Bath of the Nymph," a picture that was
given away with the Easter edition of *Photo-Bits*. See
Bloom's recollection below on pp. 216-218.]: "would I be
[when naked] like that bath of the nymph with my hair
down yes only shes younger" (753) "or Im a little like that
dirty bitch in that Spanish photo he has the nymphs used
they go about like that I asked him" (753)

2. May. Nancy Blake, an acquaintance of the old days,
dies, and Molly, mishelped by Leopold, has to write a
letter of condolence:

> that poor Nancy Blake died a month ago of acute pneu-
> monia well I didnt know her so well as all that she was
> Floeys friend more than mine its a bother having to answer
> he always tells me the wrong things and no stops to say
> like making a speech your sad bereavement sympathy I
> always make that mistake and newphew with 2 double
> yous in (758)

3. Molly and Blazes Boylan—preliminaries. It is not
clear from the text just when Molly and Boylan first met
although it appears to have been rather recently. Since
Joyce has so many other things happen in the month of
May, I am assuming that they met in May 1904.

The first meeting at the D.B.C. (one of a chain of
reasonably-priced eating places) in Dame Street, with
additional complications because of a visit to the W.C. by
Molly; Boylan was taken by her foot:

> theyre all so different Boylan talking about the shape of
> my foot he noticed at once even before he was introduced

when I was in the D B C with Poldy laughing and trying to listen I was waggling my foot we both ordered 2 teas and plain bread and butter I saw him looking with his two old maids of sisters when I stood up and asked the girl where it [the W.C.] was what do I care with it dropping out of me and that black closed breeches he [Bloom] made me buy takes you half an hour to let them down wetting all myself always with some brandnew fad every other week such a long one I did I forgot my suede gloves on the seat behind that I never got after some robber of a woman and he wanted me to put it in the Irish Times lost in the ladies lavatory D B C Dame street finder return to Mrs Marion Bloom and I saw his eyes on my feet going out through the turning door he was looking when I looked back and I went there for tea 2 days after in the hope but he wasnt now how did that excite him because I was crossing them when we were in the other room first he meant the shoes that are too tight to walk in (744-745)

c. May 23 to May 29. The prize fight and the dinner. Besides being a "bill-sticker" and a singer, Boylan is also the manager of a prize fighter, Myler Keogh, "Dublin's pet lamb," who is scheduled to fight Sergeantmajor Bennett, an Englishman out of the Portobello barracks, on May 22 (250:30-251:2). About a month before, c. April 22, Boylan had taken Keogh down to County Carlow where, as Nosey Flynn explains, he made him train hard and did not allow him to drink (173:11-21). However, as Alf Bergin further explains, Boylan caused it to be generally believed that Myles or Myler was "on the beer," thus running up the betting odds against him (318:15-16). On May 22 little Myles, Ireland, gave "the father and mother of a beating" to big Percy Bennett, England (318:23-319:19), and Boylan, so rumor has it, won a hundred pounds (318:9-10). With part of this money Boylan took the Blooms out to dinner:

the fine gentlemen in their silk hats that K C lives up somewhere this way coming out of Hardwicke lane the night he gave us the fish supper on account of winning over the boxing match of course it was for me he gave it I knew him by his gaiters and the walk and when I turned round a minute after just to see there was a woman after coming out of it too some filthy prostitute then he goes home to his wife after that (777-778)

4. May 23. Monday (Whitmonday) two important events transpire. Molly has her last menstrual, being irregular, and is also suffering from discharges:

> who knows [this is the beginning of Molly's seventh sentence] is there anything the matter with my insides or have I something growing in me getting that thing like that every week when was it last I Whit Monday yes its only about 3 weeks I ought to go to the doctor (770)

Her husband is stung by a bee: "Whit Monday is a cursed day too no wonder that bee bit him" (764) [Whitsunday, the festival that is the third most important of the great feasts of the Catholic Church, occurs on the fiftieth day after Easter, and fell on May 22 in 1904. Whitmonday— May 23 in 1904—was a bank holiday by virtue of an act passed by Parliament on May 25, 1871.]

5. May 29 (a Sunday). The Blooms attend a dance with Boylan; on the way home Boylan makes his first pass at Molly; Bloom is aware of this covert act:

> and the last time he [Bloom] came on my bottom when was it the night Boylan gave my hand a great squeeze going along by the Tolka [a river in the northern part of Dublin] in my hand there steals another I just pressed the back of his like that with my thumb to squeeze back singing the young May Moon shes beaming love because he [Bloom] has an idea about him [Boylan] and me hes not such a fool (740)

6. Early June. Bloom sends Milly to the photography
shop in Mullingar in order to get her out of the house
because of the impending love affair between her mother
and Boylan (he rationalizes this by saying that Milly
would have an inherent taste for photography because of
the hereditary Bloom interest in this craft):

> now with Milly away such an idea for him to send the
> girl down there to learn to take photographs on account of
> his grandfather instead of sending her to Skerrys academy
> where shed have to learn not like me getting all at school
> only hed do a thing like that all the same on account of
> me and Boylan thats why he did it Im certain (766)

June 1. Bloom gets a check and buys Molly only garters,
face lotion, and four cheap handkerchiefs:

> the violet pair I wore today thats all he bought me out of
> the cheque he got on the first O no there was the face
> lotion I finished the last of yesterday that made my skin
> like new I told him over and over again get that made up
> in the same place and dont forget it God only knows
> whether he did after all I said to him Ill know by the bottle
> anyway if not I suppose Ill only have to wash in my piss like
> beeftea or chickensoup with some of that opoponax and
> violet I thought it was beginning to look coarse or old a
> bit the skin underneath is much finer where it peeled off
> there on my finger after the burn its a pity it isnt all
> like that and the four paltry handkerchiefs about 6/- in
> all (750-751)

The week of June 6.

1. Molly goes out one day in this week and sees an older,
still beautiful, but waning woman:

> O well [she has been thinking of her age and of aging]
> look at that Mrs. Galbraith shes much older than me I saw
> her when I was out last week her beautys on the wane she

was a lovely woman magnificent head of hair on her down to her waist tossing it back (751)

2. Molly had worn her black dress to the dance on May 29 and subsequently sends it to the cleaners so it will be fresh and clean for the Belfast concert with Boylan. As of June 16, the dress is still at the cleaners: "Ive no clothes at all the brown costume and the skirt and jacket and the one at the cleaners 3" (751)

The week of June 13 (Bloomweek).

1. The Blooms send their daughter presents for her birthday, fifteen years of age on June 15, 1904: "She [Molly] was reading the card [from Milly which arrived on the doorstep of 7 Eccles Street on June 16], propped on her elbow. —She got the things, she said." (62) [The "things" were a tam from Bloom and a box of "creams" from Molly.]

2. Molly burns her finger: "the skin underneath is much finer where it peeled off there on my finger after the burn its a pity it isnt all like that" (751)

3. June 14 (Tuesday). Molly shows Bloom the announcement of Dignam's death; catches Bloom writing a covert letter and suspects a secret romance:

> its some little bitch or other he got in with somewhere or picked up on the sly if they only knew him as well as I do yes because the day before yesterday he was scribbling something a letter when I came into the front room for the matches to show him Dignams death in the paper as if something told me and he covered it up with blottingpaper pretending to be thinking about business so very probably that was it to somebody who thinks she has a softy in him because all men get a bit like that at his age especially getting on to forty he is now so as to wheedle any money she can out of him no fool like an old fool (739)

4. June 15 (Wednesday). Molly finishes the last of the face lotion (750:43).

Night of June 15-16; Molly has a dream about poetry, which leads her to think there is something in the cards for her and Stephen Dedalus:

> and didnt I dream something too yes there was something about poetry in it I hope he hasnt long greasy hair hanging into his eyes or standing up like a red Indian what do they go about like that for only getting themselves and their poetry laughed at (775)

Bloom on Dublin in the spring and early summer of 1904.

1. Irish nationalism at a low ebb; even Parnell's memory grows dim. On the way to the cemetery on June 16, 1904, the funeral procession passes the foundation stone for a monument which is to be erected for Parnell, and Bloom thinks of Parnell's physical breakdown (95:39-40). [This base was completed on October 8, 1899. The monument, executed by the American sculptor Augustus Saint-Gaudens, was not completed until 1910 (G.).] Later Bloom thinks of how quickly the dead are forgotten: "Even Parnell. Ivy day dying out." (111) After Dignam is interred, the mourners pay a visit to Parnell's grave. Mr. Power repeats the persistent myth that Parnell is not dead and will return. But Hynes says he will never return: peace to his ashes (112:35-113:2). Similarly, in the cab shelter a cabman repeats the myth of Parnell's return, to which Bloom gives a silent negative (649:7-17). The Citizen, naturally, still invokes the spirit of Parnell (298:2-6).

2. Foreigners are taking over: "Germans making their way everywhere. Sell on easy terms to capture trade. Undercutting." (166)

3. The sewage system is terrible: "Widower I hate to

see. Looks so forlorn. Poor man O'Connor wife and five children poisoned by mussels here. The sewage. Hopeless." (381)

4. The army is rotten with venereal disease (72:40-73:2).

5. Unsanitary conditions are ruining the Irish race, as Buck Mulligan twice explains (14:12-16; 418:33-42).

6. A rage for gambling: "Betting. Regular hotbed of it lately. Messenger boys stealing to put on sixpence. Raffle for large tender turkey. Your Christmas dinner for threepence." (86)

7. Arthur Griffith's nationalist movement, stressing passive resistance and appeal to moral force, is gathering strength; and Bloom is supposed to have been its ideologue:

> So anyhow when I got back [the Nameless One has just returned from the W.C. to the bar in Barney Kiernan's pub] they were at it dingdong, John Wyse saying it was Bloom gave the idea for Sinn Fein to Griffith to put in his paper all kinds of jerrymandering, packed juries and swindling the taxes off of the Government and appointing consuls all over the world to walk about selling Irish industries. Robbing Peter to pay Paul. Gob, that puts the bloody kybosh on it if old sloppy eyes [Bloom] is mucking up the show. Give us a bloody chance. God save Ireland from the likes of that bloody mouseabout. Mr. Bloom with his argol bargol. (335-336)

Shortly after this, Martin Cunningham, the most knowledgeable of the Dubliners, comes in and when asked if Bloom gave Griffith his ideas, he replies in the affirmative (337:17-35).

[Arthur Griffith, 1872-1922, was an Irish writer, editor, and politician. In 1899 he founded the *United Irishman,* a weekly paper. Griffith did not think separation from England possible, but he believed that such a degree of Irish independence could be effected as to make the link with the British Crown only symbolical. To this end he advocated passive resistance: payment of taxes was to be refused; and Irish members elected to the English Parliament were to absent themselves from Westminister and remain in Ireland to govern. The policy was first announced at a meeting in Dublin in October 1902. The name chosen to represent the policy was "Sinn Féin," meaning "Ourselves"—and meaning, proverbially, "Stand Together." In 1906 the *United Irishman* became *Sinn Féin.*

The opportunity for Joyce to tie the real Griffith to the fictional Bloom, his imaginary three-quarters Hungarian and one-quarter Irishman, arose from the fact that in 1905 Griffith published a pamphlet, "The Resurrection of Hungary," describing how the Hungarians of the Austro-Hungarian empire had managed to achieve autonomy and freedom by employing just the methods Griffith was advocating for Ireland. "The Resurrection of Hungary" had originally been published serially in the *United Irishman* in 1904, Bloomyear.

The improbabilities of the imaginary Bloom giving the real Arthur Griffith his basic political ideas are discussed by A. (pp. 100-104).]

Bloom thinks three times of Griffith: twice about a satiric comment that Griffith had made about *Freeman's Journal* (57:35-39; 376:27-28); and once about the fact that Griffith, unlike Parnell, is not a spellbinder (163:42-164:2). He never thinks of having given Griffith his basic political program.

8. The popular press will print anything now, as, for example, Philip Beaufoy's "Matcham's Masterstroke" in *Titbits,* which Bloom reads at stool on the morning of June 16, 1904 (69:10-17).

The Leopold Blooms; Leopold's point of view.

The loneliness of the Blooms: "From inexistence to existence he came to many and was as one received: existence with existence he was with any as any with any: from existence to nonexistence gone he would be by all as none perceived." (667-668)

Bloom on Molly.

Although his wife, and her act of adultery, is often in, and never far below, the consciousness of Bloom on June 16, 1904, his explicit thoughts about her person and character are rather rare, especially so when one considers the magnitude of the interior monologues of Bloom's which we overhear throughout the day. The frequency of his thoughts about her is miniscule in comparison to the torrent of explicit information, speculation, exasperation, desperation, and, even, admiration that are poured out by Molly about her husband in her one opportunity to do so, her concluding monologue.

Her habits and characteristic actions and reactions:

1. The morning breakfast tray and its rituals. Molly must have four slices of buttered bread and tea, for her mouth is dry in the morning (55:11-15). And the bread must be thin (56:18). She also likes yesterday's bread toasted (57:14). And sugar and cream for her tea (63:13-14).

2. Food. She gets swelled after eating cabbage (103:40). He remembers her tasting butter with her veil up (155:14).

3. The last glance in the mirror before opening the door: "Knock. Last look at mirror always before she answers the door. The hall. There? How do you?" (274) "Mirror there. Is that best side of her face? They always know. Knock at the door. Last tip to titivate." (284) The

solace of song: "Yes, joy it [music] must be. Mere fact of
music shows you are. Often thought she was in the dumps
till she began to lilt. Then know." (282) "Her high notes
and her low notes." (374) Her menstruals: "Devils they
are when that's coming on them. Dark devilish appearance. Molly often told me feel things a ton weight. Scratch
the sole of my foot. O that way! O, that's exquisite!" (369).
Her powers of intuition: "Molly great dab at seeing
anyone looking [at her]." (284)

4. The greater part of Bloom's thoughts about his wife
are concerned with her sheer physicality, especially her
amplitude and odor:

> He looked calmy down on her bulk and between her large
> soft bubs, sloping within her nightdress like a shegoat's
> udder. The warmth of her couched body rose on the air,
> minging with the fragrance of the tea she poured. (63) He
> smiled, glancing askance at her mocking eye. The same
> young eyes. (64) And the dark one [Cissy Caffrey] with the
> mop head and the nigger mouth. I knew she could whistle.
> Mouth made for that. Like Molly. (371) What is it [Gerty
> MacDowell's perfume]? Heliotrope? No, Hyacinth? Hm.
> Roses, I think. She'd [Molly] like scent of that kind. Sweet
> and cheap: soon sour. Why Molly likes opoponax. Suits her
> with a little jessamine mixed. (374) Clings [her odor] to
> everything she takes off. Vamp of her stockings. Warm
> shoe. Stays. Drawers: little kick, taking them off. Byby till
> next time. Also the cat likes to sniff in her shift on the
> bed. Know her smell in a thousand. Bathwater too. Reminds
> me of strawberries and cream. Wonder where it is really.
> There or the armpits or under the neck. Because you get
> it out of all holes and corners. (375) That's where Molly
> can knock spots off them. It is the blood of the south.
> Moorish. Also the form, the figure. Hands felt for the
> opulent. Just compare [Molly's figure] for instance [to]
> those others. (373) Petticoats for Molly. She has something

to put in them. (381) Besides he [Stephen] said the picture [of Molly] was handsome which, say what you like, it was, though at the moment she was distinctly stouter. And why not? (653-654)

5. The question of Molly's wit:

She's not exactly witty. Can be rude too. Blurt out what I was thinking. Still I don't know. She used to say Ben Dollard had a base barreltone voice. He has legs like barrels and you'd think he was singing into a barrel. Now, isn't that wit? They used to call him big Ben. Not half as witty as calling him base barreltone. (154)

Domestic events and ambiance.

1. As Milly grew up, and especially after she left home, Bloom had to concentrate on a domestic problem that had always plagued him—what to do with our wives? He tried everything from games to music to evening entertainments; he would have liked there to be a masculine brothel for her. He decided to shore up her deficient education but without success. He found, finally, that he could manage her only by indirect suggestion implying self-interest. For example: "She disliked umbrella with rain, he liked woman with umbrella, she disliked new hat with rain, he liked woman with new hat, he bought new hat with rain, she carried umbrella with new hat." (687)

2. Mrs. Fleming, the Blooms' part-time servant, mends his socks poorly: "Glad I took that bath. Feel my feet quite clean. But I wish Mrs Fleming had darned these socks better." (89)

3. The neighborhood of 7 Eccles Street in the spring and summer of 1904. Neighborhood noises, girls practicing scales: "Still always nice to hear [improvisations on the piano]. Except scales up and down, girls learning. Two together nextdoor neighbours. Ought to invent dummy pianos for that." (278)

Morning sounds: "matutinal noises, premonitions and perturbations, a clattered milkcan, a postman's double knock," (674)

An unlet house: "Blotchy brown brick houses. Number eighty still unlet. Why is that? Valuation is only twenty-eight." (61)

Hens next door: "The hens in the next garden: their droppings are very good top dressing." (68)

4. The charms of the sturdy serving girl of the Woods, the Blooms' next-door neighbors, whom Bloom observes in Dlugacz's butcher shop the morning of June 16. She appears to have joined the Woods fairly recently, and Bloom's first sight of her was, evidently, beating a carpet on the clothesline: "Whacking a carpet on the clothesline. She does whack it, by George. The way her crooked skirt swings at each whack." (59) "The crooked skirt swinging whack by whack by whack." (59) "Crooked skirt swinging, whack by." (280)

5. The Gardiner Street—Old Glynn—"Stabat Mater" complex. Sometime fairly recently—exact date never given—Molly sang in the "Stabat Mater" in the Jesuit Church on upper Gardiner Street. Bloom finagled this somehow through Father Farley, but was finally found out in his duplicity [see Molly's explanation below]. The evidence that this event transpired recently is given by the fact that Father Bernard Vaughan gave the sermon. Thus when Mrs. David Sheehy, wife of the M.P., runs into Father Conmee on the afternoon of June 16, 1904, her favorable memory of Father Vaughan's sermon appears to be still fresh. And she looks forward to his return, which Father Conmee promises: "Yes [Father Conmee is responding to a comment and a question by Mrs. Sheehy], it was very probable that Father Bernard Vaughan would come again to preach. O, yes: a very great success. A wonderful man really." (219)

Bloom arranges the matter of getting Molly into the choir: "Conmee: Martin Cunningham knows him: distinguished looking. Sorry I didn't work him about getting Molly into the choir instead of that Father Farley who looked a fool but wasn't." (80)

Molly's recollection explains Bloom's ploy:

> was it him managed it [arranging for her concert in 1903 when she sang "The Absent Minded Beggar" and wore the brooch for Lord Roberts] this time I wouldnt put it past him like he got me on to sing in the *Stabat Mater* by going around saying he was putting Lead Kindly Light to music I put him up to that till the jesuits found out he was a freemason thumping the piano lead Thou me on copied from some old opera yes (748) ["Lead Kindly Light" was a famous hymn composed by John Henry Newman.]

The organist is Old Glynn:

> Old Glynn he knew how to make that instrument talk, the *vibrato*: fifty pounds a year they say he had in Gardiner street. (82) Organ in Gardiner street. Old Glynn fifty quid a year. Queer up there in the cockloft alone with stops and locks and keys. Seated all day at the organ. Maunder on for hours, talking to himself or the other fellow blowing the bellows. Growl angry, then shriek cursing (want to have wadding or something in his no don't she cried), then all of a soft sudden wee little wee little pippy wind. (288)

Father Vaughan gives the sermon [Father Conmee's recollection]:

> Father Conmee walked and, walking, smiled for he thought on Father Bernard Vaughan's droll eyes and cockney voice.
> —Pilate! Wy don't you old back that owlin mob?
> A zealous man, however. Really he was. And really did great good in his way. Beyond a doubt. He loved Ireland,

he said, and he loved the Irish. Of good family too would
one think it? Welsh, were they not? (219-220)

Molly sings:

> Molly was in fine voice that day, the *Stabat Mater* of
> Rossini. Father Bernard Vaughan's sermon first. Christ
> or Pilate? Christ, but don't keep us all night over it. Music
> they wanted. Footdrill stopped. Could hear a pin drop. I
> told her to pitch her voice against that corner. I could feel
> the thrill in the air, the full, the people looking up:
>   *Quis est homo!* (82)

Molly singing: *"qui est homo:* Mercadante. My ear
against the wall to hear. Want a woman who can deliver
the goods." (282) [Bloom here mistakes Mercadante
(1795-1870) for Rossini (1792-1868). The opening
words of Rossini's "Stabat Mater" are "Qui est homo."
Bloom makes the slip because right after he had first
thought of Molly's performance (p. 82), he began to
think of sacred music and its composers; the first name
that came to his mind was Mercadante.]

In the cab shelter Bloom once more thinks, ecstatically,
of the great triumph for his wife in the Gardiner Street
Church (661:15-25).

Bloom's ploy unfrocked by Father Farley:

> FATHER FARLEY
> He is an episcopalian, an agnostic, an anythingarian seek-
> ing to overthrow our holy faith. (490)

6. Sometime, evidently fairly recently, Bloom runs into
Nurse Callan on a Dublin street and fails to tip his hat to
her as she bows to him. But his worry that she is
displeased with him for this is dissipated by the warm
greeting she accords him when he arrives at the hospital
on the evening of June 16 (385:25-29).

March 20. The German barque "Mona" rams the English barque, "Lady Cairns," which sinks immediately, all hands lost (236:29-36; 638:12-17).

April 4, Easter Monday. Ned Lambert pays a visit to Cork for the races and finds that an old acquaintance of his and Simon Dedalus', one Dick Tivy, has gone bald (102: 21-31).

Post-Easter (April 3); that is, April, May, and June.

The Nymph whose picture is on the wall is a witness to certain sights and sounds in the Blooms' bedchamber.

1. When the Easter number of *Photo Bits* gave away a representation of the "Bath of the Nymph," the Blooms decided to preserve it:

> The *Bath of the Nymph* over the bed. Given away with the Easter number of *Photo Bits*: Splendid masterpiece in art colours. Tea before you put milk in. Not unlike her with her hair down: slimmer. Three and six I gave for the frame. She said it would look nice over the bed. Naked nymphs: Greece: and for instance all the people that lived then. (65)

2. In an hallucination at Bella Cohen's the nymph thanks Bloom for taking her out of the evil company she was in, the gamey and disreputable pictures, stories, and advertisement of *Photo Bits* (545:11-546:2).

3. But after looking down from the Blooms' bedroom wall for three months the Nymph begins to think she has fallen into worse company:

THE NYMPH

(*Covers her face with her hand.*) What have I not seen in that chamber? What must my eyes look down on? (547)

(*Her fingers in her ears.*) And words. They are not in my dictionary. (546)

4. What the Nymph saw and heard.

Bloom administering an enema, with Wonderworker, to Molly (551:1-19). Bloom had obtained Wonderworker by mail from London: "no visitors or post ever except his cheques or some advertisement like that wonderworker they sent him addressed dear Madam" (758), and the prospectus for Wonderworker still resides in Bloom's drawer (721:38-722:20). Bloom also thinks of it elsewhere (289:16-17).

Bloom talks in his sleep, snores, and falls, or was pushed, from bed (546:12-21). The Blooms' bed is noisy and has soiled linen (547:1-7).

There is in the Blooms' bedroom an antiquated commode, which Molly had cracked by sitting on it, and an orange-colored chamberpot with one handle (547:10-15). The commode is elsewhere remarked on by both Blooms. Molly: "wheres the chamber gone [she is searching for the chamberpot in the darkened bedroom just after her menstrual has come upon her] easy Ive a holy horror of its breaking under me after that old commode" (769) Bloom had stubbed his toe against the broken commode in the morning (65:26-27), and had dispassionately contemplated it before going to bed (730:27-28).

[The occasion of Molly's cracking the leg of the commode offers some dating problems. When Bloom describes it to the Nymph (547:10-15), he says that it was not Molly's weight that caused the crack, for she weighed only eleven stone nine (154 pounds). He then says she put on nine pounds after weaning. Molly, however, weaned only once, Milly in 1889 or 1890. But it seems much more likely that the mishap occurred recently since the Nymph appears to have seen it happen and since Molly is still, on June 16, thinking of it.]

5. A Dublin romance, Bloom and the Nymph. He kisses the picture in four places and shades with a pencil her eyes her bosom and her shame (546:3-7). He feels almost like praying to her (546:8-11). He masturbates before her and then feels guilty (553:13-19). A nymph immortal, beauty, the bride of no man (727:33-34).

May 12. Bloom weighs himself: 158 pounds (668:29-34).

May 21. Bloom borrows Arthur Conan Doyle's *The Stark Munro Letters* from the Capel Street Library, his "guarantor" having been one Kearney. Since the book was due back on June 4, it is overdue by thirteen days on June 17 (64:42-65:1; 652:19-21; 708:30-34).

May 23 (Whitmonday). Bloom, sleeping in his garden, according to Dr. Dixon, is stung by a bee. He goes to the nearby Mater Hospital, where Dr. Dixon, whom he had first met in the Joe Chamberlain demonstration in 1899, dresses his wound. Since that time Dixon has transferred to the Holles Street Maternity Hospital (68:18-19; 97:28-30; 163:5-7; 386:25-33; 425:15-16; 710:37-711:4). The bee, become Brother Buzz, buzzes through hallucinations at Bella Cohen's (495:5-6; 498:6-10; 515:23, 32). [Since Bloom had been bitten in the "rere" of the premises at 7 Eccles Street, I would have assumed, knowing Joyce, that his creator would have had him stung by the bee in the "rere" as well. This is not the case, however; he was stung in the front on the lower left side (710:37-711:4), although elsewhere (386:25-30) it is said that he was stung in the chest.

May 26. Bloom lends three shillings to Hynes at Meagher's. He has since given Hynes three hints about it (119:25-34). He will remind him again (375:30-32).

May 29. The Blooms and Boylan attend a dance; Boylan and Molly begin to understand one another.

Getting dressed for the dance [Bloom in the carriage on the way to Glasnevin on June 16 sees Boylan and tries, unsuccessfully, to not think about the matter, but cannot succeed in avoiding an image of Molly's figure]: "But the shape is there. The shape is there still. Shoulders. Hips. Plump. Night of the dance dressing. Shift stuck between the cheeks behind." (92) In helping Molly to dress for the dance Bloom thinks he made an error, which proved to be an omen of ill: "Not to lace the wrong eyelet as I did the night of the bazaar dance. Bad luck. Nook in wrong tache of her . . . person you mentioned. That night she met . . . Now!" (530) Boylan is beautifully dressed: "the tie he wore, his lovely socks and turnedup trousers. He wore a pair of gaiters the night that first we met. His lovely shirt was shining beneath his what? of jet." (368) The dance itself, which features Ponchielli's "Dance of the Hours":

> the bazaar dance when May's band played Ponchielli's dance of the hours. Explain that morning hours, noon, then evening coming on, then night hours. Washing her teeth. That was the first night. Her head dancing. Her fansticks clicking. Is that Boylan well off? He has money. Why? I noticed he had a good smell off his breath dancing. No use humming then. Allude to it. (69) Evening hours, girls in grey gauze. Night hours then black with daggers and eye-masks. Poetrical idea pink, then golden, then grey, then black. Still true to life also. Day, then the night. (69) At the dance night she met him, dance of the hours. Heat brought it out. She was wearing her black and it had the per-fume of the time before. (374) [In a fantasy at Bella Cohen's the "Dance of the Hours" is performed, directed by Profes-sor Maginni (576:3-577:26)].

The three walk home by the Tolka and Boylan makes his pass:

> Wait. The full moon was the night we were Sunday fort-
> night exactly there is a new moon. Walking down by the
> Tolka. Not bad for a Fairview moon. She was humming:
> The young May moon she's beaming, love. He other side of
> her. Elbow, arm. He. Glowworm's la-amp is gleaming, love.
> Touch. Fingers. Asking. Answer. Yes.
> Stop. Stop. If it was it was. Must. (167)

May 30. Molly's boots cause welts in her calves which
she rubs the next morning: "Rubbing smartly in turn each
welt against her stocking calf. Morning after the bazaar
dance when May's band played Ponchielli's dance of the
hours." (69)

The Month of June, Bloomonth.

Two important events take place after the May 29
dance and the walk along the Tolka with Boylan.

1. Bloom decides to, and does, send Milly to Mullinger,
as noted above

2. Bloom begins, under the pseudonym of Henry
Flower, his clandestine epistolary romance with Martha
Clifford.

He placed an ad: "Wanted smart lady typist to aid
gentleman in literary work" (160; 369:32), in the *Irish
Times,* and possibly other newspapers. He picked up
forty-four responses, and there were probably more.
Passing the office of the *Irish Times* on June 16, he thinks
of going in to collect some more but decides not to (160:7-
12). Out of the forty-four, he chose, for whatever reason,
Martha Clifford for his correspondent. One of the reasons
certainly was that Martha lives in Dolphin's Barn where
Molly lived when Bloom met her and where he first kissed
her. The letter that he receives from Martha on June 16 is
the fourth such letter he has received, and at the end of his
day he adds it, (722:21-23), to the three others already

there (721:11-16). He has written her three, using some special stationery purchased for the correspondence (721: 21-23). He adds a fourth on the afternoon of June 16 (279:10-31; 279:41-280:18).

Other June events.

1. There is a prolonged drought which is to break on the night of June 16: "No good eggs with this drouth. Want pure fresh water." (56) (See also 671:10-25; 396:29-39.)

2. Bantam Lyons shaves off his moustache but (still) does not take a bath:

> Shaved off his moustache again, by Jove! [Bloom thinks as he looks at Lyons.] Long cold upper lip. To look younger. He does look balmy. Younger than I am.
>
> Bantam Lyons' yellow blacknailed fingers unrolled the baton [Bloom's newspaper]. Wants a wash too. Take off the rough dirt. Good morning, have you used Pears' soap? Dandruff on his shoulders. Scalp wants oiling. (85)

3. Bloom sees Stephen Dedalus wearing some broken-down shoes with mud on them (147:4-6).

4. Bloom sees Mr. Purefoy out with part of his large family (161:11-13).

5. c. June 1. Bloom buys Molly a pair of violet garters which she puts on, and takes off, on June 16. (57:30-31; 180:16-17; 368:33-34; 730:16-17)

6. June 1 or 2. Blooms visits the chemist and buys skin lotion for Molly (84:2-4). On June 16, Bloom returns to refill the prescription:

> —Sweet almond oil and tincture of benzoin, Mr Bloom said, and then orangeflower water . . .
> It certainly did make her skin so delicate white like wax.
> —And white wax also, he said.
> Brings out the darkness of her eyes. Looking at me, the

sheet up to her eyes, Spanish, smelling herself, when I was fixing the links in my cuffs. (84)

7. June 2. The Nameless One, having just gotten a job as a collector of bad debts, tries to collect Geraghty's debt to Moses Herzog. By June 16 he has been at it, unsuccessfully, for a fortnight (292:24-25).

8. June 2. The Derby is run, and Nosey Flynn, having taken a tip on John O'Gaunt from Ben Dollard, backs a loser. Saint Amant won the race (174:4-16).

The week of June 6th.

A bee gets into Bloom's room: "That bee last week got into the room playing with his shadow on the ceiling. Might be the one bit me, come back to see." (378) (See also 515:34-35.)

June 7 (Tuesday). A man drowns in Dublin Bay (21:28-31; 45:35-37).

June 9 (Thursday). Mr. Power sees Paddy Dignam for the last time (95:16-19).

June 9 or 10 (Thursday or Friday). M'Coy sees Dignam for the last time (74:23-25).

June 11 (Saturday). Dignam goes to what is to be his last confession to Father Conroy (251:35-252:2).

June 12 (Sunday). Dignam, preparing to go out on what will be his last drunk, can't find one of his boots (251:34-37). However, in the afterlife he remembers that it was under the commode in the return room and that it should be sent to Cullen's to be resoled—only—since the heels were still good. [Dignam makes a brief reappearance from the land of the dead in a séance in Barney Kiernan's (302:5-13).]

The week of June 13 (Bloomweek).

1. Sometime, fairly recently, Bloom scraped his left

forearm on a pin that Molly had stuck in a curtain. It is virtually healed by June 16 (168:23-25).

2. Bloom visits the office of Long John Fanning, the subsheriff of Dublin (375:16-17).

3. Long John Fanning is going to back Nannetti for Lord Mayor (119:19-20).

4. Bob Cowley, unable to pay his debts, barricades himself in his room to avoid the duns (243:33-244:12).

5. Wren, the auctioneer, offers a lady's bicycle at auction. (99: 17-18).

June 13 (Monday).

1. Dignam, dying, tells his son Patrick to be a good son to his mother; he tries to say more but becomes inaudible; he expires and his red face turns grey, as a fly walks over his eye; he is coffined (251:28-35, 38-42). Bloom tries to imagine Dignam's last conversation with his son: "I owe three shillings to O'Grady." (103) "Monday he died." (111)

2. Bloom tries to observe a young woman fixing her garter in a Eustace Street hallway, but a friend of the young woman, displaying "esprit de corps," covers for her (74:31-32).

3. Lady Fingall puts on a concert for Irish industries (663:9-11).

4. Bloom sees outside Cramer's, a musical establishment, a widow who appears to be progressing favorably on her widow's mite (380:39-381:1).

5. Stephen Dedalus sees a literary woman looking at a book shop window (48:38-49:3).

June 14 (Tuesday).

1. Nosey Flynn sees Bloom getting cream for Molly:

—I met him [says Nosey to Davy Byrne] the day before yesterday and he coming out of that Irish farm dairy John Wyse Nolan's wife has in Henry street with a jar of cream in his hand taking it home to his better half. She's well nourished, I tell you. Plovers on toast. (177)

The jar is now in the Bloom cupboard (675:21). And the cream is served to Stephen Dedalus on June 17 (677:5-6).

2. Zoe, a whore at Bella Cohen's, reports that a priest who tried unsuccessfully to disguise himself, visited the establishment but was unable to make a connection and therefore had only a "dry rush" (519:18-21; 520:6-15).

3. Ned Lambert catches a cold (231:35-41).

4. Bloom wonders if he wrote "Ballsbridge" on the envelope he used to cover the letter to Martha that Molly caught him writing (107:37-39). [See Molly's recollection of this on p. 206 above.]

5. Mrs. Purefoy goes into the lying-in hospital (158:42-159:2).

6. Bags Comiskey, a disreputable friend of Stephen Dedalus, gets drunk and is arrested (618:28-33).

June 15 (Wednesday).

1. Bloom is slightly constipated (69:6-7).

2. Milly becomes fifteen years old (66:19-20).

3. Milly is seeing a young student named Bannon in Mullingar (66:12-15; 693:20-23, 31-32). Her father, remembering that her mother had her first sexual experience at fifteen, wonders if his daughter will go the way of all flesh:

O well: she knows how to mind herself. But if not? No, nothing has happened. Of course it might. Wait in any case till it does. [. . . .] Destiny. Ripening now. Vain: very.

He smiled with troubled affection at the kitchen window. (66) Still, she's a dear girl. Soon be a woman. Mullingar.

Dearest Papli. Young student. Yes, yes: a woman too. Life. Life. (89)

Mullingar. Who knows? Ways of the world. Young student. (372)

4. For her birthday Milly wears her new tam. Bannon, who carries about an inscribed picture of her, describes with rapture to the revellers at the hospital (and to Bloom) how ravishing she looked on her name day with her new coquette cap (404:28-405:8). But to Mulligan he gives a more earthy description: "a skittish heifer, big of her age and beef to the heel" (397). And in the drunken babble at Burke's pub she is called: "Bold bad girl from the town of Mullingar." (425) However, Milly is still a virgin (414:29-41). But she has been embraced (542:14-19).

5. A man at the Ship, a pub, tells Buck Mulligan that Stephen Dedalus is crazy (6:19-21).

The evening of June 15.

1. Mr. Deasy writes a letter about foot-and-mouth disease to Mr. Field, M.P., who, he hopes, will lay it before the meeting of the cattle traders association, which is meeting at the City Arms Hotel on June 16. He also hopes Stephen Dedalus can arrange to have a copy of the letter published in a newspaper (35:19-32).

2. M'Coy learns of Dignam's death. M'Coy was in Conway's, a pub, with Bantam Lyons and Bob Doran, who was on his annual drunk. Hoppy Hollohan comes in for "a wet" and announces the demise of Paddy (73:28-30; 74:1-26).

3. Dan Dawson makes a patriotic speech which is published in the morning paper on June 16 (91:8-14). The speech is full of sentimentalities, inanities, and Irish rhetoric at its worst. In the office of *Freeman's Journal* on

June 16 Ned Lambert reads parts of it aloud, to the amused derision of his auditors (123:25-126:5 *passim*), who call its author "Doughy Daw." Bloom, however, thinks otherwise, as usual:

> All very fine to jeer at it now in cold print but it goes down like hot cake that stuff. He was in the bakery line too wasn't he? Why they call him Doughy Daw. Feathered his nest well anyhow. Daughter engaged to that chap in the inland revenue office with the motor. Hooked that nicely. Entertainments open house. Big blow out. Wetherup always said that. Get a grip of them by the stomach. (126)

[Dan Dawson is one of the more mysterious of the minor off-stage figures in the novel, although he is an important figure in the social panorama of Joyce's Dublin. "Mysterious" he is because, unlike most of the other minor figures in the book, no real-life prototype has been found for him. For example, Wetherup, who is quoted above as a sage by Bloom, and again in the cab shelter (660:8-9) was one W. Wetherup who served for awhile with John Joyce in the office of the Collector-General of Rates (A., p. 217). Padraic Colum informed Gifford that he had a vague memory that Dawson was "one of Dublin's merchant politicians," and this is all we know of him, at least so far.

But he is a key figure in Joyce's Dublin because of the fact that he is a worldly and social success and evidently has been on the rise for some time, since he gave a speech at the Glencree Reformatory banquet in 1894, as Lenehan tells McCoy on June 16, 1904 (234:6). Bloom, then, gives above a capsule description of Dawson's career: beginning as a baker he had made enough money to become a figure in the Dublin "establishment," as merchant-politician, speech-maker, and social entertainer, with a marriageable daughter properly placed. He is thus completely outside of Joyce's world of "losers," of which the social fabric of *Ulysses* is almost completely composed, for Joyce has peopled his fictional world, both past and present, with the fallen or the falling or the never-to-rise. A figure of contempt in their eyes, Dawson may yet be, as Bloom shrewdly remarks, much more canny than the inanities of his speech on the night of June 15 would indicate.]

4. Paddy Hooper, a journalist, comes over to Dublin from England (130:7-8).

5. One Seymour, an acquaintance of Buck Mulligan's, who has chucked medicine and is going into the army, spends the evening on the pier "spooning" with one Lily, a redhead and the daughter of a wealthy man (22:10-24).

6. Tom Kernan was pompously "immense" at some social gathering, and Paddy Leonard imitated him to his face (90:39-91:7).

7. The Blooms go out together and hear a kind of strange music: "Strange kind of music that last night. The mirror was in shadow. She rubbed her handglass briskly on her woollen vest against her full wagging bub. Peering into it. Lines in her eyes. It wouldn't pan out somehow." (69)

8. When the Blooms return home, Bloom lights the nightly incense which the next day smells like foul flower water (63:33-34). In the early morning of June 17 he repeats the ritual (707:4-19).

9. When Bloom undresses on the night of June 15, he forgets to remove the house key from his trousers. He remembers this the next morning, when he has on other trousers, but won't go into the bedroom to retrieve the key because the wardrobe creaks and the noise might disturb his half-asleep wife (57:1-3; 668:4-15). He then forgets about it again, and does not re-remember until he returns home the next day.

June 15-16.

1. Bloom has a strange dream about Molly, in which she appears in a Turkish costume, with slippers and red trousers (381:11-12; 397:27-30; 439:81-441:12).

2. Denis Breen has a nightmare: the ace of spades is walking up the stairs (158:4-8).

3. In the Martello Tower, an Englishman named Haines who is living with Stephen Dedalus and Buck Mulligan sees a black panther in a nightmare and takes a shot at it with a revolver. This disturbance interrupts a recurrent Oriental dream of Dedalus's (47:4-9; 217:32-34).

Bloomsday, June 16 (Thursday).
[There are woven into the text six references to the day of the month and nine references to the day of the week. June 16: 183:6; 229:18; 322:34; 396:28; 617:37-38; 711:9; Thursday: 26:24; 56:9; 97:40; 109:37; 191:35; 349:15; 440:17; 465:30; 562:8-10.]

Sixteen Years of Marriage for the Blooms:

Eh! I have sixteen years of black slave labour behind me. And would a jury give me five shillings alimony tomorrow, eh? (554) God here we are as bad as ever after 16 years how many houses we were in at all (772)

June 16.

Molly Bloom's day, early morning until 4:00 P.M.

1. Breakfasts in bed and reads Milly's card and Boylan's letter (62 ff.): "Reading lying back now, counting the strands of her hair, smiling, braiding." (67)

2. Bloom finishes dressing in the bedroom: "Looking at me, the sheet up to her eyes, Spanish, smelling herself,

when I was fixing the links in my cuffs." (84) "Her eyes over the sheet, a yashmak." (281) Before Bloom leaves he tells her he will be out for the evening: "he said Im dining out and going to the Gaiety" (740)

3. Tells her fortune in cards and foresees Stephen Dedalus there:

> wait by God yes wait yes hold on he was on the cards this morning when I laid out the deck union with a young stranger neither dark nor fair you met before I thought it meant him but hes no chicken [Boylan] nor a stranger either besides my face was turned the other way what was the 7th card after that the 10 of spades for a Journey by land then there was a letter on its way and scandals too the 3 queens and the 8 of diamonds for a rise in society yes wait it all came out and 2 red 8s for new garments look at that (774-775)

Foresees some ill fortune for her husband:

> so well he may sleep and sigh the great Suggester Don Poldo de la Flora if he knew how he came out on the cards this morning hed have something to sigh for a dark man in some perplexity between 2 7s too in prison for Lord knows what he does that I dont know (778)

4. Shortly after 10:00 A.M.; has still not arisen: "Mrs Marion Bloom. Not up yet [thinks Bloom]. Queen was in her bedroom eating bread and. No book. Blackened court cards laid along her thigh by sevens. Dark lady and fair man. Cat furry black ball. Torn strip of envelope [Boylan's letter]." (75)

5. Post-11:00 A.M.; she has arisen: "Twenty past eleven. Up. Mrs Fleming is in to clean. Doing her hair, humming: *voglio e non vorrei*. No: *vorrei e non.* Looking at the tips of her hairs to see if they are split." (93) Dons the violet garters: "the violet pair I wore today" (750)

6. Does some cleaning up on a hot day:

stifling it was today Im glad I burned the half of those old Freemans and Photo bits leaving things like that lying around hes getting very careless and threw the rest of them up in the WC (754-755) and all those old overcoats I bundled out of the hall making the place hotter than it is (755) a good job I found that rotten old smelly dishcloth that got lost [by Mrs. Fleming] behind the dresser I knew there was something and opened the window to let out the smell (768)

7. Some tradesmen call: "and the coalmans bell that noisy bugger trying to swindle me with the wrong bill he took out of his hat what a pair of paws" (758) "and pots and pans and kettles to mend any broken bottles for a poor man today" (758)

8. Considered returning a pair of ruined stockings to Lewers but did not:

and the second pair of silkette stockings is laddered after one days wear I could have brought them back to Lewers this morning and kick up a row and made that one change them only not to upset myself and run the risk of walking into him [Bloom?] and ruining the whole thing (750)

9. Rearranges some furniture: "the room looks all right since I changed it the other way" (779), thereby causing her husband to bump his head upon reentering the house around 2:00 A.M. after parting with Stephen Dedalus (705:23-706:5; 706:31-707:3).

10. Goes out to the pork butchers for a chop and has that and tea for a midday repast, causing flatulence:

that was a relief [Molly has just broken wind] wherever you be let your wind go free who knows if that pork chop I took with my cup of tea after was quite good with the heat I couldnt smell anything off it Im sure that queerlooking man in the porkbutchers is a great rogue (763)

11. Puts fresh sheets on the bed (731:13).

12. Spends some time cultivating her charms for the benefit of Boylan: "after my hours dressing and perfuming and combing" (742)

13. 3:00 P.M. Throws a coin to the crippled sailor (225:10-11, 38—226:3): "when I threw the penny to that lame sailor for England home and beauty when I was whistling there is a charming girl I love" (747)

14. 3:15 P.M. Sees two Dedalus girls: "it was 1/4 after 3 when I saw the 2 Dedalus girls coming from school" (747)

15. Between 3:15 and 4:00 P.M. A messenger arrives bearing gifts from Boylan, but she worries about whether the donor himself will arrive:

> you have to peep out through the blind like the messenger-boy today I thought it was a putoff first him sending the port and the peaches first and I was just beginning to yawn with nerves thinking he was trying to make a fool of me . . . he must have been a bit late (747)

4:00 P.M. and after. A Dublin romance; Molly Bloom and Blazes Boylan.

There are in *Ulysses* four versions of the encounter between Molly and Boylan: three in Bloom's imagination; one, the real thing, in Molly's memory. On his way to his assignation at 7 Eccles Street, Boylan stops for a drink at the Ormond bar, where Bloom is having dinner. After Boylan departs, Bloom, by an act of the imagination, accompanies his wife's lover-to-be as he proceeds through Dublin streets in a hackney car on his way to Eccles Street. Bloom imagines the knock on the door and Molly giving a last glance at herself in the mirror before opening the door for Boylan. Watching a barmaid operate a beerpull, Bloom recreates, by analogy, the adulterous act:

On the smooth jutting beerpull laid Lydia hand lightly, plumply, leave it to my hands. All lost in pity for croppy. Fro, to: to, fro: over the polished knob (she knows his eyes, my eyes, her eyes) her thumb and finger passed in pity: passed, repassed and, gently touching, then slid so smoothly, slowly down, a cool firm white enamel baton protruding through their sliding ring.

With a cock with a carra. (286)

There are two much more explicit Bloom fantasies about the encounter between Molly and Boylan at Bella Cohen's (541:12-22; 563:26-567:11).

Molly and Boylan: fact, Molly's account.

An exact chronology for these tumultuous events is difficult to establish; Molly is not remarkable for her consistency.

1. Anticipatory activities: had not had time for certain niceties: "I hadnt even put on my clean shift or powdered myself or a thing" (747)

2. But did powder her face: "I looked a bit washy of course when I looked close in the handglass powdering a mirror never gives you the expression" (749)

3. Boylan knocks: "when I knew his tattarrattat at the door" (747)

4. Has to peep out, as she always does, to see who it is at her door: "nobody to say youre out you have to peep out through the blind like the messengerboy today" (747)

5. Boylan is beautifully dressed: "lovely stuff in that blue suit he had on and stylish tie and socks with the skyblue silk things on them hes certainly welloff I know by the cut his clothes have and his heavy watch" (749)

6. Has a flower in his buttonhole and smells of a sweet liquid:

who gave him that flower he said he bought he smelt of some kind of drink [Boylan had had a sloe gin at the Ormond bar] not whiskey or stout or perhaps the sweety kind of paste they stick their bills up with some liquor Id like to sip those richlooking green and yellow expensive drinks those stagedoor johnnies drink with the opera hats I tasted one with my finger dipped out of that American that had the squirrel talking stamps with father (741)

7. They smoke cigarettes and sing, among other things, "Love's Old Sweet Song." Earlier Molly had told her husband they were going to sing *La ci darem* with J. C. Doyle and "Love's Old Sweet Song" (63:29-32). Upon Bloom's return he finds cigarette debris and the sheet music for "Love's Old Sweet Song" open to the last page (706:21-30). Boylan is in good form: "he was in great singing voice" (742)

The Encounter.

1. Molly sits in his lap: "I wonder was I too heavy sitting on his knee" (769) "he was so busy where he oughtnt to be he never felt me I hope my breath was sweet after those kissing comfits" (770)

2. Clothes are removed. Molly:

I made him sit on the easychair purposely when I took off only my blouse and skirt first in the other room (769-770) Hugh the ignoramus . . . thats what you get for not keeping them in their proper place pulling off his shoes and trousers there on the chair before me so barefaced without even asking permission and standing out that vulgar way in the half of a shirt they wear to be admired like a priest or a butcher or those old hypocrites in the time of Julius Caesar (776)

3. Boylan enticed by her breasts: "O well I suppose its because they were so plump and tempting in my short petticoat he couldnt resist they excite myself sometimes its well for men all the amount of pleasure they get off a womans body were so round and white for them" (776)

4. Molly pulls down the blinds and disrobes: "I took off all my things with the blinds down" (742) Boylan sees her beautiful thighs: "I bet he never saw a better pair of thighs than that look how white they are the smoothest place is right there between this bit here how soft like a peach" (770)

5. Boylan huge:

> yes because he must have come 3 or 4 times with that tremendous big red brute of a thing he has I thought the vein or whatever the dickens they call it was going to burst though his nose is not so big . . . like iron or some kind of a thick crowbar standing all the time he must have eaten oysters I think a few dozen . . . no I never in all my life felt anyone had one the size of that to make you feel full up he must have eaten a whole sheep after whats the idea making us like that with a big hole in the middle of us like a Stallion driving it up into you because thats all they want out of you with that determined vicious look in his eye I had to halfshut my eyes (742)

6. Birth control: "still he hasn't such a tremendous amount of spunk in him when I made him pull it out and do it on me considering how big it is so much the better in case any of it wasnt washed out properly" (742)

7. The bed is so noisy that they transfer the seat of operations to the floor: "this damned old bed too jingling like the dickens I suppose they could hear us away over the other side of the park till I suggested to put the quilt on the floor with the pillow under my bottom I wonder is it nicer in the day I think it is" (769)

8. Oral Boylan sucks her breasts:

> yes [this is the beginning of Molly's third sentence] I think
> he made them a bit firmer sucking them like that so long he
> made me thirsty titties he calls them I had to laugh (753)
> much an hour he was at them Im sure by the clock like some
> kind of a big infant I had at me they want everything in
> their mouth all the pleasure those men get out of a woman
> I can feel his mouth (754)

9. Boylan bites her nipple: "theres the mark of his teeth
still where he tried to bite the nipple I had to scream out
arent they fearful trying to hurt you" (754)

10. Boylan is heavy and hot: "scrooching down on me
like that all the time with his big hipbones hes heavy too
with his hairy chest for this heat always having to lie
down for them better for him put it into me from behind
. . . like the dogs do it" (749)

11. Ecstasy. Molly spends twice, the second time, she
thinks, for five minutes:

> I can feel his mouth OLord I must stretch myself I wished
> he was here or somebody to let myself go with and come
> again like that I feel all fire inside me or if I could dream
> it when he made me spend the 2nd time tickling me behind
> with his finger I was coming for about 5 minutes with my
> legs round him I had to hug him after O Lord I wanted to
> shout out all sorts of things fuck or shit or anything at all
> only not to look ugly or those lines from the strain who
> knows the way hed take it you want to feel your way with a
> man theyre not all like him thank God some of them want
> you to be so nice about it I noticed the contrast he does it
> and doesnt talk I gave my eyes that look with my hair a bit
> loose from the tumbling and my tongue between my lips up
> to him the savage brute Thursday Friday one Saturday two
> Sunday three O Lord I cant wait till Monday [when Boylan
> is supposed to return and come again] (754)

12. How many times did Boylan ejaculate? Three or four? Four or five? Five or six?

> yes because he must have come 3 or 4 times (742) see if they [other Dublin women] can excite a swell with money that can pick and choose whoever he wants like Boylan to do it 4 or 5 times locked in each others arms (763) his [Bloom's] wife is fucked yes and damn well fucked too up to my neck nearly not by him 5 or 6 times handrunning theres the mark of his spunk on the clean sheet I wouldnt bother to even iron it out (780)

13. The last time he finishes in her: "the last time I let him finish it in me nice invention they made for women for him to get all the pleasure but if someone gave them a touch of it [pregnancy] themselves theyd know what I went through" (742)

14. If she is pregnant [which she isn't] by Boylan the product would be all right: "supposing I risked having another not off him though still if he was married Im sure hed have a fine strong child" (742)

15. Sometime during the festivities Molly lit the lamp: "yes when I lit the lamp yes" (742)

Aftermath.

1. The two lovers eat together and Boylan almost falls asleep: "he had all he could do to keep himself from falling asleep after the last time we took the port and potted meat it had a fine salty taste yes" (741)

[Upon Bloom's return he finds an empty pot of Plumtree's potted meat, a wicker basket with one Jersey pear, and a half-empty bottle of port (675:12-16). When he eases himself into the marital bed, he finds the new clean bed linen, additional odors, the imprint of a male form and some flakes of potted meat. (731:12-16).]

2. Boylan compliments her: "what did he say I could give 9 points in 10 to Katty Lanner and beat her what does that mean I asked him I forget what he said" (745)

[The reader should be as mystified by this obscure compliment as Molly since Katti Lanner (1829-1915) was a Viennese ballet mistress and choreographer who had retired in 1877 (A., G., and T.)]

3. Boylan goes out to get the newspaper: "I forget what he said because the stoppress edition just passed" (745) [It is by now after 8:00 P.M. since Bloom, on the beach at this time, also hears the newsboys crying up the stop-press edition of the *Evening Telegraph* (379:15-16).]

4. A perusal of the *Evening Telegraph* reveals an account of Dignam's funeral: "this is the fruits of Mr Paddy Dignam yes they were all in great style at the grand funeral in the paper Boylan brought in" (773) The newspaper also reveals that Boylan had not placed his money on the winner of the Gold Cup horse race, that his friend Lenehan had given him a bad tip, and that Molly is a loser as well. Boylan, in a rage, tears up the tickets:

> but he was like a perfect devil for a few minutes after he came back with the stop press tearing up the tickets and swearing blazes because he lost 20 quid [two, according to Lenehan] he said he lost over that outsider that won and half he put on for me on account of Lenehans tip cursing him to the lowest pits that sponger (749-750)

The Nameless One, who knows, or who gets to know, everything, had interrogated Lenehan in Barney Kiernan's pub on the outcome of the Gold Cup race. When Lenehan came into Kiernan's, Nameless knew there was something wrong by the look on Lenehan's face. It turns out that Throwaway, a rank outsider at twenty-to-one, had won the race. Sceptre, Lenehan's tip, upon whom

Boylan had placed two pounds, one for Molly and one for himself, was, as the saying goes, still running. "Frailty, thy name is Sceptre," says Lenehan who will now no longer be able to sponge off Boylan (325:27-40). When Bloom returns home, he finds on the dresser two lacerated scarlet betting tickets (675:30-33).

5. As Boylan leaves he slaps her behind:

> one thing I didn't like his slapping me behind going away so familiarly in the hall though I laughed Im not a horse or an ass am I (741)
>
>   no thats no way [this is the beginning of Molly's eighth and last sentence] for him has he no manners nor no refinement nor no nothing in his nature slapping us behind like that on my bottom because I didnt call him Hugh the ignoramus that doesnt know poetry from a cabbage thats what you get for not keeping them in their proper place (776)

6. Some further thoughts and questions on "Hugh." Was he satisfied: "I wonder was he satisfied with me" (741) Is he thinking of her: "I wonder is he awake thinking of me or dreaming am I in it" (741) Does he really like her: "if I could find out whether he likes me" (749) Will he write her a real love letter: "I hope hell write me a longer letter the next time if its a thing he really likes me . . . I wish somebody would write me a loveletter his wasnt much and I told him he could write what he liked yours ever Hugh Boylan" (758) She will answer his letter lying in bed: "I could write the answer in bed to let him imagine me [in bed] short just a few words not those long crossed letters" (758) What is his opinion on, and preferences about, women's drawers: "but I dont know what kind of drawers he likes none at all I think didnt he say yes" (750) He gives her some heart: "O

thanks be to the great God I got somebody to give me what I badly wanted to put some heart up into me youve no chances at all in this place like you used long ago" (758) But, finally, one might as well be in bed with a lion: "of course hes right enough in his way to pass the time as a joke sure you might as well be in bed with what with a lion God Im sure hed have something better to say for himself an old Lion would O well" (776)

Molly solo.
1. Washes herself, without benefit of bathtub: "after washing every bit of myself back belly and sides if we had even a bath itself" (763)

2. Pops into bed and falls asleep: "yes because I felt lovely and tired myself and fell asleep as sound as a top the moment I popped straight into bed" (741)

3. Post-10:00 P.M. A crack of thunder resounds over Dublin: "till that thunder woke me up as if the world was coming to an end God be merciful to us I thought the heavens were coming down about us to punish when I blessed myself and said a Hail Mary like those awful thunderbolts in Gibraltar" (741)

4. Sometime before Bloom and Stephen arrive at 7 Eccles Street, Molly turns on a light in the front room (669:29-30).

5. Post-2:00 A.M. In bed with his wife Bloom experiences an "approximate" erection; he kisses her rump and his erection becomes "proximate" (734:35-735:5). His wife then interrogates him, as she has been doing now for nine months and a day (since September 15, 1903), about what he has done that day (735:6-8; 736:20-29). His account of his day's activities is partly true, partly false, and incomplete (735:9-31). Bloom falls asleep.

Molly begins her great silent monologue in the dark.

1. Bloom has also told her of meeting Josie Powell Breen, setting off a train of thought by Molly about her old friend and her sad fate:

> I suppose it was meeting Josie Powell and the funeral and thinking about me and Boylan set him off well he can think what he likes now if thatll do him any good (742) then let him go to her she of course would only be too delighted to pretend shes mad in love with him that I wouldnt so much mind Id just go to her and ask her do you love him and look her square in the eye she couldnt fool me but he might imagine he was and make a declaration with his plabbery kind of a manner to her like he did to me (743) I wonder what shes got like now after living with that dotty husband of hers she had her face beginning to look drawn and run down the last time I saw her she must have been just after a row with him because I saw on the moment she was edging to draw down a conversation about husbands and talk about him to run him down what was it she told me O yes that sometimes he used to go to bed with his muddy boots on when the maggot takes him just imagine having to get into bed with a thing like that that might murder you any moment what a man well its not the one way everyone goes mad . . . and now hes going about in his slippers to look for £10000 for a postcard up up O Sweetheart May wouldnt a thing like that simply bore you stiff to extinction actually too stupid even to take his boots off now what could you make of a man like that (744) as for her Denis as she calls him that forlornlooking spectacle you couldn't call ːm a husband (773) I wonder was it her Josie off her head ʋith my castoffs hes such a born liar too no hed never have the courage with a married woman thats why he wants me and Boylan (773)

2. Molly's menstrual begins:

wait O Jesus wait yes that thing has come on me yes now
wouldnt that afflict you of course all the poking and rooting
and ploughing he had up in me now what am I to do Friday
Saturday Sunday [on Monday Boylan is supposed to come
back again] wouldnt that pester the soul out of a body
(769) anyhow he didnt make me pregnant as big as he is
(769)

3. Some final thoughts on her husband in the early
morning hours of June 17, 1904. The lateness of his
return: "coming in at 4 in the morning it must be if not
more" (764) [Later Molly realizes that it was not this
late.]

hawking him [Stephen Dedalus] down into the dirty old
kitchen now is he right in his head I ask pity it wasn't
washing day my old pair of drawers might have been
hanging up too on the line on exhibition for all hed ever
care with the ironmould mark the stupid old bundle [Mrs.
Fleming] burned on them he might think was something
else (768)

Did he bring home her lotion: "I told him over and over
again get that made up in the same place and dont forget it
God only knows whether he did after all I said to him Ill
know by the bottle anyway" (751) But he is still consider-
ate of her: "still he had the manners not to wake me"
(764) However, he's a liar and perhaps a philanderer:

wait theres Georges church bells wait 3 quarters the hour
wait 2 oclock well thats a nice hour of the night for him
to be coming home at to anybody climbing down into the
area if anybody saw him Ill knock him off that little habit
tomorrow first Ill look at his shirt to see or Ill see if he
has that French letter [condom] still in his pocketbook I
suppose he thinks I dont know deceitful men all their 20

> pockets arent enough for their lies then why should we tell
> them even if its the truth they dont believe you (772)

What has he been doing? To her knowledge he has not ejaculated since May 29: "and the last time he came on my bottom when was it the night Boylan gave my hand a great squeeze going along by the Tolka" (740) But he could not abstain this long: "because he couldnt possibly do without it that long so he must do it somewhere" (740) So she knows he has ejaculated since then: "yes he came somewhere Im sure by his appetite anyway love its not or hed be off his feed thinking of her" (738) Possibilities—a whore: "either it was one of those night women if it was down there he was really and the hotel story he made up a pack of lies to hide it planning it Hynes kept me" (738-739) "hes sleeping hard had a good time somewhere still she must have given him great value for his money of course he has to pay for it from her" (771-772) Some little bitch: "if its not that its some little bitch or other he got in with somewhere or picked up on the sly if they only knew him as well as I do yes" (739) "yes its some little bitch hes got in with" (773) Not a married woman: "no hed never have the courage with a married woman" (773) She does not care, but would still like to find out: "not that I care two straws who he does it with or knew before that way though Id like to find out so long as I dont have the two of them under my nose all the time" (739) But she will not inquire right now: "I hate having a long wrangle in bed" (739) Does he think she's finished, a nothing: "I supposed he thinks Im finished out and laid on the shelf well Im not no nor anything like it well see well see" (766) "I suppose Im nothing any more" (773) This day he has made an adulteress of her: "hed never have the courage with a married woman thats why he wants me and Boylan" (773)

theres the mark of his [Boylan's] spunk on the clean sheet
I wouldnt bother to even iron it out that ought to satisfy
him if you dont believe me feel my belly unless I made him
stand there and put him into me Ive a mind to tell him every
scrap and make him do it in front of me serve him right its
all his own fault if I am an adulteress as the thing in the
gallery said (780) [The gallery reference is to a performance
of *The Wife of Scarli,* which the Blooms saw in 1897.]

And what harm is there in it, really:

O much about it if thats all the harm ever we did in this
vale of tears God knows its not much doesnt everybody only
they hide it I suppose thats what a woman is supposed to be
there for or He wouldnt have made us the way He did so
attractive to men (780) anyhow its done now once and for
all with all the talk of the world about it people make its
only the first time after that its just the ordinary do it and
think no more about it why cant you kiss a man without
going and marrying him first you sometimes love to wildly
when you feel that way so nice all over you cant help
yourself (740)

But he will not make a whore of her: "can you feel him
trying to make a whore of me what he never will" (740)

Bloom asleep: "then tucked up in bed like those babies
in the Aristocrats Masterpiece he brought me another
time" (772) [A reference to *Aristotle's Masterpiece,* a
compendium of sexual and medical lore, falsely attributed
to Aristotle, which Bloom once brought home. One of its
features was pictures of malformed babies. Bloom looks at
it in the bookstore on the afternoon of June 16 (235:19-
22).] Molly also remembers it well:

the Aristocrats Masterpiece he brought me another time as
if we hadnt enough of that in real life without some old
Aristocrat or whatever his name is disgusting you more
with those rotten pictures children with two heads and no

legs thats the kind of villainy theyre always dreaming about
with not another thing in their empty heads they ought to
get slow poison the half of them (772)

His cold feet: "I wish hed sleep in some bed by himself
with his cold feet on me" (763) It is best not to wake him:
"better go easy not wake him have him at it again
slobbering" (763) Still he has spunk: "if he [Boylan] was
married Im sure hed have a fine strong child but I dont
know Poldy has more spunk in him yes" (742) Maybe she
will give him a real surprise in the future: "I think Ill cut
all this hair [pubic] off me there scalding me I might look
like a young girl wouldnt he get the great suckin the next
time he turned up my clothes on me Id give anything to
see his face" (769)

THE IMMEDIATE FUTURE FOR THE BLOOMS

Milly.

June 18 (Saturday). A concert in the Greville Arms
(66:11-12).

June 20 (Monday). A scrap picnic with a few friends at
lough Owel (66:8-9).

July 15 (St. Swithin's day). Alec Bannon will leave
Mullingar (397:14-17).

Molly.

Alternative plans and hopes for Friday, June 17.

1. The most important thing that Bloom has said to
Molly is that she should get his breakfast in bed on the
morning of June 17. Her reactions—outrage:

YES BECAUSE HE [this is the opening of Molly's first
sentence] NEVER DID A THING LIKE THAT BEFORE
AS ASK to get his breakfast in bed with a couple of eggs
since the *City Arms* hotel (738) then he starts giving us

his orders for eggs and tea Findon haddy and hot buttered toast I suppose well have him sitting up like the king of the country pumping the wrong end of the spoon up and down in his egg wherever he learned that from (764) then tea and toast for him buttered on both sides and newlaid eggs I suppose Im nothing any more (772-773) and Im to be slooching around down in the kitchen to get his lordship his breakfast while hes rolled up like a mummy will I indeed did you ever see me running Id just like to see myself at it show them attention and they treat you like dirt (778)

Acquiescence: "then Ill throw him up his eggs and tea in the moustachecup she [Milly] gave him to make his mouth bigger I suppose hed like my nice cream too" (780) [Since this is Molly's last thought about the matter of breakfast in bed for Bloom, we may assume that she will comply.] According to *Finnegans Wake* she did, in fact, get Bloom's breakfast on June 17, 1904: "And an odd time she'd cook him up blooms of fisk and lay to his heartsfoot her meddery eygs, yayis, and staynish beacons on toasc and a cupenhave so weeshywashy of Greenland's tay . . . (*F.W.*, 199). Anna Livia continues on to describe other delicacies. And, according to *Finnegans Wake*, Molly also sang to her husband: "And then she'd esk to vistule a hymn, *The Heart Bowed Down* or *The Rakes of Mallow* or Chelli Michele's *La Calumnia è un Vermicelli* or a balfy bit ov *old Jo Robison*" (ibid.).

But Molly also has several other tentative plans for the morning of June 17.

2. Perhaps a visit to the market:

Ill get up early in the morning . . . in any case I might go over to the markets to see all the vegetables and cabbages and tomatoes and carrots and all kinds of splendid fruits all coming in lovely and fresh who knows whod be the 1st

man Id meet theyre out looking for it in the morning Mamy
Dillon used to say they are and the night too (780)

3. Or buying some fish:

what a robber too that lovely fresh plaice I bought I
think Ill get a bit of fish tomorrow or today is it Friday yes
I will with some blancmange with black currant jam like
long ago not those 2 lb pots of mixed plum and apple from
the London and Newcastle Williams and Woods goes twice
as far only for the bones I hate those eels cod yes Ill get
a nice piece of cod Im always getting enough for 3 forgetting
anyway Im sick of that everlasting butchers meat from
Buckleys loin chops and leg beef and rib steaks and scrag
of mutton and calfs pluck the very name is enough (764)

4. Strategies for getting some money from her husband to go shopping, involving displays of flesh and parts, and even some action, after she gets his breakfast:

I know what Ill do Ill go about rather gay not too much
singing a bit now and then mi fa pietà Masetto then Ill
start dressing myself to go out presto non son più forte
Ill put on my best shift and drawers let him have a good
eyeful out of that to make his micky stand for him Ill let
him know if thats what he wanted that his wife is fucked
. . . then if he wants to kiss my bottom Ill drag open my
drawers and bulge it right out in his face as large as life
he can stick his tongue 7 miles up my hole as hes there my
brown part then Ill tell him I want £1 or perhaps 30/- Ill
tell him I want to buy underclothes then if he gives me that
well he wont be too bad I dont want to soak it all out of
him like other women do . . . besides he wont spend it
Ill let him do it off on me behind provided he doesnt smear
all my good drawers O I suppose that cant be helped Ill do
the indifferent 1 or 2 questions Ill know by the answers
when hes like that he cant keep a thing back I know every
turn in him Ill tighten my bottom well and let out a few

smutty words smellrump or lick my shit or the first mad
thing comes into my head then Ill suggest about yes O wait
now sonny my turn is coming Ill be quite gay and friendly
over it O but I was forgetting this bloody pest of a thing
. . . no Ill have to wear the old things so much the better
itll be more pointed hell never know whether he did it nor
not there thats good enough for you any old thing at all
then Ill wipe him off me just like a business his omission
then Ill go out Ill have him eyeing up at the ceiling
where is she gone now make him want me thats the only
way (780-781)

5. Perhaps a picnic with Boylan, Bloom, and Mrs.
Fleming:

or a picnic suppose we all gave 5/- each and or let him
pay and invite some other woman for him who Mrs
Fleming and drive out to the furry glen or the strawberry
beds wed have him examining all the horses toenails first
like he does with the letters no not with Boylan there yes
with some cold veal and ham mixed sandwiches there are
little houses down at the bottom of the banks there on
purpose [for sexual intercourse] . . . he says not a bank
holiday anyhow . . . better the seaside (764)

6. Will see if Stephen Dedalus is in the cards: "Ill throw
them the 1st thing in the morning till I see if the wishcard
comes out or Ill try pairing the lady herself and see if he
comes out" (776)

7. A household task for Bloom: "Ill get him to cut them
[old Freeman and Photo bits] tomorrow for me instead of
having them there for the next year to get a few pence for
them have him asking wheres last Januarys paper" (755)

June 20 (Monday). Boylan will pay a visit:

I hope hell come on Monday as he said at the same time
four (747) Thursday Friday one Saturday two Sunday three

> O Lord I cant wait till Monday (754) what am I to do Friday Saturday Sunday wouldnt that pester the soul out of a body [her menstrual] unless he likes it some men do (769)

June 23 (Thursday). Molly and Boylan will go to Belfast for the concert: "this day week were to go to Belfast" (747) Bloom will not go:

> it wouldnt be pleasant if he did suppose our rooms at the hotel were beside each other and any fooling went on in the new bed I couldnt tell him to stop and not bother me with him in the next room or perhaps some protestant clergyman with a cough knocking on the wall then he wouldnt believe next day we didnt do something its all very well a husband but you cant fool a lover after me telling him we never did anything of course he didnt believe me no its better hes going where he is [Bloom is going to go to Ennis for his father's vigil] besides something always happens with him (747-748)

Will Boylan wish to do it on the train: "I wonder will he take a 1st class for me he might want to do it in the train by tipping the guard well O I suppose therell be the usual idiots of men gaping at us with their eyes as stupid as ever they can possibly be" (748) Will Boylan buy her things:

> he could buy me a nice present up in Belfast after what I gave theyve lovely linen up there or one of those nice kimono things I must buy a mothball like I had before to keep in the drawer with them it would be exciting going around with him shopping buying those things in a new city (749) my hand is nice like that if I only had a ring with the stone for my month [September] a nice aquamarine Ill stick him for one and a gold bracelet (745)

How can they disguise their relationship:

> better leave this ring behind want to keep turning and turning to get it over the knuckle there or they might bell

it round the town in their papers or tell the police on me
but theyd think were married O let them all go and smother
themselves for the fat lot I care he has plenty of money
and hes not a marrying man so somebody better get it out
of him (749)

Suppose they elope: "suppose I never came back what
would they say eloped with him that gets you on on the
stage" (748) Suppose she divorces Bloom and marries
Boylan: "suppose I divorced him Mrs Boylan" (761)
Molly, in her imagination, in front of the footlights at the
Belfast concert:

> Frseeeeeeeeeeeeeeeeeeeeeefrong [the sound of a train] that
> train again weeping tone once in the dear deaead days be-
> yond recall close my eyes breath my lips forward kiss sad
> look eyes open piano ere oer the world the mists began I
> hate that istsbeg comes loves sweet ssooooooong Ill let
> that out full when I get in front of the footlights again
> (762) ["dear deaead days beyond recall" and "loves sweet
> sooooooong" are phrases from "Love's Old Sweet Song,"
> which Molly and Boylan practised singing together.]

Music and sex:

> the left side of my face the best (760) comes looooves old
> deep down chin back not too much make it double My Ladys
> Bower is too long for an encore about the moated grange
> at twilight and vaulted rooms yes Ill sing Winds that blow
> from the south that he gave after the choirstairs perfor-
> mance Ill change that lace on my black dress to show off my
> bubs and Ill yes by God Ill get that big fan mended make
> them [other female singers] burst with envy (763) [Molly
> here, anticipating success, foresees a call from the audience
> for an encore. "My Lady's Bower" is too long; "Winds
> That Blow From the South" will then be her choice.]

June 27. Bloom will go to Ennis: "just as well he has to
go to Ennis his fathers anniversary the 27th" (747)

September 8, her birthday: "for the 4 years more I have
of life up to 35 no Im what am I at all Ill be 33 in
September [actually she'll be 34] will I what" (751)

Bloom. June through September.

June 17. Considers a visit to Howth: "She kissed me. My
youth. Never again. Only once it comes. Or hers. Take the
train there [to Howth] tomorrow. No. Returning not the
same. Like kids your second visit to a house." (377)
Will get Molly's lotion: "I was just going back for that
lotion whitewax, orangeflower water. Shop closes early
on Thursday. But the first thing in the morning." (440)

June 25. (Saturday). Molly off to Belfast for her concert:

—She's going to sing at a swagger affair in the Ulster
hall, Belfast, on the twentyfifth [says Bloom to McCoy].
(75)

—She's engaged for a big tour end of this month. You
may have heard perhaps [says Bloom to Nosey Flynn].
(172) And Belfast. I won't go. Race there, race back to
Ennis. Let him. (382)

Apprehensions over the smallpox: "I hope that smallpox
up there doesn't get worse. Suppose she wouldn't let
herself be vaccinated again." (76) [There was, in histori-
cal fact, an outbreak of smallpox in Belfast at this time.]

June 27 (Monday) at his father's grave: "Twentysev-
enth I'll be at his grave. Ten shillings for the gardener. He
keeps it free of weeds. Old man himself. Bent down
double with his shears clipping. Near death's door." (113)

August. Bloom wants Keyes's ad to run for three
months; it will thus be running in August during the
Dublin horseshow: "Three months' renewal. Want to get
some wind off my chest first. Try it anyhow. Rub in
August: good idea: horseshow month. Ballsbridge. Tour-

ists over for the show." (122) But Keyes agrees to renew only for two months (146:23-24). May pay a visit to Milly in Mullingar:

> Might take a trip down there. August bank holiday, only two and six return. Six weeks off however. Might work a press pass. Or through M'Coy. (67) Damn it. I might have tried to work M'Coy for a pass to Mullingar. (80) considering the fare to Mullingar where he figured on going was five and six there and back. (626) [The fare to Mullingar has gone from two and six in Calypso to five and six in Eumaeus, constituting another item in the vast web of errors built into the Eumaeus section.]

September 8. Molly's birthday. Bloom thinks four times of his wife's birthday and the present he will get her. His change of mind in this matter is characteristic. He begins with two practical ideas: since she is always sticking pins all over the place, and he recently got stuck by one, he thinks of buying her a pincushion, but decides she might not like it (168:26-28); or a plait workbasket, but she hates sewing (181:37-38). He finally settles on violet silk petticoats (260:42-261:1). She has something to put in them (381:15-16).

Autumn. There will be a total eclipse (166:40-41).

FUTURE POSSIBILITIES, INTENTIONS, AND FANTASIES
(These could happen tomorrow, next year, or never)

Molly. Possible lovers—Stephen Dedalus. Molly does not begin to think of Stephen Dedalus until her sixth sentence where there is one brief, and neutral, reference to him. However she soon grows to like the idea of him, and he appears quite prominently in sentence seven; slightly less so in sentence eight. In general, as Penelope goes on to its conclusion Boylan fades out and Stephen comes on—hope springs eternal. And Bloom is always there, no matter what. The first reference in sentence six is even slightly hostile: "bringing in his friends to entertain them ... especially Simon Dedalus son his father such a criticiser . . . and his son that got all those prizes for whatever he won them in the intermediate" (768) But things are to warm up in sentences seven and eight. If he had stayed, Molly could have gotten him breakfast in bed:

> what a pity he didnt stay Im sure the poor fellow was dead tired and wanted a good sleep badly I could have brought him in his breakfast in bed with a bit of toast so long as I didnt do it on the knife for bad luck or if the woman was going her rounds with the watercress and something nice and tasty there are a few olives in the kitchen he might like I never could bear the look of them in Abrines I could do the criada (779) [Abrines is a bakery on Gibraltar; criada is Spanish for "maid" (G.).]

Perhaps Bloom will bring him back, in which case she'll get some flowers and clean up the house and the piano, on which she will accompany him as he sings:

> as I can get up early Ill go to Lambes there beside Findlaters and get them to send us some flowers to put about the place in case he brings him home tomorrow today I mean no no Fridays an unlucky day first I want to do the place up someway the dust grows in it I think while Im asleep then we can have music and cigarettes I can accompany him first I must clean the keys of the piano with milk whatll I wear shall I wear a white rose or those fairy cakes in Liptons (781)

There is no reason why he couldn't stay with the Blooms, sleeping in Milly's bed, writing at Bloom's unused writing desk, and having his breakfast served in bed by Bloom:

> itd be great fun supposing he stayed with us why not theres the room upstairs empty and Millys bed in the back room he

could do his writing and studies at the table in there for all the scribbling he [Bloom] does at it and if he wants to read in bed in the morning like me as hes [Bloom] making the breakfast for 1 he can make it for 2 (779) [The desk, in fact, is not used for writing (542:23-24); but it is stalked over by the cat (55:20-21).]

Stephen could have stayed the night and slept on the sofa, from which vantage point he could have heard her making acoustical sounds on the chamber pot: "he could easy have slept in there on the sofa in the other room I suppose he was as shy as a boy he being so young hardly 20 of me in the next room hed have heard me on the chamber arrah what harm Dedalus I wonder its like those names in Gibraltar" (779)

If he had stayed, she could have had an amusing meeting with him, perhaps pretending they were in Spain:

Id have to introduce myself not knowing me from Adam very funny wouldnt it Im his wife or pretend we were in Spain with him half awake without a Gods notion where he is dos huevos estrellados senor ["two fried eggs, sir"] Lord the cracked things come into my head sometimes itd be great fun" (779)

In any event her intuition has told her on three counts that he is about to come into her life: he was in a dream (775:6-10); he was in the cards the morning of June 16 (774:41-775:1); and something stronger than housewifery led her to rearrange the furniture on June 16: "the room looks all right since I changed it the other way you see something was telling me all the time" (779) He's running wild at present: "I suppose hes running wild now out at night away from his books and studies and not living at home on account of the usual rowy house I suppose well its a poor case that those that have a fine son like that theyre not satisfied and I none" (778) A university professor-to-be, who will give her lessons in Italian: "now I wonder what sort is his [Simon Dedalus's] son he [Bloom] says hes an author and going to be a university professor of Italian and Im to take lessons what is he driving at" (774)

The question of respective ages and life-styles:

> I wonder is he too young hes about wait 88 I was married 88 Milly is 15 yesterday 89 what age was he then at Dillons 5 or 6 about 88 I suppose hes 20 or more Im not too old for him if hes 23 or 24 I hope hes not that stuck up university student sort no otherwise he wouldnt go sitting down in the old kitchen with him [Bloom] taking Eppss cocoa and taking of course he pretended to understand it all probably he [Bloom] told him he was out of Trinity college hes very young to be a professor I hope hes not a professor like Goodwin was he was a patent professor of John Jameson (775)

He's a poet and poets write about their mistresses:

> they all write about some woman in their poetry well I suppose he wont find many like me where softly sighs of love the light guitar where poetry is in the air (775) Im sure itll be grand if I can only get in with a handsome young poet at my age . . . then hell write about me lover and mistress publicly too with our 2 photographs in all the papers when he becomes famous O but then what am I going to do about him [Bloom] though (776)

Mutual pedagogy:

> Ill read and study all I can find or learn a bit off by heart if I knew who he likes so he wont think me stupid if he thinks all women are the same (776) I can tell him the Spanish and he tell me the Italian then hell see Im not so ignorant (779) itll be a change the Lord knows to have an

intelligent person to talk to about yourself (775) Id love to
have a long talk with an intelligent welleducated person
(780)

For these conversations Molly imagines herself in the
following attire: "Id have to get a nice pair of red slippers
like those Turks with the fez used to sell or yellow and a
nice semitransparent morning gown that I badly want or
a peachblossom dressing jacket like the one long ago in
Walpoles only 8/6 or 18/6" (780) Carnal embraces: "and
I can teach him the other part Ill make him feel all over
him till he half faints under me" (776)
Youth and intellect: "Im sure hes very distinguished Id
like to meet a man like that God not those other ruck
besides hes young" (775)

Other possible sexual encounters—a boy:

> unless I paid some nicelooking boy to do it since I cant do it
> myself a young boy would like me Id confuse him a little
> alone with him if we were Id let him see my garters the new
> ones and make him turn red looking at him seduce him I
> know what boys feel with that down on their cheek doing
> that frigging drawing out the thing by the hour (740)

A gypsy:

> or one of those wildlooking gipsies in Rathfarnham had
> their camp pitched near the Bloomfield laundry to try and
> steal our things if they could I only sent mine there a few
> times for the name model laundry sending me back over and
> over some old ones old stockings that blackguardlooking
> fellow with the fine eyes peeling a switch attack me in the
> dark and ride me up against the wall without a word (777)

Some man or other: "I wish some man or other would
take me sometime when hes there and kiss me in his arms
theres nothing like a kiss long and hot down to your soul

almost paralyses you" (740-741) A priest: "Id like to be embraced by one in his vestments and the smell of incense off him like the pope besides theres no danger with a priest if youre married hes too careful about himself then give somthing to H H the pope for a penance" (741) The Greek ideal:

> those fine young men I could see down in Margate strand bathing place from the side of the rock standing up in the sun naked like a God or something and then plunging into the sea with them why arent all men like that thered be some consolation for a woman like that lovely little statue he bought I could look at him all day long curly head and his shoulders his finger up for you to listen theres real beauty and poetry for you I often felt I wanted to kiss him all over also his lovely young cock there so simply I wouldnt mind taking him in my mouth if nobody was looking as if it was asking you to suck it so clean and white he looked with his boyish face I would too in 1/2 minute even if some of it went down what its only like gruel or the dew theres no danger besides hed be so clean compared with those pigs of men I suppose never dream of washing it from 1 years end to the other the most of them only thats what gives the women the moustaches (775-776)

A sailor: "sometimes by the Lord God I was thinking would I go around by the quays there some dark evening where nobodyd know me and pick up a sailor off the sea thatd be hot on for it and not care a pin whose I was only to do it off up in a gate somewhere" (777) Anybody: "of course a woman wants to be embraced 20 times a day almost to make her look young no matter by who so long as to be in love or loved by somebody if the fellow you want isnt there" (777) "or a murderer anybody" (777)

Some other matters for the future. Must buy a mothball: "I must buy a mothball like I had before to keep in the drawer with them [the clothes she hopes Boylan will buy her in Belfast]" (749) A study of the human body and medicinal matters: "I often wanted to study up that myself what we have inside us in that family physician" (743) Since she is irregular, perhaps she should visit a doctor: "who knows [the beginning of her 7th sentence] is there anything the matter with my insides or have I something growing in me getting that thing like that every week when was it last I Whit Monday yes its only about 3 weeks I ought to go to the doctor" (770) Weight-reducing. Giving up the stout: "my belly is a bit too big Ill have to knock off the stout at dinner or am I getting too fond of it the last they sent from ORourkes was as flat as a pancake" (750) Breathing exercises: "or I must do a few breathing exercises" (750) Patent medicine: "I wonder is that antifat any good might overdo it thin ones are not so much the fashion now" (750) Further develop her breasts: "Ill get him [Boylan] to keep that up [sucking her breasts] and Ill take those eggs beaten up with marsala fatten them out for him" (753) Mrs. Fleming is old and incompetent, has terrible problems with her paralyzed husband, and will probably have to be replaced:

> she never even rendered down the fat I told her and now shes going such as she was on account of her paralyzed husband getting worse theres always something wrong with them [men] disease or they have to go under an operation or if its not that its drink and he beats her Ill have to hunt around again for someone (768)

Will she ever find peace? No, not on this side of the grave: "every day I get up theres some new thing on sweet God sweet God well when Im stretched out dead in my grave I suppose Ill have some peace" (768-769) And menstruals: "God knows theres always something wrong with us 5 days every 3 or 4 weeks usual monthly auction isnt it simply sickening" (769) Could the world be a better place? Yes, if it were run by women:

> I dont care what anybody says itd be much better for the world to be governed by the women in it you wouldnt see women going and killing one another and slaughtering when do you ever see women rolling around drunk like they do or gambling every penny they have and losing it on horses yes because a woman whatever she does she knows where to stop sure they wouldnt be in the world at all only for us they dont know what it is to be a woman and a mother how could they where would they all of them be if they hadnt all a mother to look after them what I never had (778)

Molly's ultimate doubt is who her mother "what I never had" (778) actually was: "my mother whoever she was" (761)

Bloom.

Will have his grey suit turned by Mesias (110:17).

Some thoughts on a hoped-for, but most unlikely, future relationship with Stephen Dedalus—pedagogy. Stephen will give Bloom lessons in Italian; Molly will give Stephen singing lessons; there will be intellectual dialogues between Bloom and Stephen at various places, indoors and out-of-doors, in Dublin (696:1-16).

The purchase of tea from Tom Kernan (71:24; 161: 20-21).

On the next visit to the trotting matches will bring a paper goblet in order to get some of the lovely cool water from the well at the Ashtown Gate (79:14-17; 672:14-16). [The Ashtown Gate is one of the entrances to Phoenix Park.]

Will fix the noisy brass quoits of the marital bed (56:28).

A visit to the Guinness brewery:

> Be interesting some day get a pass through Hancock to see the brewery. Regular world in itself. Vats of porter, wonderful. Rats get in too. Drink themselves bloated as big as a collie floating. Dead drunk on the porter. Drink till they puke again like christians. Imagine drinking that! Rats: vats. Well of course if we knew all the things. (152)

Must get his old field glasses set right (166:20-21).

The ultimate question—leaving Molly: "Leave her: get tired. Suffer then. Snivel. Big Spanishy eyes goggling at nothing. Her wavyavyeavyheavyeavyevyevy hair un comb: 'd." (277) "Divorce, not now." (733)

Perhaps learn to play a musical instrument. After leaving the Ormond Hotel Bloom sees a melodeon in a music shop for sale for six shillings. Since it is so cheap, he entertains the thought of buying it (290:18-21).

He must begin doing his Sandow's exercises again (61:25-26; 435:24-25).

Some work in the garden:

> He bent down to regard a lean file of spearmint growing by the wall. Make a summerhouse here. Scarlet runners. Virginia creepers. Want to manure the whole place over, scabby soil. A coat of liver of sulphur. All soil like that without dung. Household slops. Loam, what is this that is? The hens in the next garden: their droppings are very good top dressing. Best of all though are the cattle, especially when they are fed on those oilcakes. Mulch of dung. Best thing to clean ladies kid gloves. Dirty cleans. Ashes too. Reclaim the whole place. Grow peas in that corner there. Lettuce. Always have fresh greens then. Still gardens have their drawbacks [they attract bees]. (68)

Perhaps a literary enterprise: "Might manage a sketch. By Mr and Mrs L. M. Bloom. Invent a story for some proverb which? Time I used to try jotting down on my cuff what she said dressing." (69)

In the cabman's shelter Bloom thinks of writing a sketch, "My Experiences in a Cabman's Shelter" (647:2-7).

A visit to Dunsink:

> Now that I come to think of it, that ball falls at Greenwich time. It's the clock is worked by an electric wire from Dunsink. Must go out there some first Saturday of the month. If I could get an introduction to professor Joly or learn up something about his family. That would do to: man always feels complimented. Flattery where least expected. Nobleman proud to be descended from some king's mistress. His foremother. Lay it on with a trowel. Cap in hand goes through the land. Not go in and blurt out what you know you're not to: what's parallax? Show this gentleman the door. (167)

[The time ball (a ball on a pole dropped to indicate some point in mean time) of the Ballast Office is referred to. Just previous to this (154) Bloom had noticed the time ball on the ballast was down, to indicate it was 1:00 P.M. Actually the ball falls at the Dunsink Observatory in Dublin, not at Greenwich. The correct time, second by second, was sent by an electric wire from Greenwich Observatory in England to Dunsink. Charles Joly was Astronomer Royal of Ireland, Andrew Professor of Astronomy at Trinity College, and director of the Observatory at Dunsink (G.).]

A trip to London (a prospect which reveals that Bloom had once crossed St. George's Channel and landed at Holyhead in Wales. This is the only reference in the book to this important matter):

a long-cherished plan he meant to one day realise some Wednesday or Saturday of travelling to London *via* long sea not to say that he had ever travelled extensively to any great extent but he was at heart a born adventurer though by a trick of fate he had consistently remained a land-lubber except you call going to Holyhead which was his longest. Martin Cunningham frequently said he would work a pass through Egan but some deuced hitch or other eternally cropped up with the net result that the scheme fell through. (626)

Pay a visit to the Huguenot churchyard (84:6-7).

A visit to the grounds of Trinity College:

"There's Hornblower standing at the porter's lodge. Keep him on hands: might take a turn in there on the nod. How do you do, Mr Hornblower? How do you do, sir?" (86)

The larger future.

All readers of *Ulysses* wonder about the future of the Blooms, and many ingenious, and usually groundless, hypotheses about it have been advanced by critics and scholars. In the *Odyssey* after Ulysses has won his way back to Ithaca, slaughtered the 108 suitors, overcome Penelope's doubts about his identity, and the reunited husband and wife kiss and embrace, Ulysses declares: "Dear wife, we have not yet come to the limit of all our trials. There is unmeasured labor left for the future, both difficult and great, and all of it I must accomplish." (Book XXIII, 248-250, Lattimore translation.) I believe that Joyce, had he written a continuation of the life of the Blooms, would surely have followed his Homeric arche-type.

The evolution and devolution of Leopold Bloom:

"From infancy to maturity he had resembled his maternal procreatrix. From maturity to senility he would increasingly resemble his paternal creator." (708)

The end: "One must go first: alone under the ground: and lie no more in her warm bed." (102)

THE PAST

Undatable memories of the past for Molly:

1. Bloom brings her a copy of Defoe's *Moll Flanders,* which she does not like: "I dont like books with a Molly in them like that one he brought me about the one from Flanders a whore always shoplifting anything she could cloth and stuff and yards of it" (756)

2. On a rainy Sunday afternoon Bloom takes her to see a statue of an Indian God in the Kildare Street Museum:

> breathing [Bloom is asleep in the early morning of June 17, 1904] with his hand on his nose like that Indian god he took me to show one wet Sunday in the museum in Kildare street all yellow in a pinafore lying on his side on his hand with his ten toes sticking out that he said was a bigger religion than the jews and Our Lords both put together all over Asia imitating him as hes always imitating everybody I suppose he used to sleep at the foot of the bed too with his big square feet up in his wifes mouth (771)

3. Hornblower, the porter of Trinity College, lets the Blooms, Molly, Milly, and Leopold, into the college grounds to see the races, and Bloom ogles the girls:

> when I was with him with Milly at the College races that Hornblower with the childs bonnet on the top on his nob let us into by the back way he was throwing his sheeps eyes at those two doing skirt duty up and down I tried to wink at him first no use of course (773)

4. Molly remembers Simon Dedalus; as a singer:

and Simon Dedalus too he was always turning up half screwed singing the second verse first the old love is the new was one of his so sweetly sang the maiden on the hawthorn bough he was always on for flirtyfying too when I sang Maritana with him at Freddy Mayers private opera he had a delicious glorious voice Phoebe dearest goodbye *sweet*heart he always sang it not like Bartell dArcy sweet *tart* goodbye of course he had the gift of the voice so there was no art in it all over you like a warm shower-bath O Maritana wildwood flower we sang splendidly though it was a bit too high for my register even trans-posed and he was married at the time to May Goulding but then hed say or do something to knock the good out of it hes a widower now (774)

At a cricket match: "Simon Dedalus . . . such a criticizer with his glasses up with his tall hat on him at the cricket match and a great big hole in his sock one thing laughing at the other" (768)

5. A picnic on Killiney hill: "clothes we have to wear whoever invented them expecting you to walk up Killiney hill then for example at that picnic all staysed up you cant do a blessed thing in them in a crowd run or jump out of the way" (755)

6. An overheard pseudo dirty joke:

my uncle John has a thing long I heard those cornerboys saying passing the corner of Marrowbone lane my aunt Mary has a thing hairy because it was dark and they knew a girl was passing it didnt make me blush why should it either its only nature and he puts his thing long into my aunt Marys hairy etcetera and turns out to be you put the handle in a sweepingbrush men again all over (776-777)

7. Bloom brings home a lovely little statue [of Narcis-sus]: "like that lovely little statue he bought I could look at him all day long curly head and his shoulders his finger up

for you to listen theres real beauty and poetry for you"
(775)

8. Bloom brings home a copy of Rabelais:

> like some of those books he brings me the works of
> Master François somebody supposed to be a priest about a
> child born out of her ear because her bumgut fell out a nice
> word for any priest to write and her a—e as if any fool
> wouldnt know what that meant I hate that pretending of
> all things with the old blackguards face on him anybody
> can see its not true . . . like the infant Jesus in the crib
> at Inchicore in the Blessed Virgins arms sure no woman
> could have a child that big taken out of her (751-752)

9. Bloom twice brings home for her James Lovebirch's
Fair Tyrants: "and Fair Tyrants he brought me that twice
I remember when I came to page 50 the part about where
she hangs him up out of a hook with a cord flagellate"
(751-752) [But Bloom remembers getting *Fair Tyrants*
for Molly only once (235:37-38).]

10. A dog barking in Bell Lane: "yes he used to break his
heart at me taking off the dog barking in bell lane poor
brute and it sick" (755)

11. Molly has some thoughts of past performances
while squatting on the chamber pot: "easy God I remember one time I could scout it out straight whistling like a
man almost easy O Lord how noisy" (770)

Bloom's undatable memories of the past.

1. Molly's intuitive powers; the hurdy-gurdy boy:
"With look to look: songs without words. Molly that
hurdy-gurdy boy. She knew he meant the monkey was
sick. Or because so like the Spanish. Understand animals
too that way." (285) And the man with the false arm:
"Sharp as needles they are. When I said to Molly the man

at the corner of Cuffe street was goodlooking, thought she might like, twigged [guessed] at once he had a false arm. Had too. Where do they get that?" (371-372)

2. Molly and the farmer at the horseshow: "Shame [Molly's pretence of] all put on before third person. More put out about a hole in her stocking. Molly, her underjaw stuck out head back, about the farmer in the riding boots and spurs at the horse show." (374) In the list of Molly's "lovers" there appears a farmer at the Royal Dublin Society's Horse Show (731:27-28).

3. Molly draws a graffiti: "(*He* [Bloom] *gazes ahead reading on the wall a scrawled chalk legend* Wet dream *and a phallic design.*)
Odd! Molly drawing on the frosted carriagepane at Kingstown." (452)

4. Molly tells him she'd like to visit a whore house and to satisfy other outré urges: "(*Looks behind.*) She often said she'd like to visit. Slumming. The exotic, you see. Negro servants too in livery if she had money. Othello black brute." (443)

5. One night Bloom brings home a song for Molly: "*Blumenlied* I bought for her. The name. Playing it slow, a girl, night I came home, the girl. Door of the stables near Cecilia street." (278)

6. Bloom the householder and furnisher: "Aunt Hegarty's [his mother's older sister] armchair, our classic reprints of old masters." (542) "[. . .] the Brusselette carpet you bought at Wren's auction [. . . .] the little statue you carried home in the rain for art for art's sake." (543)

> What caused him consolation in his sitting posture?
> The candour, nudity, pose, tranquillity, youth, grace, sex, counsel of a statue erect in the centre of the table, an image of Narcissus purchased by auction from P. A. Wren, 9 Bachelor's Walk. (710)

your ten shilling brass fender from Hampton Leedom's.
(543)

7. Bloom picks up a second-hand raincoat from the lost-property office: "His hand took his hat from the peg over his initialled heavy overcoat, and his lost property office secondhand waterproof." (56)

8. Bloom takes notes on what Molly says while dressing:

> Time I used to try jotting down on my cuff what she said dressing. Dislike dressing together. Nicked myself shaving. Biting her nether lip, hooking the placket of her skirt. Timing her. 9.15. Did Roberts pay you yet? 9.20. What had Gretta Conroy on? 9.23. What possessed me to buy this comb? 9.24. I'm swelled after that cabbage. A speck of dust on the patent leather of her boot. (69)

9. Sees a "spread" at the Master of the Rolls' banquet:

> Spread I saw down in the Master of the Rolls' kitchen area. Whitehatted *chef* like a rabbi. Combustible duck. Curly cabbage *à la duchesse de Parme.* Just as well to write it on the bill of fare so you can know what you've eaten too many drugs spoil the broth. (175)

[The Master of the Rolls from 1883 to 1907 was Sir Andrew Marshall Porter, who resided at 42 Merrion Square East (G.).]

10. Bloom and Drago, the barber:

> Drago's shopbell ringing. Queer I was just thinking that moment. Brown brilliantined hair over his collar. Just had a wash and brushup. (68) The cane [Bloom is helping a blind stripling across the street] moved out trembling to the left. Mr Bloom's eye followed its line and saw again the dye-works' van drawn up before Drago's. Where I saw his brilliantined hair just when I was. (180-181) Wish I could see his face [Simon Dedalus is singing in the bar of the Ormond

where, in another room, Bloom is eating], though. Explain better. Why the barber in Drago's always looked my face when I spoke his face in the glass. (275) Course everything is dear if you don't want it. That's what good salesman is. Make you buy what he wants to sell. Chap sold me the Sweedish razor he shave me with. Wanted to charge me for the edge he gave it. (290)

11. Once tried vegetarianism:

His [Bloom's] eyes followed the high figure in homespun, beard and bicycle [George Russell, the poet, known as AE], a listening woman at his side. Coming from the vegetarian. Only weggebobbles and fruit. Don't eat a beefsteak. If you do the eyes of that cow will pursue you through all eternity. They say its healthier. Wind and watery though. Tried it. Keep you on the run all day. Bad as a bloater. Dreams all night. (165-166)

12. Once wrote a letter to the *Irish Cyclist*:

BLOOM

Keep to the right, right, right [Bloom is in Nighttown on his way to Bella Cohen's]. If there is a fingerpost planted by the Touring Club at Stepaside who procured that public boon? I who lost my way and contributed to the columns of the *Irish Cyclist* the letter headed, *In darkest Stepaside*. Keep, keep, keep to the right. (436)

13. Bloom almost shot: "If I had passed Truelock's window that day two minutes later would have been shot. Absence of body. Still if bullet only went through my coat get damages for shock, five hundred pounds. What was he? Kildare street club toff. God help his gamekeeper." (452) [There were two Dublin gun dealers with the name of Truelock (G.).]

14. A quack doctor, Hy Franks, who offered cures for venereal disease:

> That quack doctor for the clap used to be stuck up in all the greenhouses. Never see it now. Strictly confidential. Dr Hy Franks. Didn't cost him a red like Maginni the dancing master self advertisement. Got fellows to stick them up or stick them up himself for that matter on the q.t. running in to loosen a button. Fly by night. Just the place too. POST NO BILLS. POST 110 PILLS. Some chap with a dose burning him. (153)

15. A feat in cricket: "Still Captain Buller broke a window in the Kildare street club with a slog to square leg. Donnybrook fair more in their line." (86)

16. M'Coy sees Bloom buy either Sir Robert Ball's *The Story of the Heavens* (708:27) or *A Handbook of Astronomy* (709:11-14):

> He's dead nuts on sales, M'Coy said. I was with him one day and he bought a book from an old one in Liffey street for two bob. There were fine plates in it worth double the money, the stars and the moon and comets with long tails. Astronomy it was about. (233)

17. Goes to midnight mass and sees a woman:

"Something going on [Bloom is entering a Catholic Church]: some sodality. Pity so empty. Nice discreet place to be next some girl. Who is my neighbour? Jammed by the hour to slow music. That woman at midnight mass. Seventh heaven." (80)

18. Bloom scolds a tram driver for mistreating his horse: "(*Enthusiastically.*) A noble work! I scolded that tramdriver on Harold's cross bridge for illusing the poor horse with his harness scab. Bad French I got for my pains. Of course it was frosty and the last tram." (454)

19. Visits the wax museum in Henry Street:

> In those waxworks in Henry street I myself saw some Aztecs, as they are called, sitting bowlegged. They couldn't

straighten their legs if you paid them because the muscles here, you see, he proceeded, indicating on his companion [Stephen Dedalus] the brief outline, the sinews, or whatever you like to call them, behind the right knee, were utterly powerless from sitting that way so long cramped up, being adored as gods. There's an example again of simple souls. (636)

20. Davy Byrne once cashed a check for Bloom:
"He entered Davy Byrne's. Moral pub. He doesn't chat. Stands a drink now and then. But in leapyear once in four. Cashed a cheque for me once." (171)

21. Mervyn Brown told Bloom an interesting fact about the dead:

Air of the place maybe. Looks full up of bad gas. Must be an infernal lot of bad gas round the place. Butchers for instance: they get like raw beefsteaks. Who was telling me? Mervyn Brown. Down in the vaults of saint Werburgh's lovely old organ hundred and fifty they have to bore a hole in the coffins sometimes to let out the bad gas and burn it. Out it rushes: blue. One whiff of that and you're a goner. (103-104)

22. Mrs. O'Connor and her five children die of poisoned mussels: "Widower I hate to see. Looks so forlorn. Poor man O'Connor wife and five children poisoned by mussels here. The sewage. Hopeless. Some good matronly woman in a pork pie hat to mother him. Take him in tow, platter face and a large apron." (381)

23. Bloom remembers a quaint and interesting name:

Wouldn't mind being a waiter in a swell hotel. Tips, evening dress, halfnaked ladies. May I tempt you to a little more filleted lemon sole, miss Dubedad? Yes, do bedad. And she did bedad. Huguenot name I expect that. A miss Dubedat lived in Killiney I remember. *Du, de la,* French. (175)

24. Simon Dedalus's sayings and anecdotes: "It's the droll way he comes out with the things. Knows how to tell a story too." (152) On Larry O'Rourke: "Simon Dedalus takes him off to a tee with his eyes screwed up. Do you know what I'm going to tell you? What's that, Mr O'Rourke? Do you know what? The Russians, they'd only be an eight o'clock breakfast for the Japanese." (58) On William Brayden, the owner of the *Weekly Freeman and National Press* and the *Freeman's Journal and National Press*:

> Mr Bloom turned and saw the liveried porter raise his lettered cap as a stately figure entered between the newsboards of the *Weekly Freeman and National Press* and the *Freeman's Journal and National Press*. Dullthudding Guinness's barrels. It passed stately up the staircase steered by an umbrella, a solemn beardframed face. The broadcloth back ascended each step: back. All his brains are in the nape of his neck, Simon Dedalus says. Welts of flesh behind on him. Fat folds of neck, fat, neck, fat, neck. (117)

On Martin Cunningham's drunken wife:

> And that awful drunkard of a wife of his. Setting up house for her time after time and then pawning the furniture on him every Saturday almost. Leading him the life of the damned. Wear the heart out of a stone, that. Monday morning start afresh. Shoulder to the wheel. Lord, she must have looked a sight that night, Dedalus told me he was in there. Drunk about the place and capering with Martin's umbrella:
> *And they call me the jewel of Asia,*
> *Of Asia,*
> *The geisha.*   (96)
> [See also 568:26-569:6.]

25. Corny Kelleher gets a job with the undertaker, O'Neill:

And past Nichols' the undertaker's. At eleven it is. Time enough. Daresay Corny Kelleher bagged that job for O'Neill's. Singing with his eyes shut. Corney. Met her once in the park. In the dark. What a lark. Police tout. Her name and address she then told with my tooraloom tooraloom tay. O, surely he bagged it. Bury him cheap in a whatyoumaycall. With my tooraloom, tooraloom, tooraloom, tooraloom. (71)

26. Certain Bloomian customary psychic, mental, physical idiosyncracies; vulnerable to hypnotic suggestion, somnambulism, and irrational fears:

From hypnotic suggestion: once, waking, he had not recognised his sleeping apartment: more than once, waking, he had been for an indefinite time incapable of moving or uttering sounds. From somnambulism: once, sleeping, his body had risen, crouched and crawled in the direction of a heatless fire and, having attained its destination, there, curled, unheated, in night attire had lain, sleeping. (692)

27. Once, evidently fairly recently, Bloom, suffering from dysentery, defecated into a bucket of porter in Beaver Street:

THE GAFFER

(*Crouches, his voice twisted in his snout.*) And when Cairns came down from the scaffolding in Beaver Street what was he after doing it into only into the bucket of porter that was there waiting on the shavings for Derwan's plasterers.

THE LOITERERS

(*Guffaw with cleft palates.*) O jays!
(*Their paintspeckled hats wag. Spattered with size and lime of their lodges they frisk limblessly about him.*)

BLOOM

Coincidence too. They think it funny. Anything but that. Broad daylight. Trying to walk. Lucky no woman.

THE LOITERERS

Jays, that's a good one. Glauber salts. O jays, into the men's porter. (450)

In an hallucination, Bloom is charged with this "crime" and is cross-examined about it in the witness chair:

PROFESSOR MACHUGH

(The crossexamination proceeds re Bloom and the bucket. A large bucket. Bloom himself. Bowel trouble. In Beaver street. Gripe, yes. Quite bad. A plasterer's bucket. By walking stifflegged. Suffered untold misery. Deadly agony. About noon. Love or burgundy. Yes, some spinach. Crucial moment. He did not look in the bucket. Nobody. Rather a mess. Not completely. A Titbits *back number.)* *(Uproar and catcalls. Bloom, in a torn frockcoat stained with whitewash, dinged silk hat sideways on his head, a strip of sticking-plaster across his nose, talks inaudibly.)* (462-463)

Other events of the past.

1. Mary Shortall, a whore, got both the pox and a child from Jimmy Pidgeon. The child died, and all the whores of Bella Cohen's subscribed to the funeral (520:28-31).

2. Garryowen, the Citizen's dog, attacked a constable in Santry (295:19-21).

3. The now deceased wife of Mr. Deasy threw soup in the face of a waiter at the Star and Garter (132:22-25).

4. The Citizen took over the property of an evicted tenant (328:15-19).

Appendix A
BLOOM'S ADDRESSES

1866. Born at 52 Clanbrassil Street, where he lives until the 1880s (see p. 28, 31, 32, 38 above).

1881. Still at 52 Clanbrassil, although there is no reference to his residing there after this year (see p. 41-42 above).

1881-
1887. No addresses indicated. By 1886 his father owns the Queen's Hotel in Ennis, Clare (see p. 71 above). In that same year both his mother and father die (see p. 72-73 above). Clearly he no longer lives at Clanbrassil Street by this time.

1888. Molly and Leopold, newly married, are living on Pleasants Street (see p. 103 above).

1888-
1892. Pleasants Street, presumably, although they may also have lived at Arbutus Place at some time during this period (see 60:38).

1892. Lombard Street West (see p. 121-122 above).

1893. Lombard Street West (see p. 123-129 above).

Spring of
1893. Raymond Terrace (see p. 129-131 above).

1893. The City Arms Hotel (see p. 131-137 above).

1894. The City Arms Hotel (see p. 137-154 above).

1895. Holles Street, "on the rocks" (see p. 161-167 above).

1896. Holles Street (see p. 167 above).

1897. Ontario Terrace (see p. 169-172 above).

1898. Ontario Terrace (see p. 172 above).

1899-
1904. There is almost no evidence in the text for the residences of these years. However, VI. C.7 (1) puts them at Eccles Street by 1903. There is some textual evidence to support this (see p. 179-181 above).

Appendix B
BLOOM'S JOBS

1881. Working for his father as a house-to-house salesman of trinkets (see p. 41-42 above), "baubles," and "penny diamonds" (see p. 70 above). One must assume that this activity continued on after 1881, at least until his father went into the business of loaning money unsecured (see p. 70 above).

Middle
1880s. Working for Kellet's, a mail-order house, where he ties packages for mailing (see p. 44 above).

1886. Working as a traveling salesman, house to house, which necessitates his traveling around the suburbs of Dublin by third-class rail (see p. 76 above).

1886-
1888. Involved in politics in some fashion: employed by or helping Alderman John Hooper (see p. 49, 76-77 above); there is also a suggestion that he worked for Valentine Dillon, an attorney and politician (see p. 77 above); he also was supposed to run for M.P. (see p. 49 above).

1888. Working for Wisdom Hely, a stationer and printer (see p. 102 above).

1889. Still with Hely (see p. 102 above).

1889-
1893. Presumably still working for Hely, although he could have quit or been dismissed sometime during this period.

1893. Working as an actuary for Joe Cuffe, the cattleman (see p. 131, 141 above).

1894. Still working for Cuffe but is fired some time this year (see p. 148, 151-152 above); Molly tries, unsuccessfully, to get him rehired (see p. 152 above); he is rehired by Hely. One of his jobs now is to collect the accounts of convents (see p. 153-154 above).

1895. Fired by Hely and is now jobless (see p. 161, 163-164 above).

1896. In the employ of Drimmie, insurance, according to VI. C.7 (1).

1897. Still with Drimmie (see p. 171 above).

1898-
1904. All the text shows is that by 1904 Bloom is an advertising canvasser for the *Freeman's Journal.* Joyce's chronological notes give the following evidence for this period: "Insurance 1901-02" (which would indicate he was still with Drimmie), V.A.8; "Freeman 1902-1904," V.A.8; "Freeman 1902-04," VI.C.7 (2); and "1903 L B Freeman's," VI.C.7 (1). On June 16 Davy Byrne thinks Bloom is still in insurance, but Nosey Flynn tells him that Bloom left that "long ago" and is working now for the *Freeman* (177:5-7).

   The most puzzling date to pin down is when Bloom worked for Thom's. My surmises are 1886 or 1888 or 1892-93-94 or sometime previous to June 16, 1904 (see p. 149-150 above).

Index